P I X A R

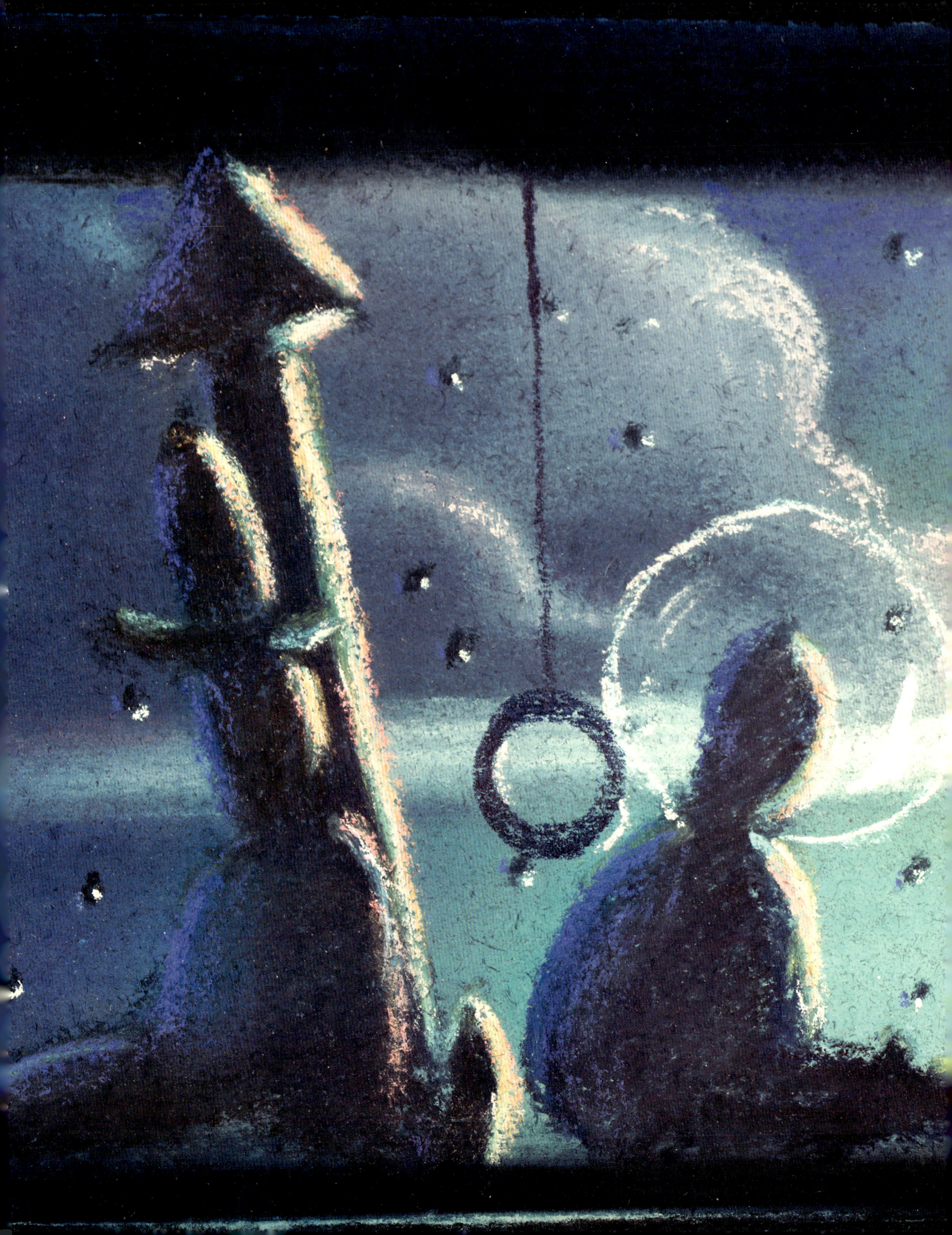

P I X A R

AT THE MUSEUM OF MODERN ART

CHRONICLE BOOKS
San Francisco

**A very special thanks to
the Intel Corporation and Porsche AG
for their generous support of
the *Pixar* exhibition at MoMA.**

**Special thanks to The Walt Disney Company
for their cooperation in this exhibition.**

Published on the occasion
of the exhibition *Pixar: 20 Years of Animation*
organized by Steven Higgins, Curator,
and Ronald S. Magliozzi, Assistant Curator,
Department of Film and Media,
at The Museum of Modern Art,
New York, December 14, 2005–February 6, 2006.

Page 176 constitutes a continuation of the copyright page.

ISBN 10: 0-8118-5216-4
ISBN 13: 978-0-8118-5216-6

Manufactured in the United States

Designed by
Andy Dreyfus and DeAnn Cobb
Typesetting and composition by
Patrick David Barber

10 9 8 7 6 5 4 3 2 1

Chronicle Books LLC
85 Second Street
San Francisco, California 94105

www.chroniclebooks.com

cover:
Tia Kratter
Sullivan fur pattern studies (detail)
MONSTERS, INC.
Mixed media
10½ x 11⅛

page 2:
Ralph Eggleston
Colorscript (detail)
TOY STORY
Pastel
5 x 27

TABLE OF CONTENTS

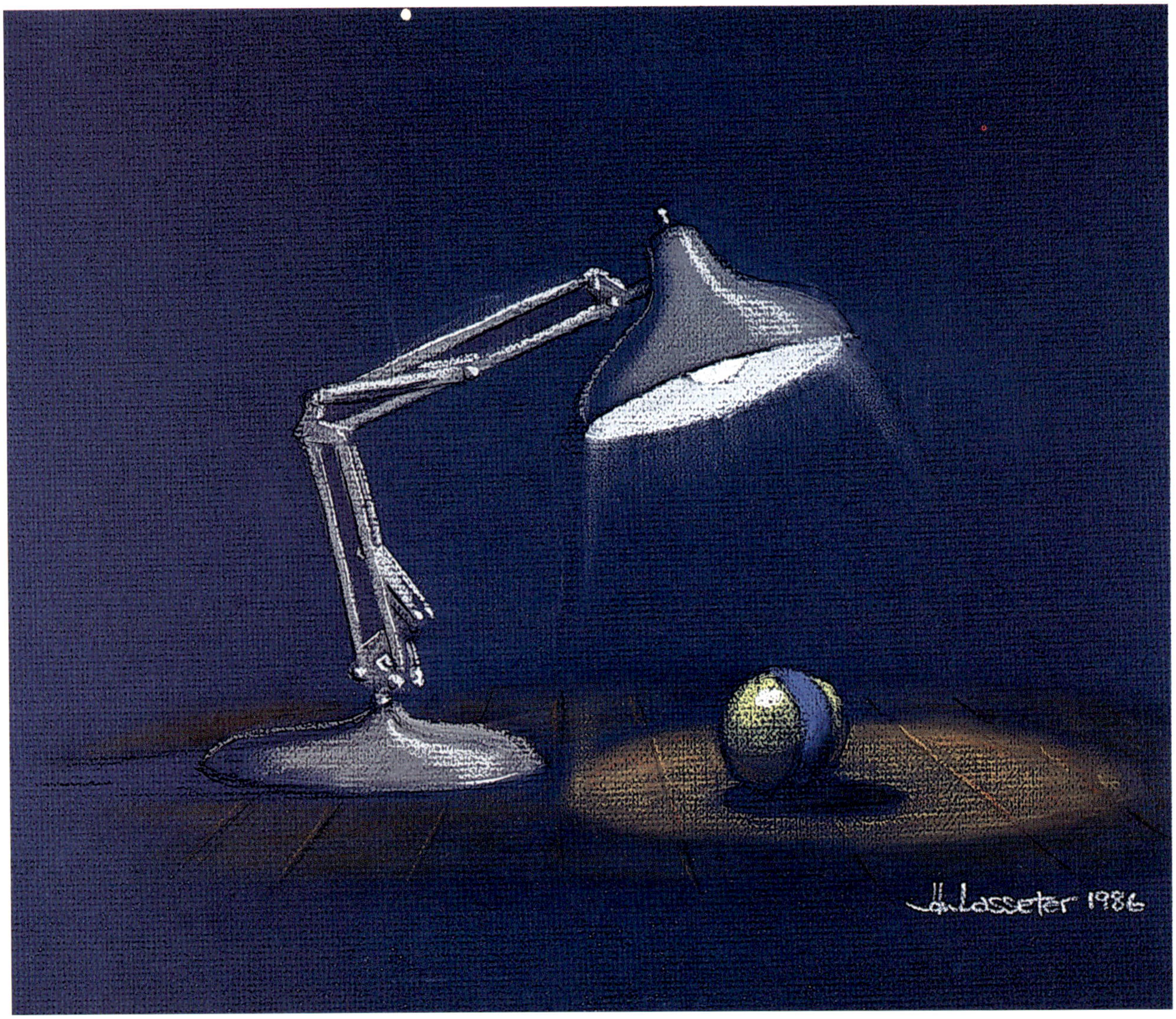

John Lasseter
Luxo
LUXO JR.
Pastel
14¾ x 17¾

FOREWORD

EVEN THOSE knowledgeable about Pixar's animated films—*Toy Story*, *A Bug's Life*, *Toy Story 2*, *Monsters, Inc.*, *Finding Nemo*, and *The Incredibles*—often need to be reminded that computer animation is not driven primarily by technology. Despite the studio's own best efforts to explain their work through the media and "extras" on their DVD releases, the notion lingers that computer animation is created through the push of a button. While it is true that 3-D animation does not make use of the many layers of photographed paper and celluloid that has served as the basic medium for virtually all 2-D cel animation over the past ninety years, the pioneering system of digital animation used by Pixar Animation Studios produces a wealth of preparatory material that is sculpted, painted, and drawn. Each piece of framed art and media in MoMA's exhibition *Pixar* is another window into the extraordinary process by which that studio conceives and develops the worlds, characters, and stories that become their films or, as their teams of artists fondly describe them during production, their "shows."

"Proof of concept" is a phrase that elegantly expresses the nature of the studio's commitment to creativity and its willingness to give its artists the freedom to test the limits of their imagination. Art generated in the early stages of production shapes the final films in surprising and rewarding ways. In addition to the time-honored animation storyboards and character model sheets familiar to every student of the genre, digital filmmaking requires colorscripts; lighting, shading, and texture studies; displacement maps; and 3-D models. Perspective, color, and light studies of the type developed by artists Tia Kratter, Robin Cooper, and Bill Cone for the natural world of *A Bug's Life* and Dominique R. Louis for the artificial world of *Monsters, Inc.* typify the kinds of crucial research done to find just the right visual style for each new story. The visions of a film noir world treated in the charcoal and pencil drawings of Simón Varela for *Finding Nemo* resonate through the finished film, although they do not appear on the screen. Character development art by Ricky Nierva, Nicolas Marlet, Harley Jessup, and Bob Pauley for *Monsters, Inc.* exists in an astounding range of delightful works on paper and in a unique series of over two dozen sculptures for the oversized lead, Sullivan. The evolution of "E," the diminutive secondary character in *The Incredibles,* is documented in art that crosses the borders of race and gender, resulting in a scene-stealing, iconic creation that seems destined to live well beyond the "show" itself.

An important aspect of seeing original Pixar animation art in person is the recognition of its handmade quality. In creating their art, studio employees make use of a remarkable range of traditional media, including but not limited to pencil, pen and marker, gouache, acrylic and clay, scissors and paste. Consider Pete Docter's whimsically precise marker sketch of "Sulley and Mike" and Geefwee Boedoe's wacky mixed media concept art for *Monsters, Inc.*, Ralph Eggleston's majestic pastel colorscripts for *Toy Story* and *Finding Nemo*, Teddy Newton's textured photo-realistic collages for *The Incredibles*, and the tribal-looking maquettes which are sometimes digitized for computer modeling purposes by Jerome Ranft and Greg Dykstra. As trained artists like Glenn Kim, John Lee, Lou Romano, and Bill Cone take up digital tools to create the paintings and colorscripts for *The Incredibles* and *Cars*, they bring a painterly sensibility to computer graphics. "Artscape," the media piece created for the Museum's Yoshiko and Akio Morita Gallery by artist/director Andrew Jimenez and legendary sound designer Gary Rydstrom, invites viewers to reexperience the handcrafted originals in the exhibition as touchstones in a digital installation. The quality of the concept and process art produced at Pixar rises above being merely useful at a particular point in the production of the studio's releases. In the act of exploring the symbiotic relationship between story and art for each new project, the artists included in *Pixar* have created work that has an expressive life all its own.

Pixar is the largest exhibition devoted to animation that The Museum of Modern Art has ever presented, and it is the first time that the original art created at Pixar has been seen outside the studio. It is a tribute to a company of artists whose work has reinvented the genre through a technology unique to the late twentieth century and whose possibilities in the twenty-first century can only be imagined. On the occasion of the studio's twentieth anniversary, with six successful features and ten shorts already to its credit, Pixar has demonstrated beyond doubt that giving free rein to artists within the disciplined structure of a major animation studio is the key to producing outstanding popular art—a "proof of concept" if ever there was one.

STEVEN HIGGINS
Curator, Department of Film and Media
The Museum of Modern Art

RONALD S. MAGLIOZZI
Assistant Curator, Department of Film and Media
The Museum of Modern Art

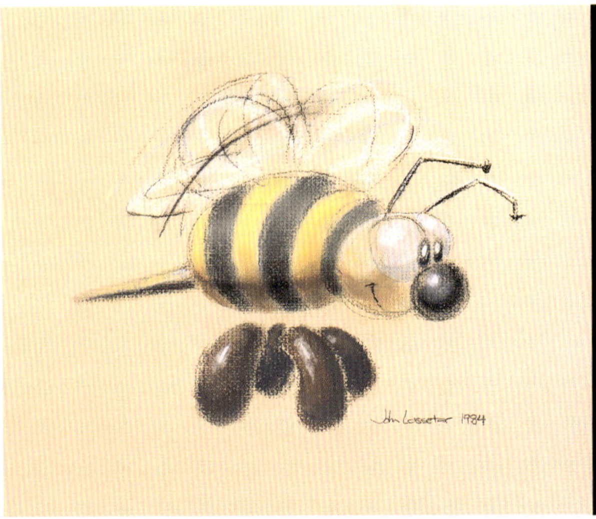

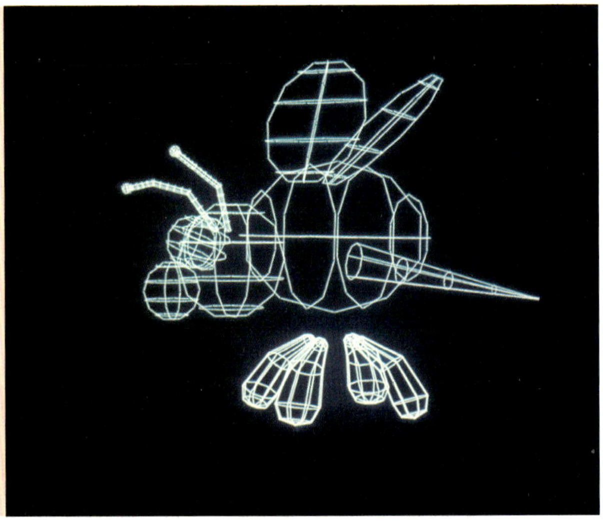

"The art challenges technology and the technology inspires the art."

JOHN LASSETER

John Lasseter
Wally B.
THE ADVENTURES OF ANDRÉ & WALLY B.
Pastel
10 x 12

Edwin Catmull, John Lasseter, Eben Ostby, Alvy Ray Smith
Wally B. wireframe
THE ADVENTURES OF ANDRÉ & WALLY B.
Digital

INTRODUCTION

MANY PEOPLE don't realize that we have almost as many artists at Pixar working in traditional media—hand drawing, painting, pastels, sculpture—as we do in digital media. Most of their work takes place during the development of a project, when we're working out the story and the look of the film. The wealth of beautiful art created for each movie is rarely seen outside the studio, but the finished film we send around the world would never be possible without it.

Computer animation is simultaneously an extraordinarily liberating and incredibly challenging medium. While it contains no limits except those that you choose for yourself, it also contains nothing, down to the smallest detail, that you do not create. You can have anything you want—as long as you are willing to design and build and shade and light it all from scratch. There are never any lucky accidents in the computer, only hard-won victories.

So the development stage, the time before we build our digital world, is the time when we're most free. We encourage our artists to explore as much as possible; to give their creativity free rein. In turn, their art inspires our directors to new heights. In the early days of computer animation, people used to ask us if the computer made the film. Fortunately, we've come a long way since then. It is gratifying that The Museum of Modern Art has recognized our medium for the art form that it is.

The work you will see here represents the abundant wellspring of every movie that we make—the world of open possibilities and the visions ultimately realized. We are proud of Pixar's many talented artists, and we are thrilled to finally be able to present their work to the public in this exhibit.

JOHN LASSETER
Executive Vice President, Creative
Pixar

ED CATMULL
President
Pixar

Victor Navone
Edna Mode (aka "E") animation thumbnail
THE INCREDIBLES
Digital. Original, pencil

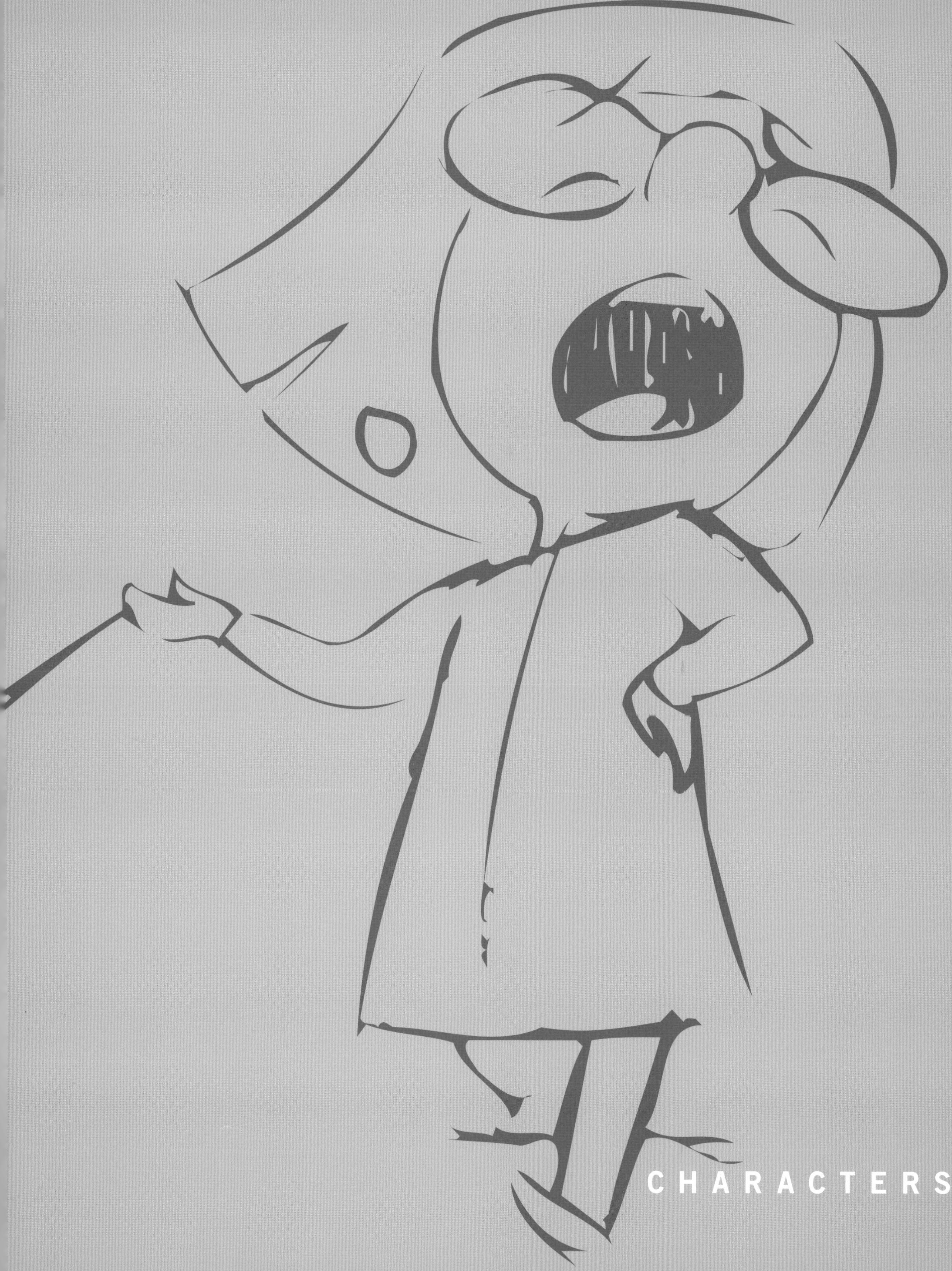

CHARACTERS

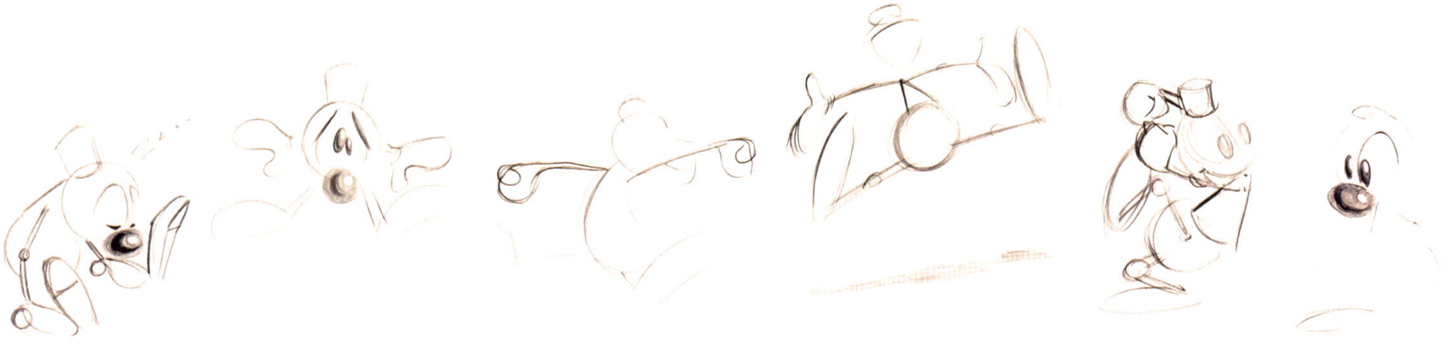

above:
John Lasseter
André animation drawings
THE ADVENTURES OF ANDRÉ & WALLY B.
Digital wall application. Original, pencil
Dimensions vary

opposite:
Dan Lee
Boo movement studies
MONSTERS, INC.
Pencil
11 x 8½

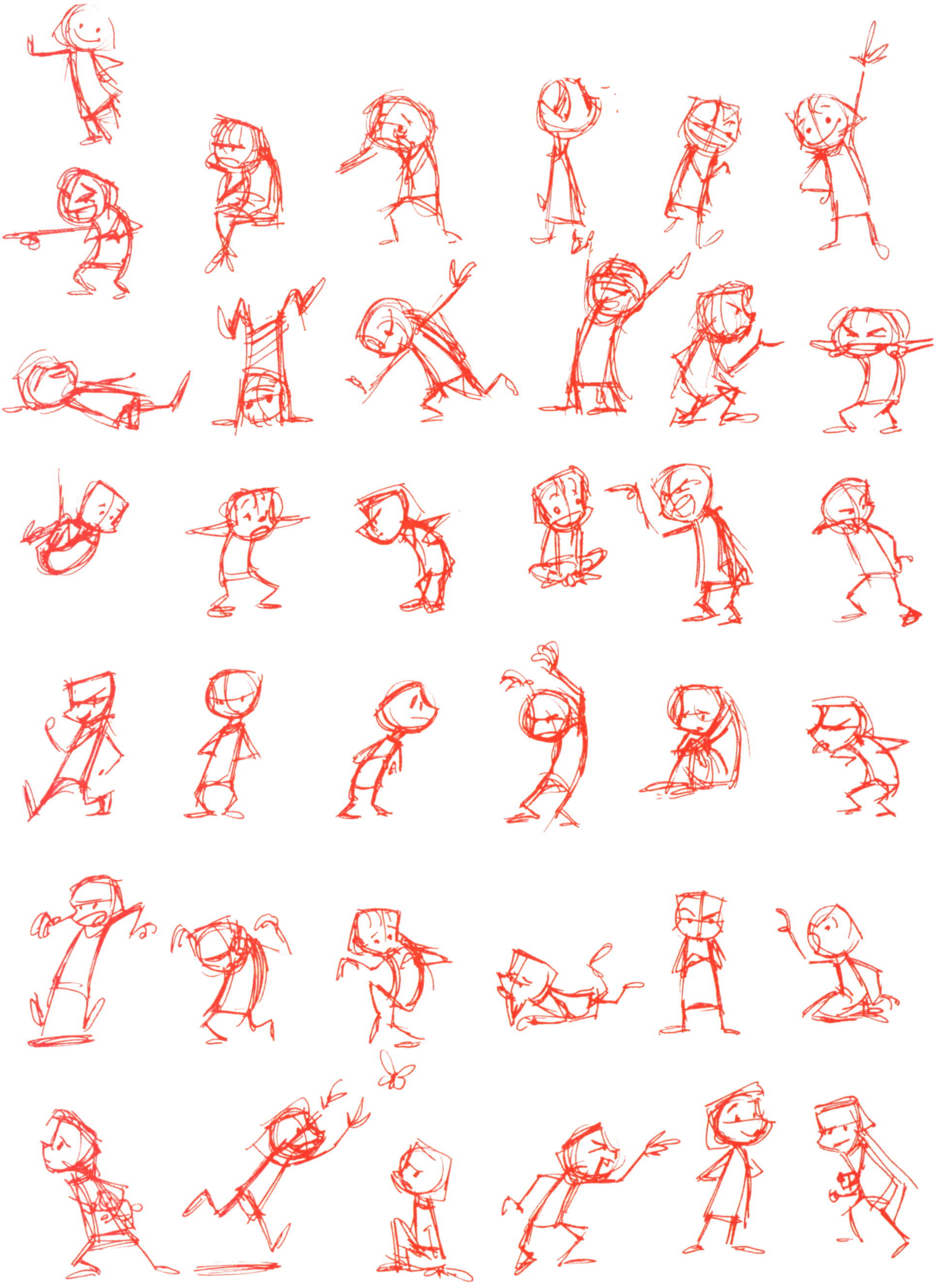

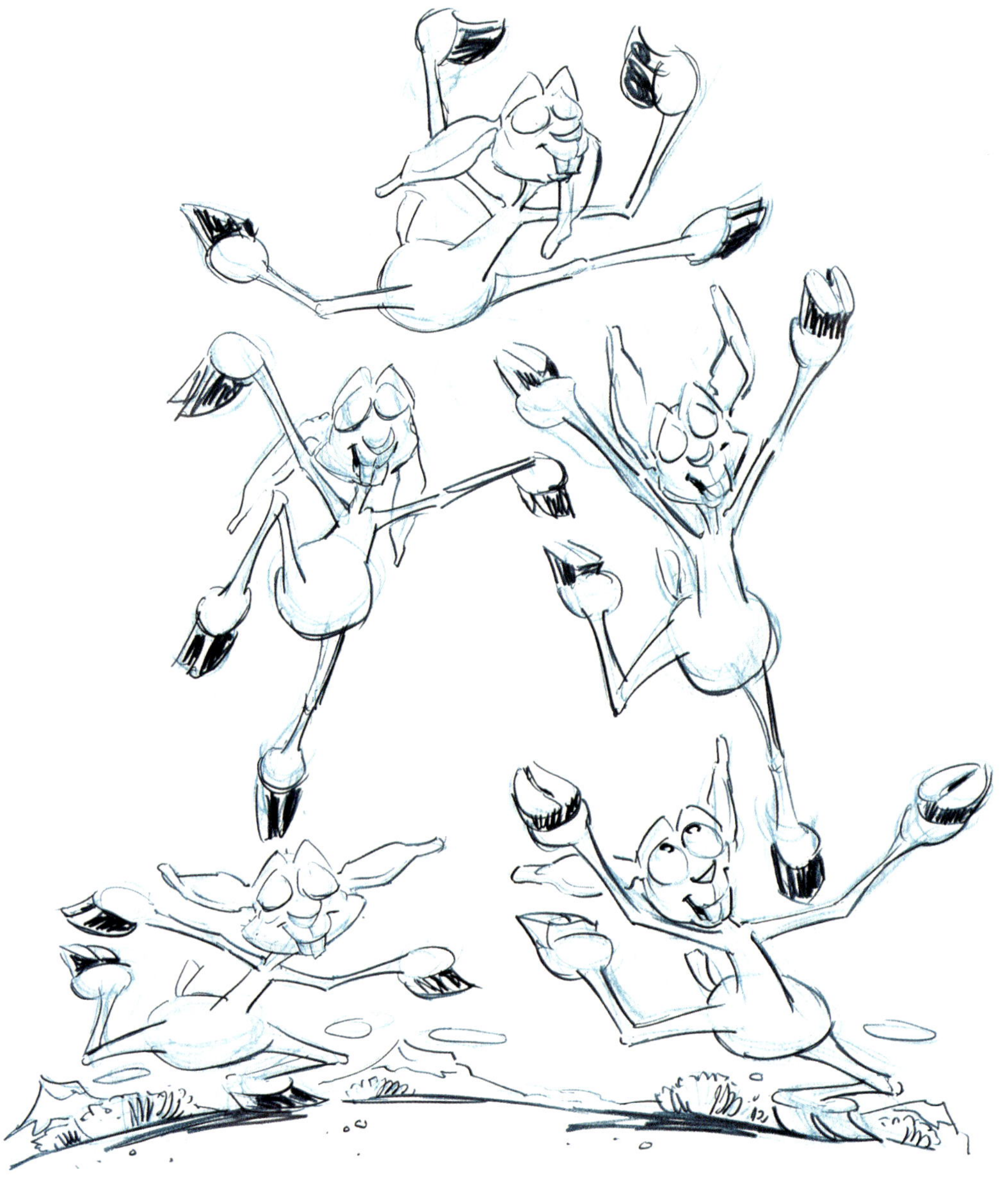

Bud Luckey
Lamb in a bound
BOUNDIN'
Pencil
17 x 14

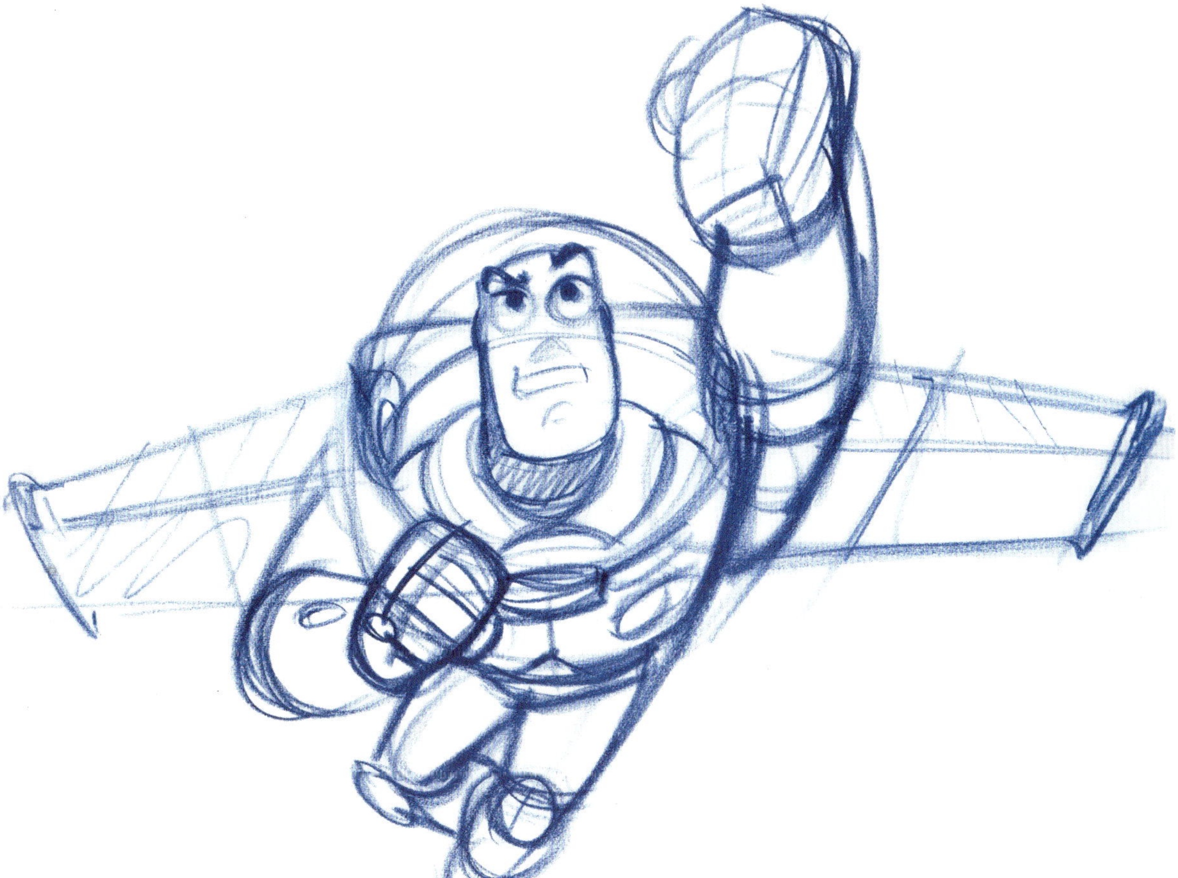

Bob Pauley
Buzz
TOY STORY
Pencil
13⅞ x 10⅞

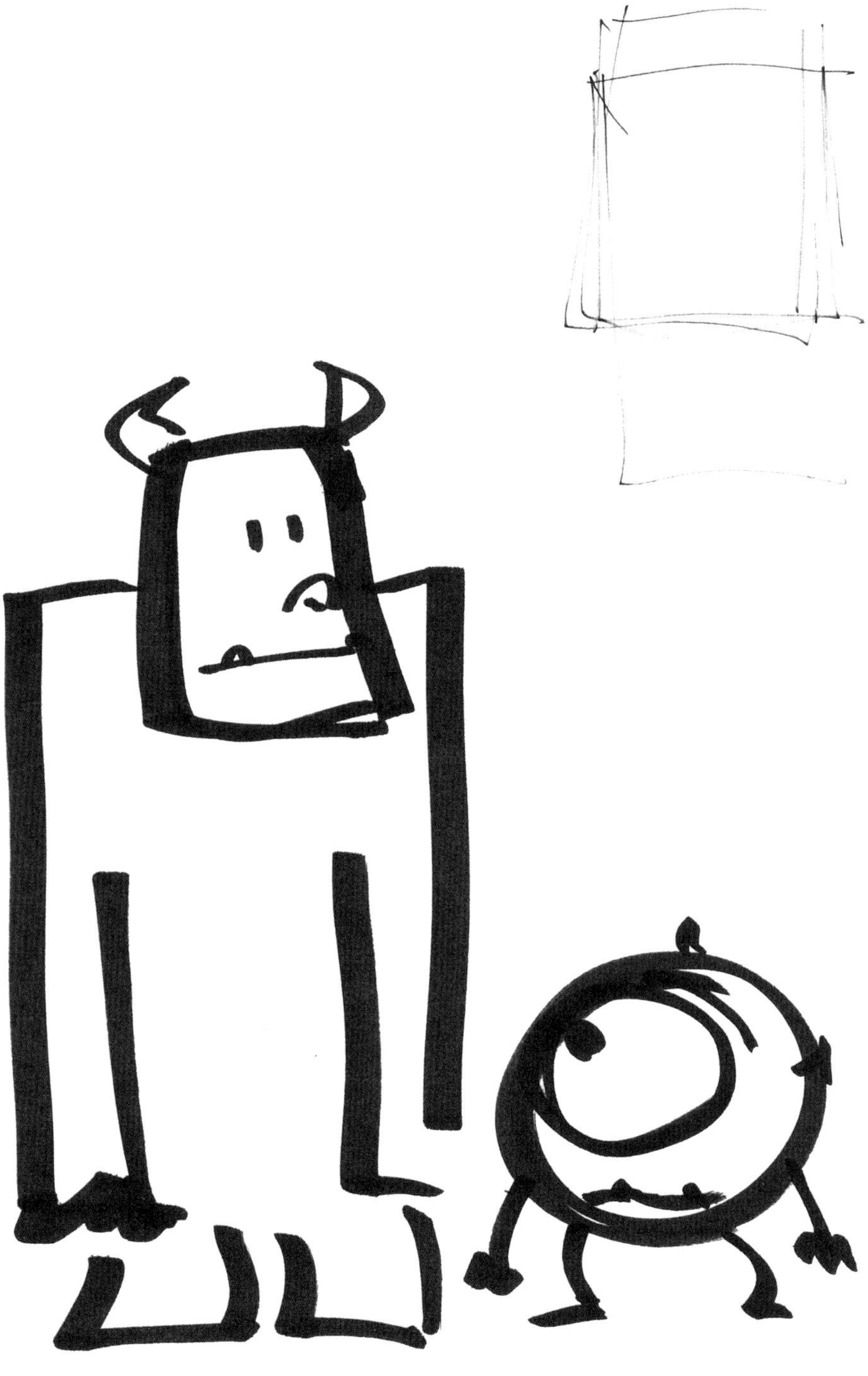

Pete Docter
Sullivan and Mike
MONSTERS, INC.
Marker
11 x 8½

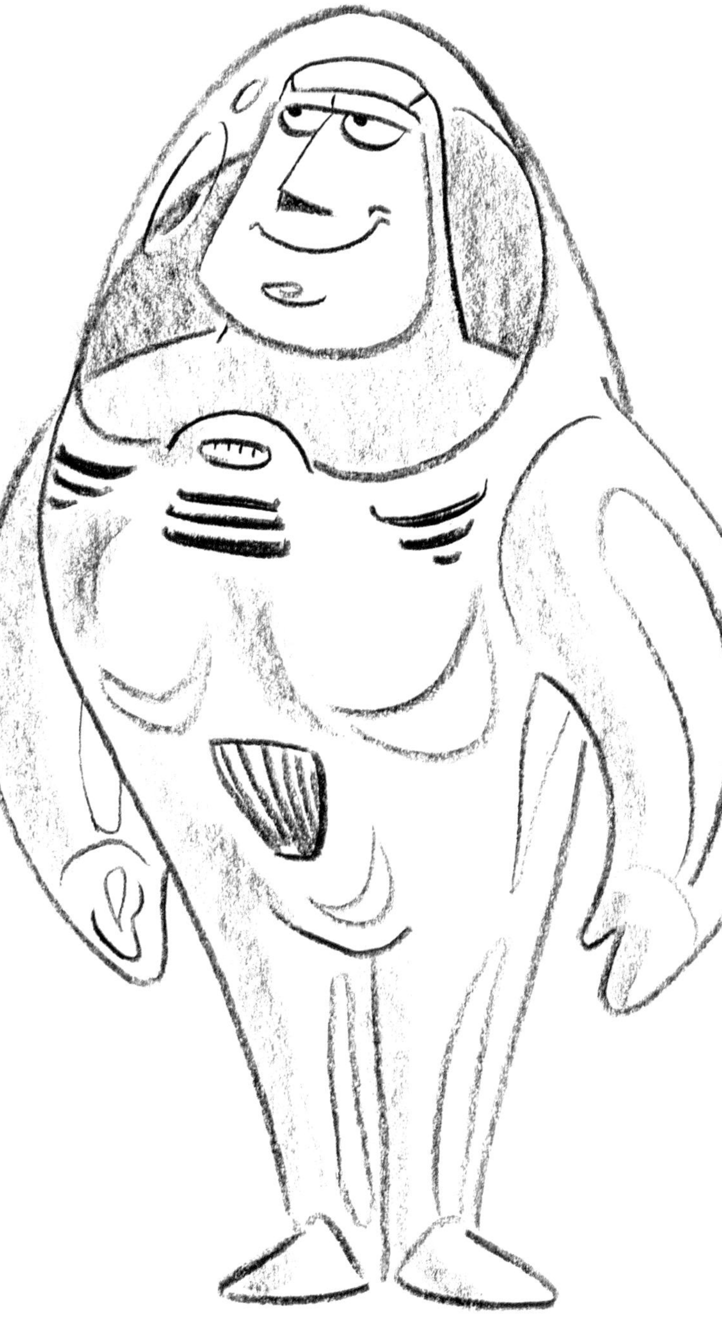

Jeff Pidgeon
Buzz
TOY STORY
Pencil
7¼ x 5

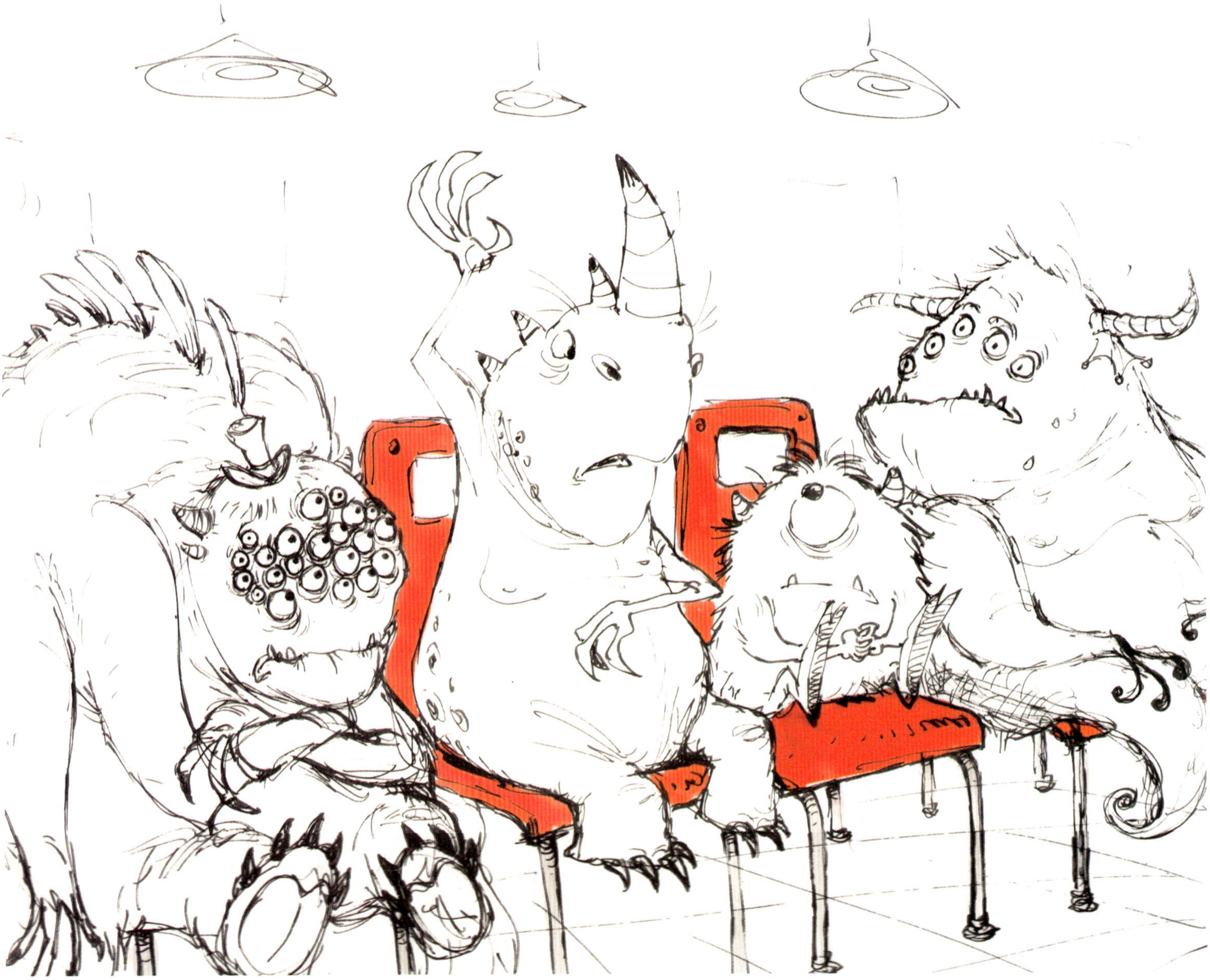

Ricky Nierva
Monsters, Inc. orientation
MONSTERS, INC.
Marker and ink
11 x 14

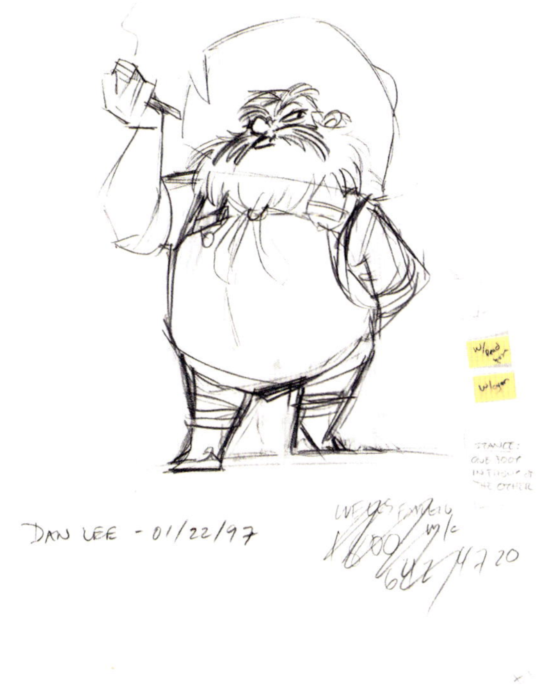

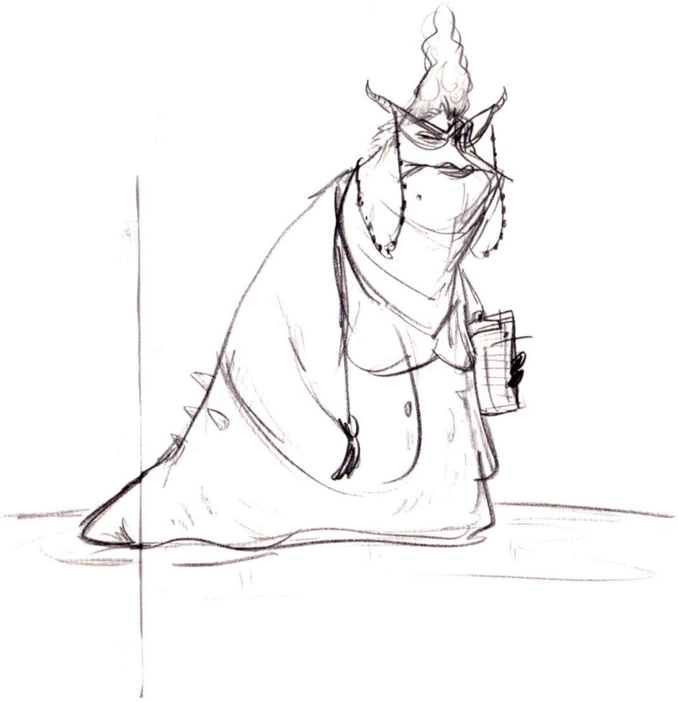

above, left:
Dan Lee
Prospector
TOY STORY 2
Pencil
11 x 8½

above, right:
Ricky Nierva
Roz
MONSTERS, INC.
Pencil
13⅛ x 14⅝

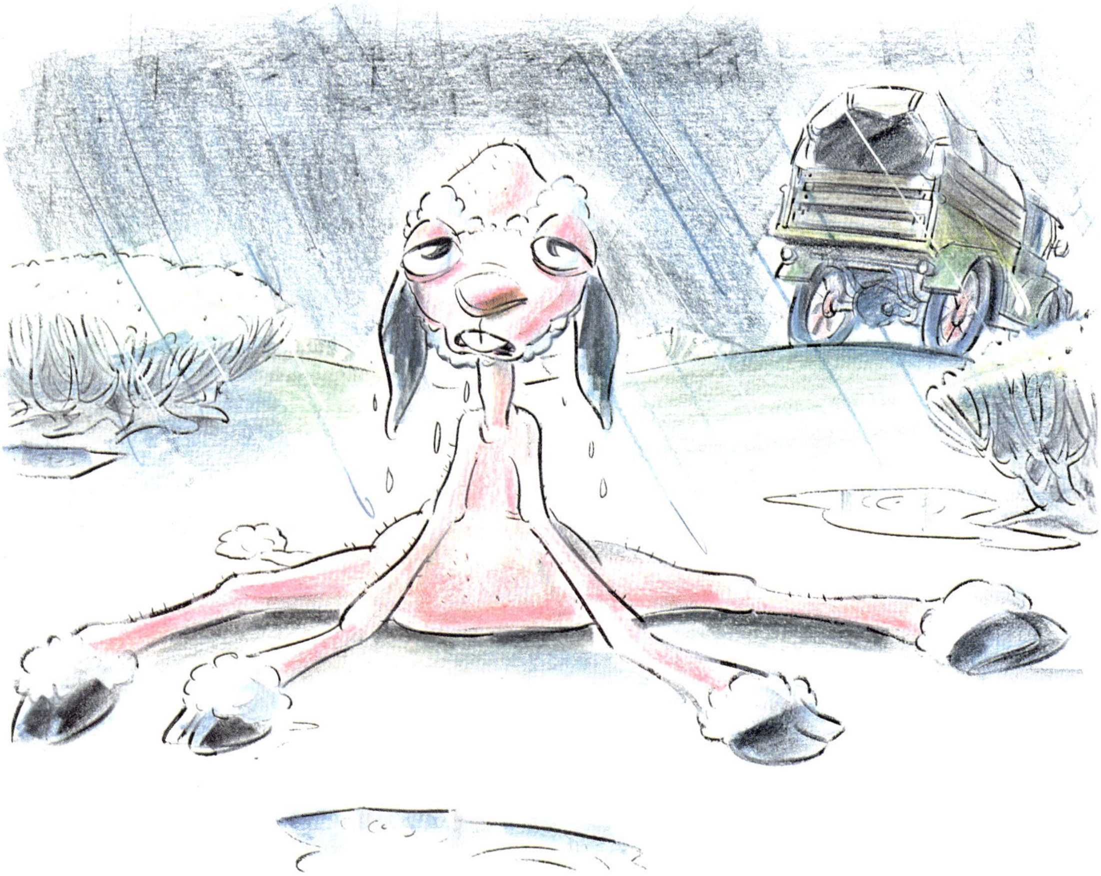

Bud Luckey
What happened?
BOUNDIN'
Pencil
8½ x 11

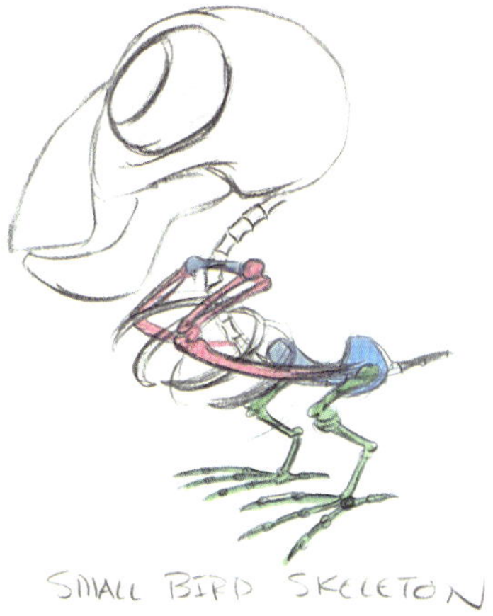

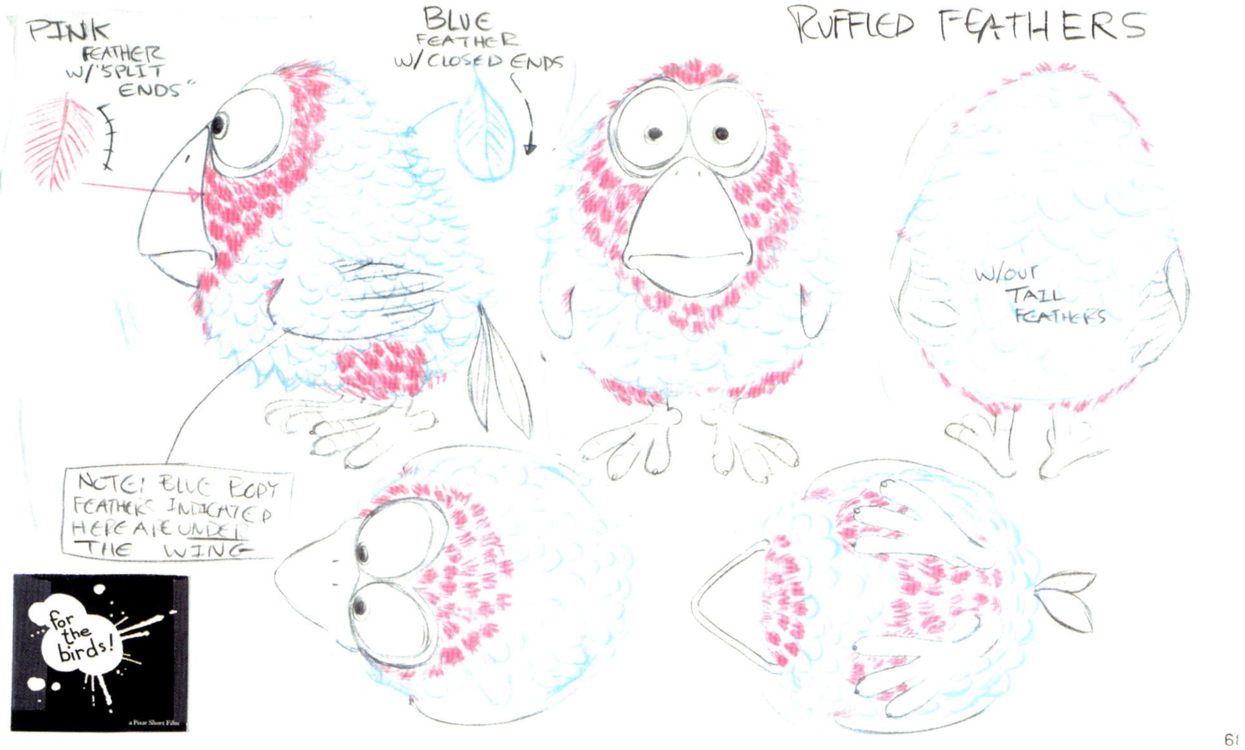

top:
Ralph Eggleston
Norm skeleton (detail)
FOR THE BIRDS
Mixed media
11 x 17

above:
Ralph Eggleston
Norm feathers
FOR THE BIRDS
Mixed media
11 x 17

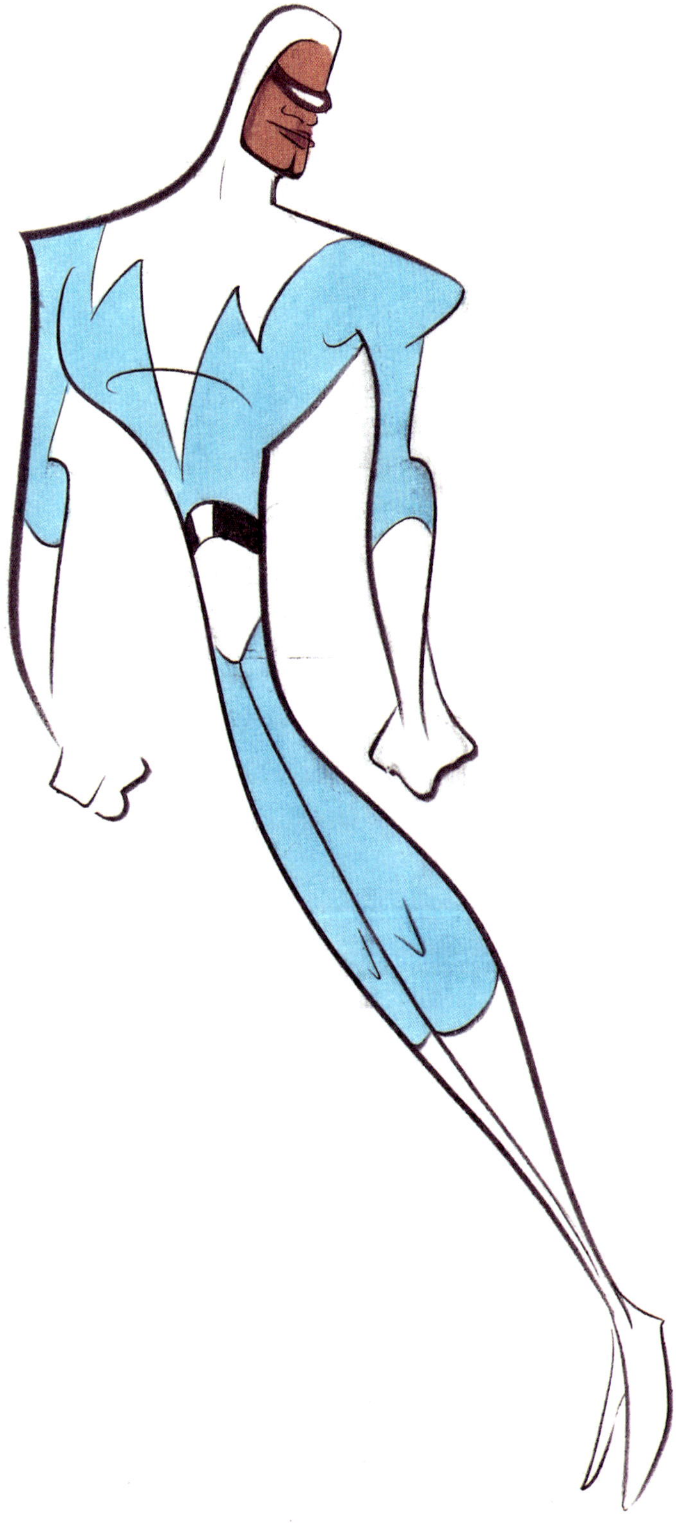

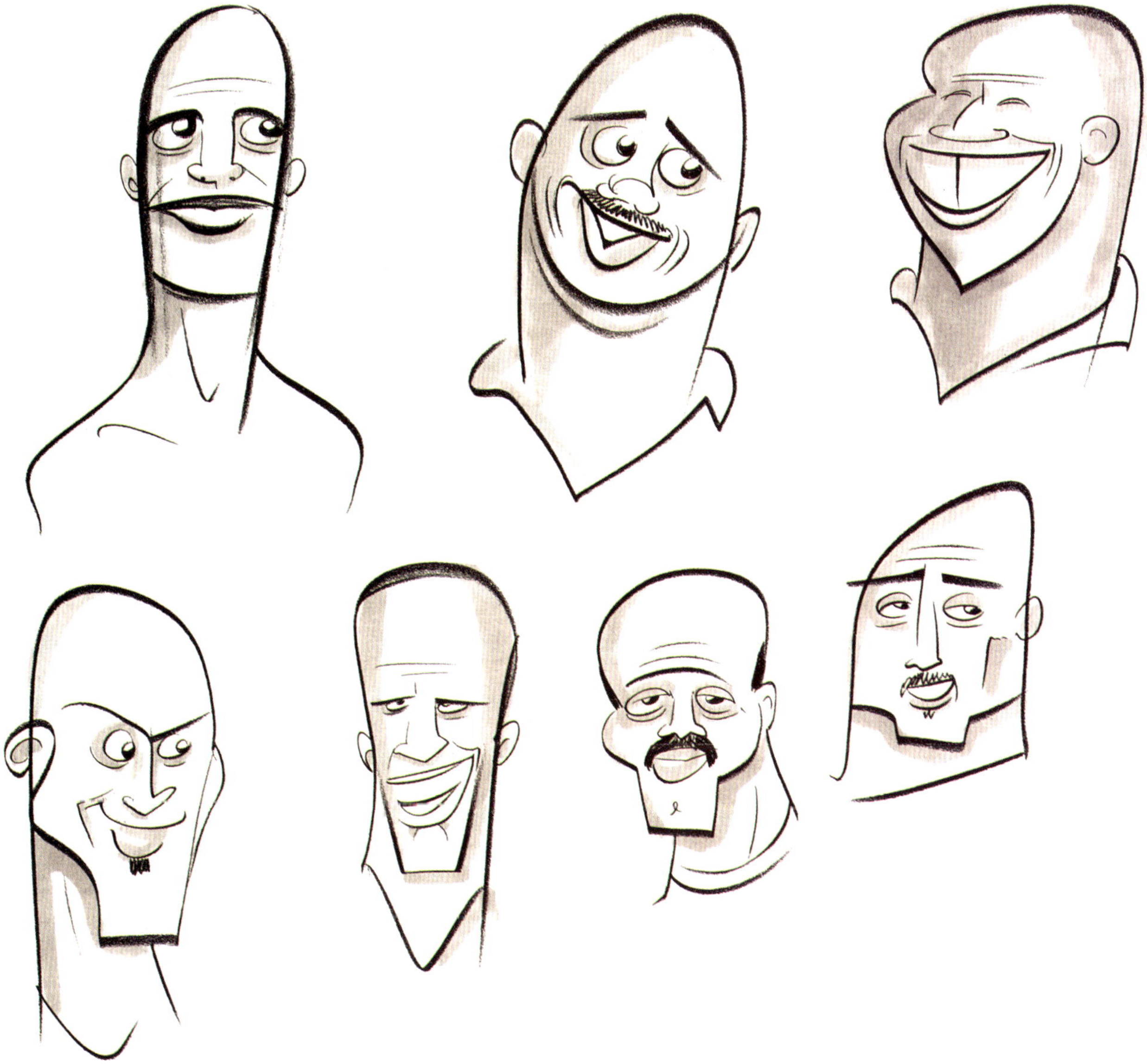

opposite:
Teddy Newton
Frozone
THE INCREDIBLES
Marker and pencil
11 x 8½

above:
Teddy Newton
Frozone facial explorations
THE INCREDIBLES
Marker and pencil
8½ x 10¼

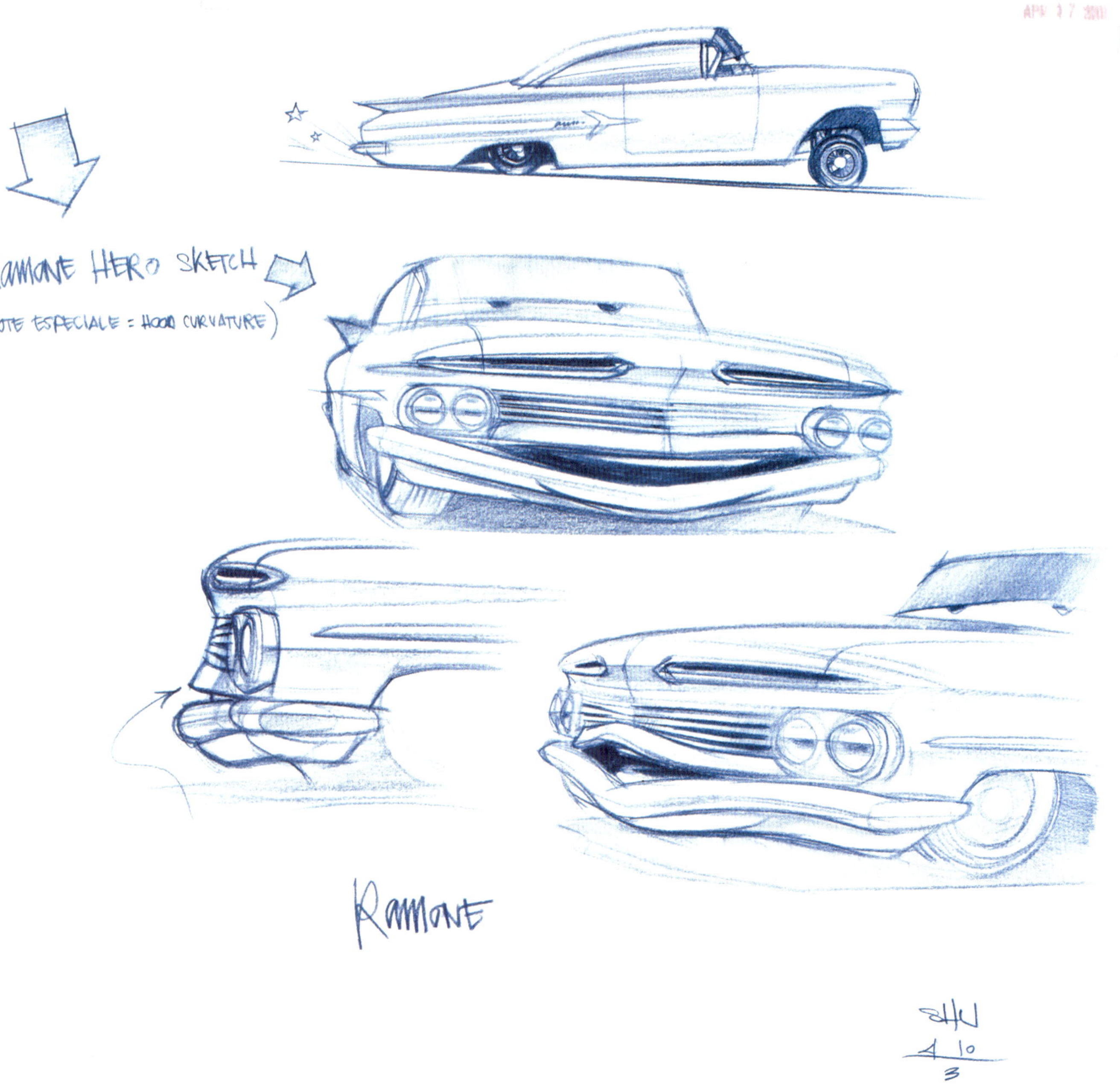

Jay Shuster
Ramone
CARS
Pencil
12½ x 17

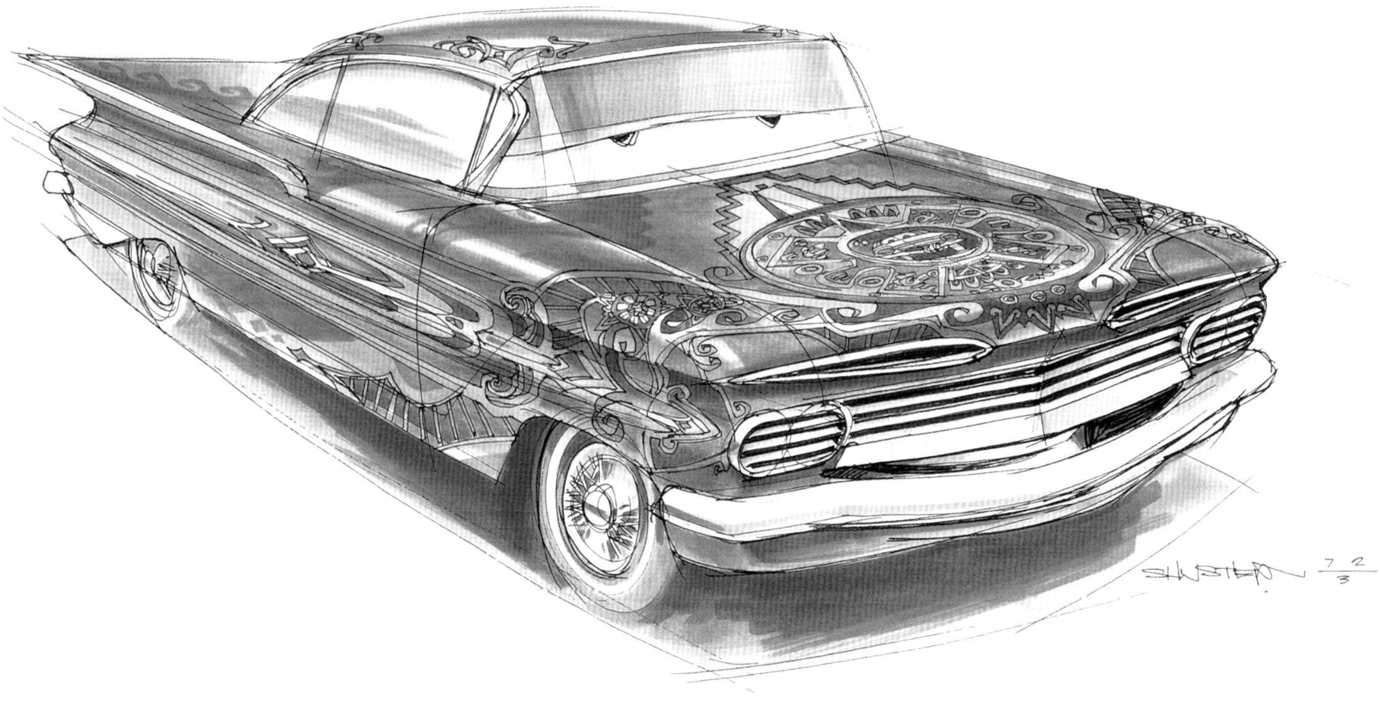

Jay Shuster
Ramone
CARS
Marker and pen
11 x 17

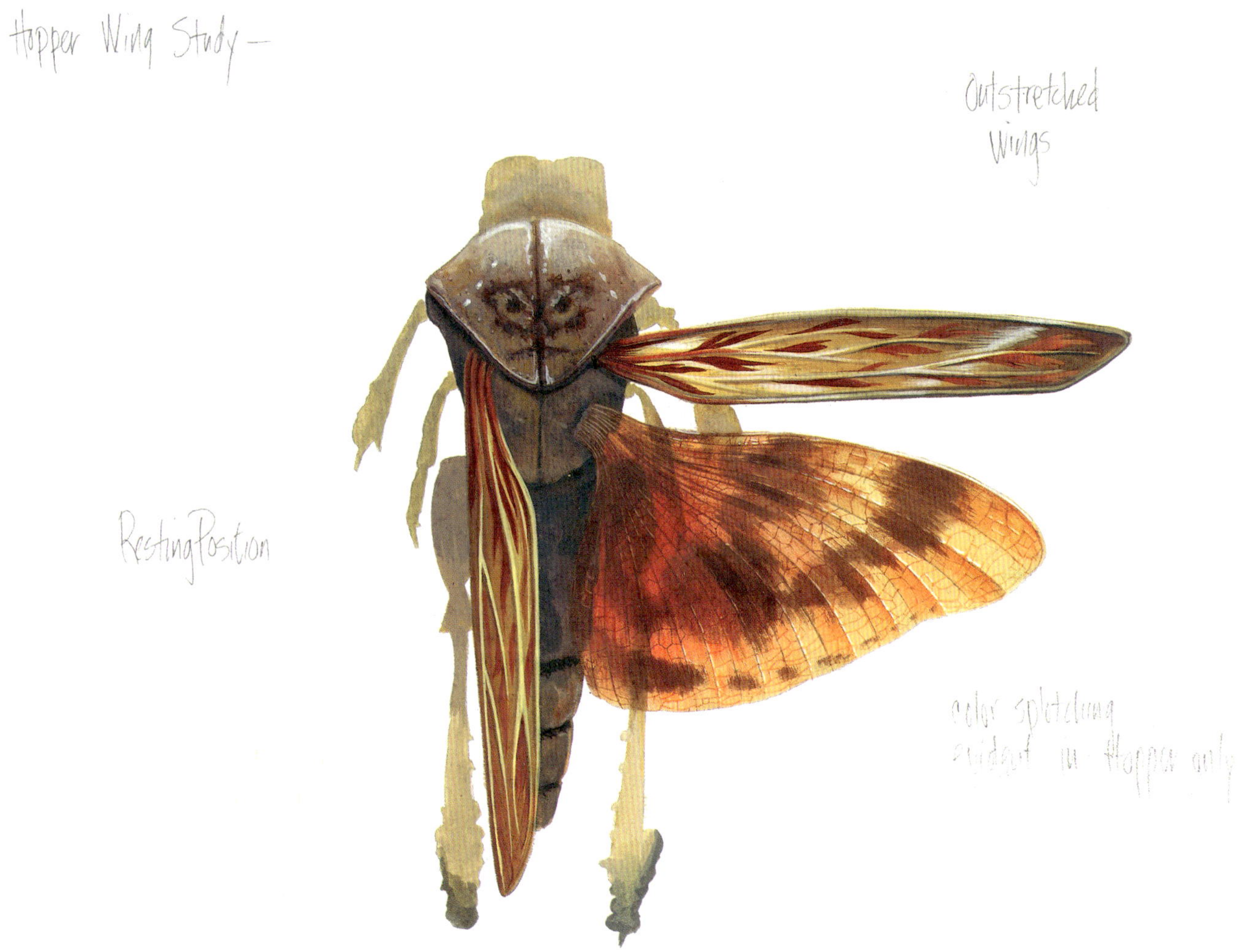

Tia Kratter
Hopper
A BUG'S LIFE
Acrylic
8½ x 11

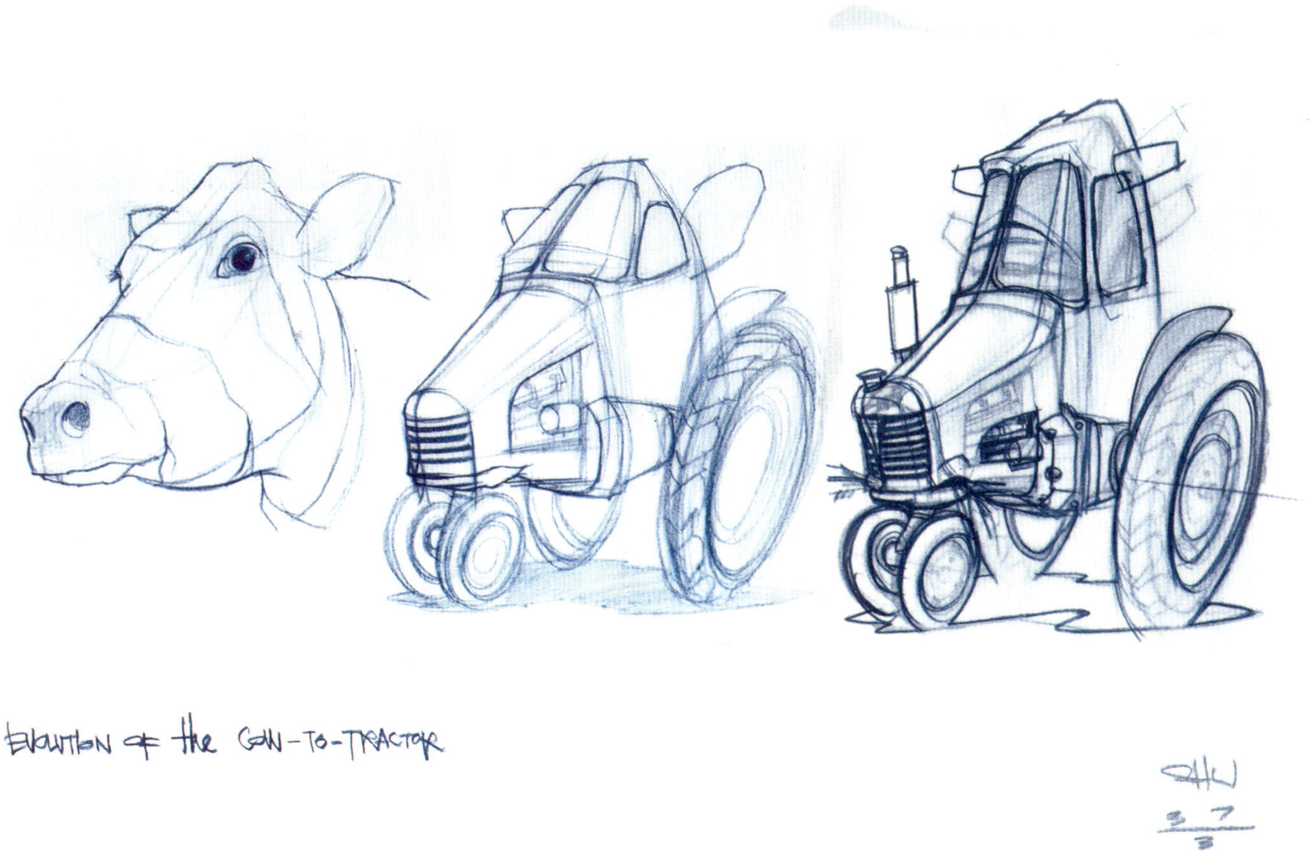

Jay Shuster
Evolution of the cow-to-tractor
CARS
Pencil
11 x 17

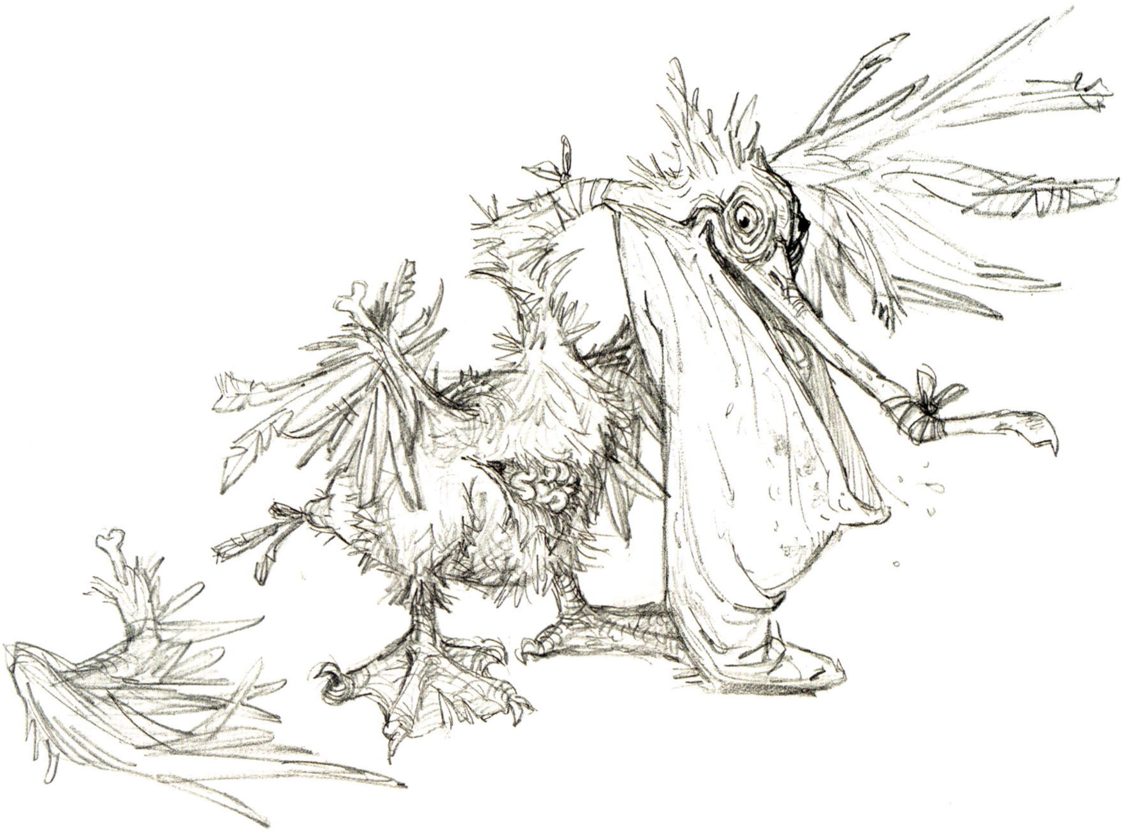

Geefwee Boedoe
Gerald
FINDING NEMO
Pencil
12½ x 17

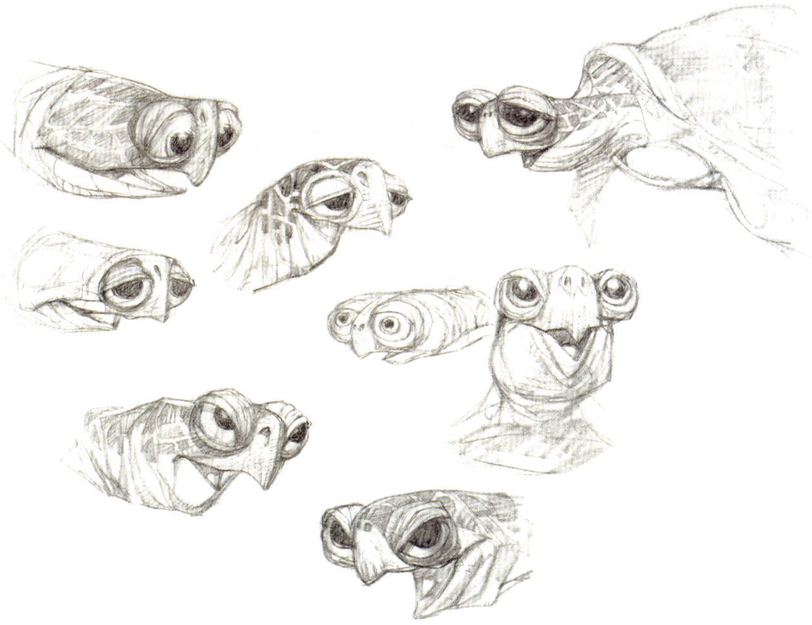

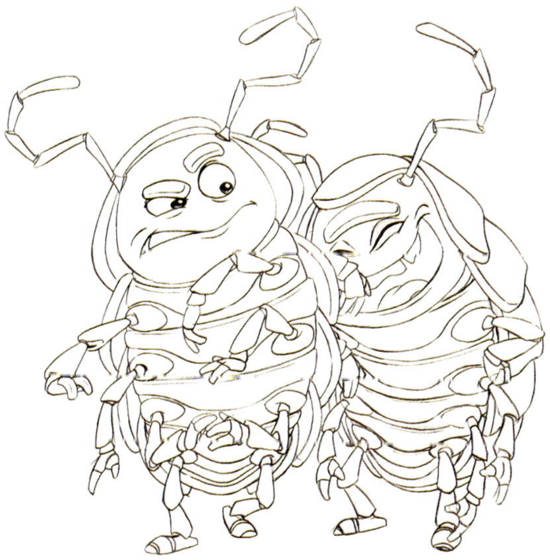

top:
Peter de Sève
Crush
FINDING NEMO
Pencil
14 x 17

above:
Dan Lee
Tuck and Roll
A BUG'S LIFE
Pencil
10½ x 13

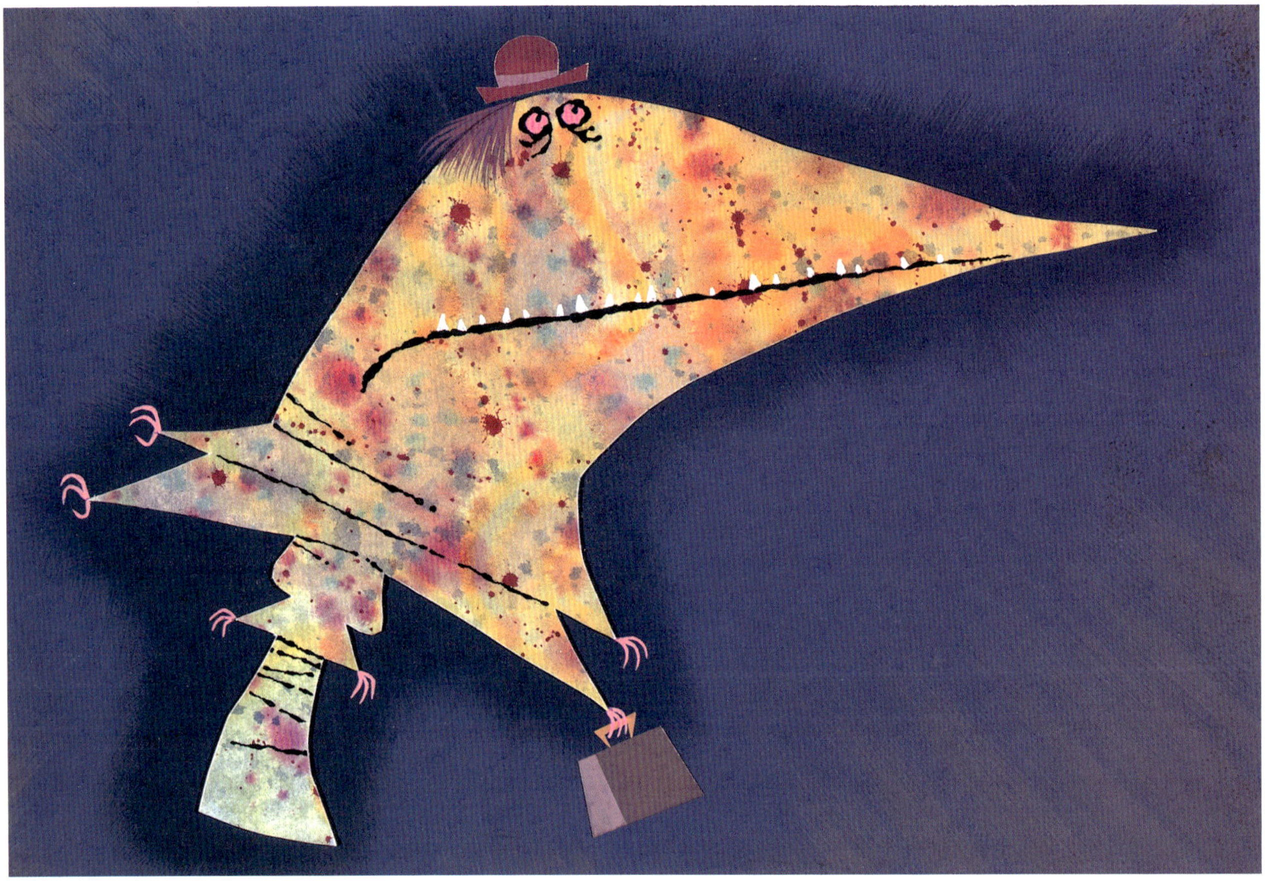

Geefwee Boedoe
Miscellaneous monster
MONSTERS, INC.
Mixed media
9¾ x 14

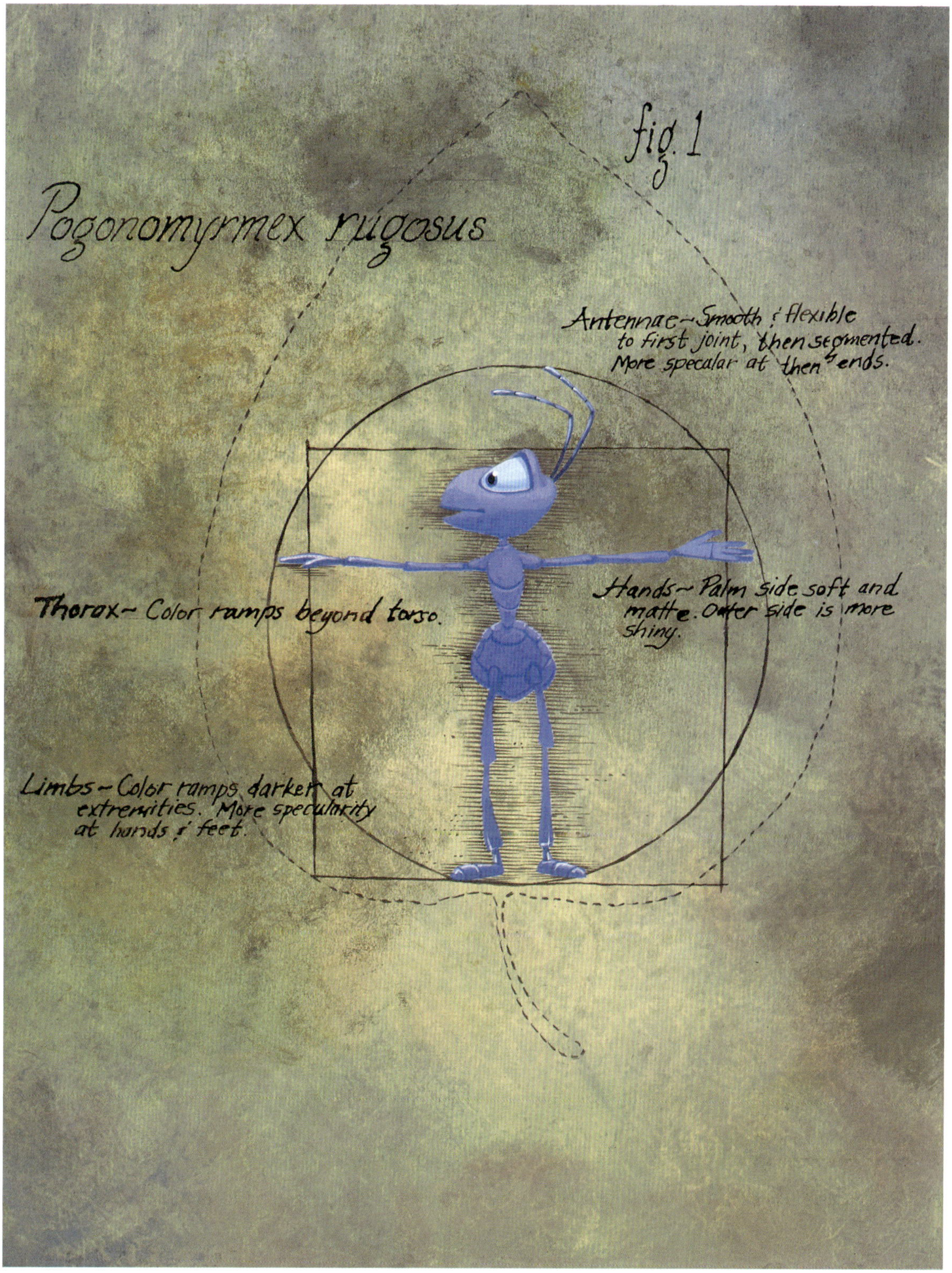

Tia Kratter
Flik
Layout by Bob Pauley
A BUG'S LIFE
Acrylic
11 x 8½

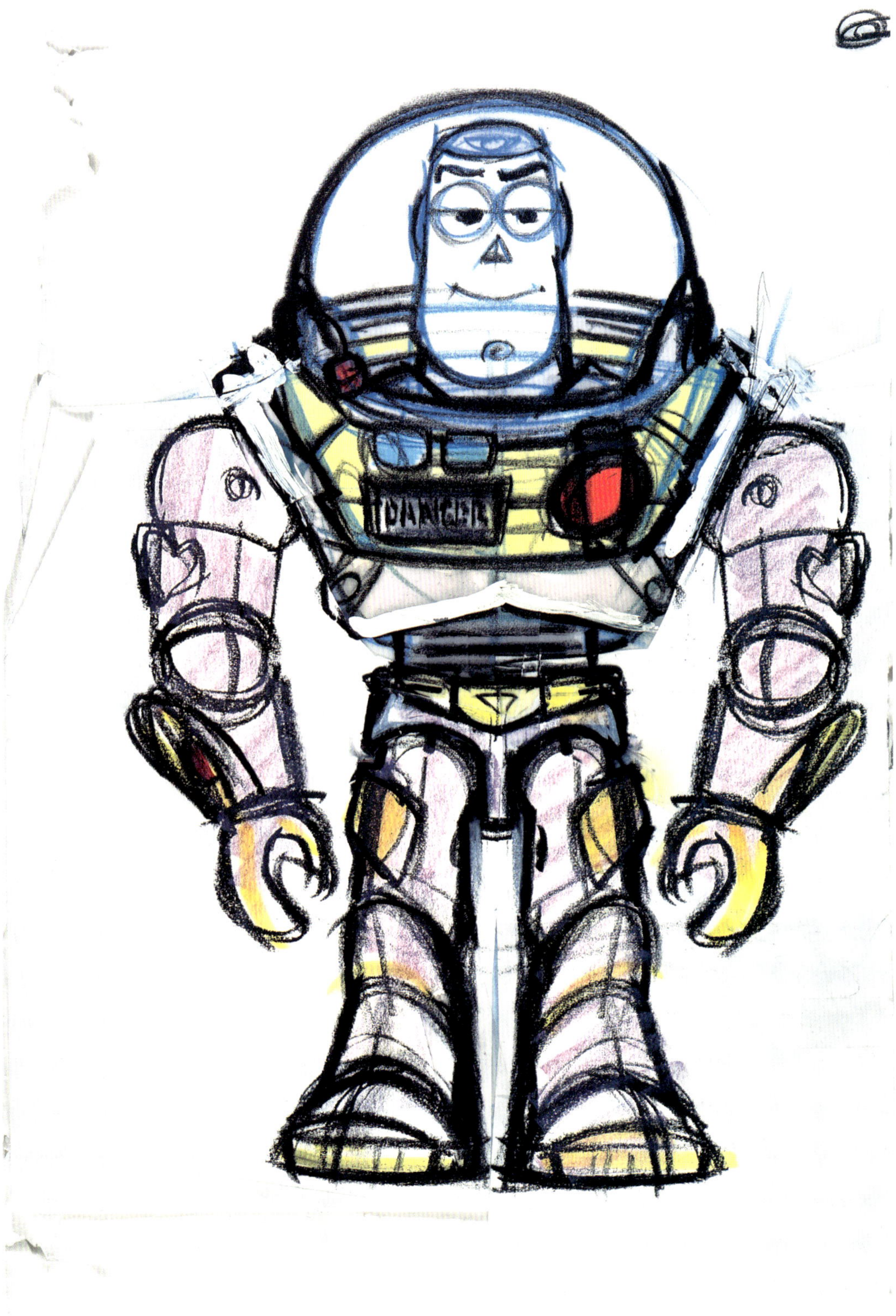
DANGER

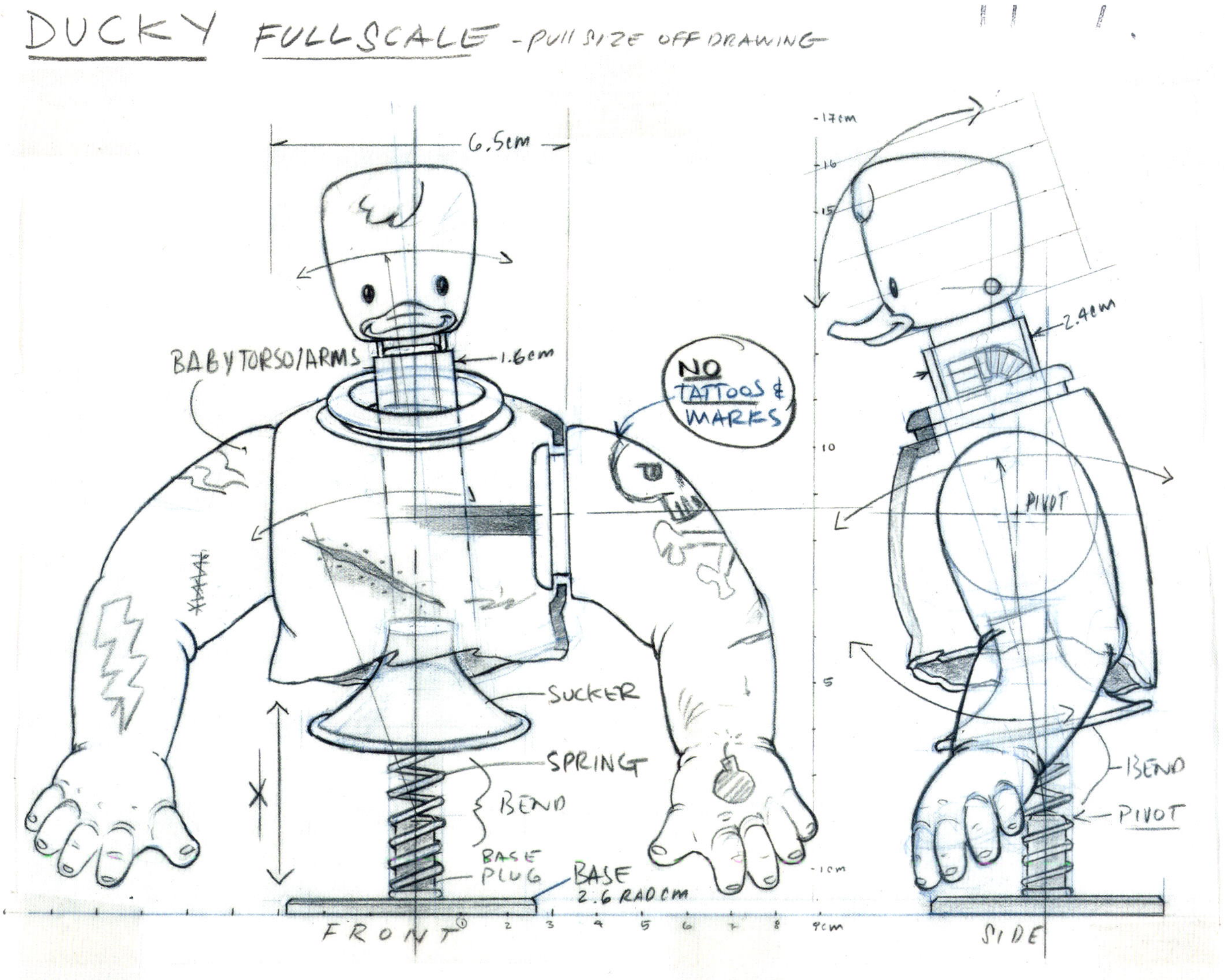

opposite:
Bob Pauley
Buzz
TOY STORY
Mixed media
13¾ x 9½

above:
Bob Pauley
Ducky model packet drawing
TOY STORY
Pencil
8½ x 11

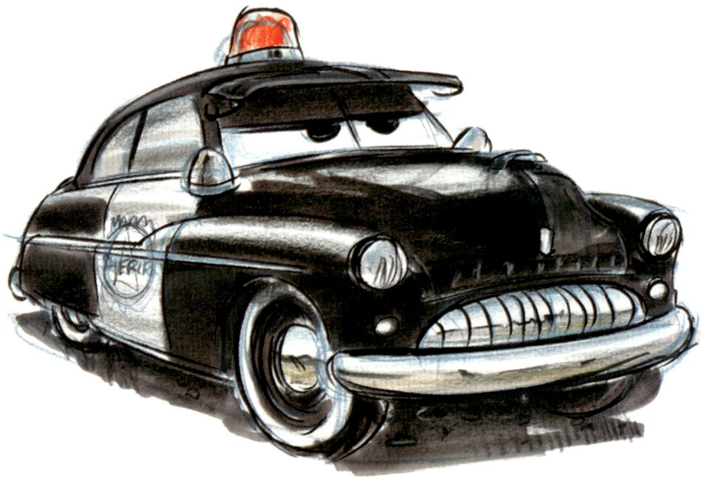

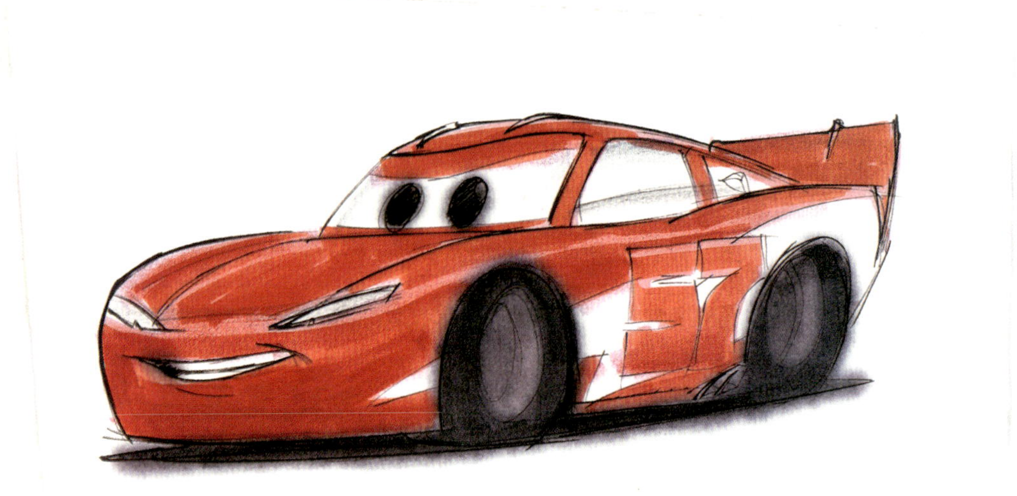

top:
Bob Pauley
Sheriff
CARS
Marker and pencil
11 x 17

above:
Bob Pauley
Lightning McQueen
CARS
Mixed media
11 x 17

opposite:
Bob Pauley
Woody and Buzz
TOY STORY
Pencil
16¾ x 13¾

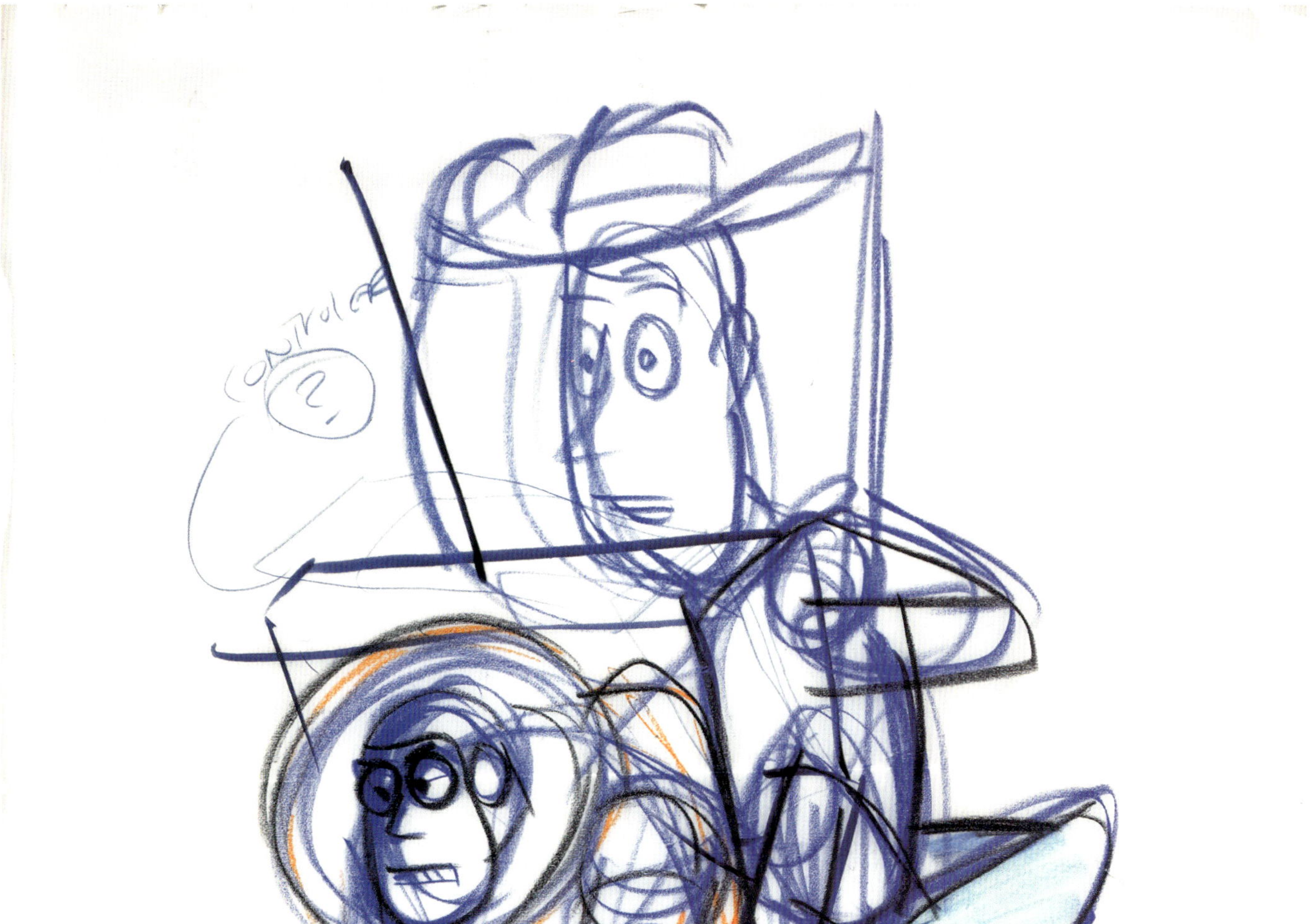

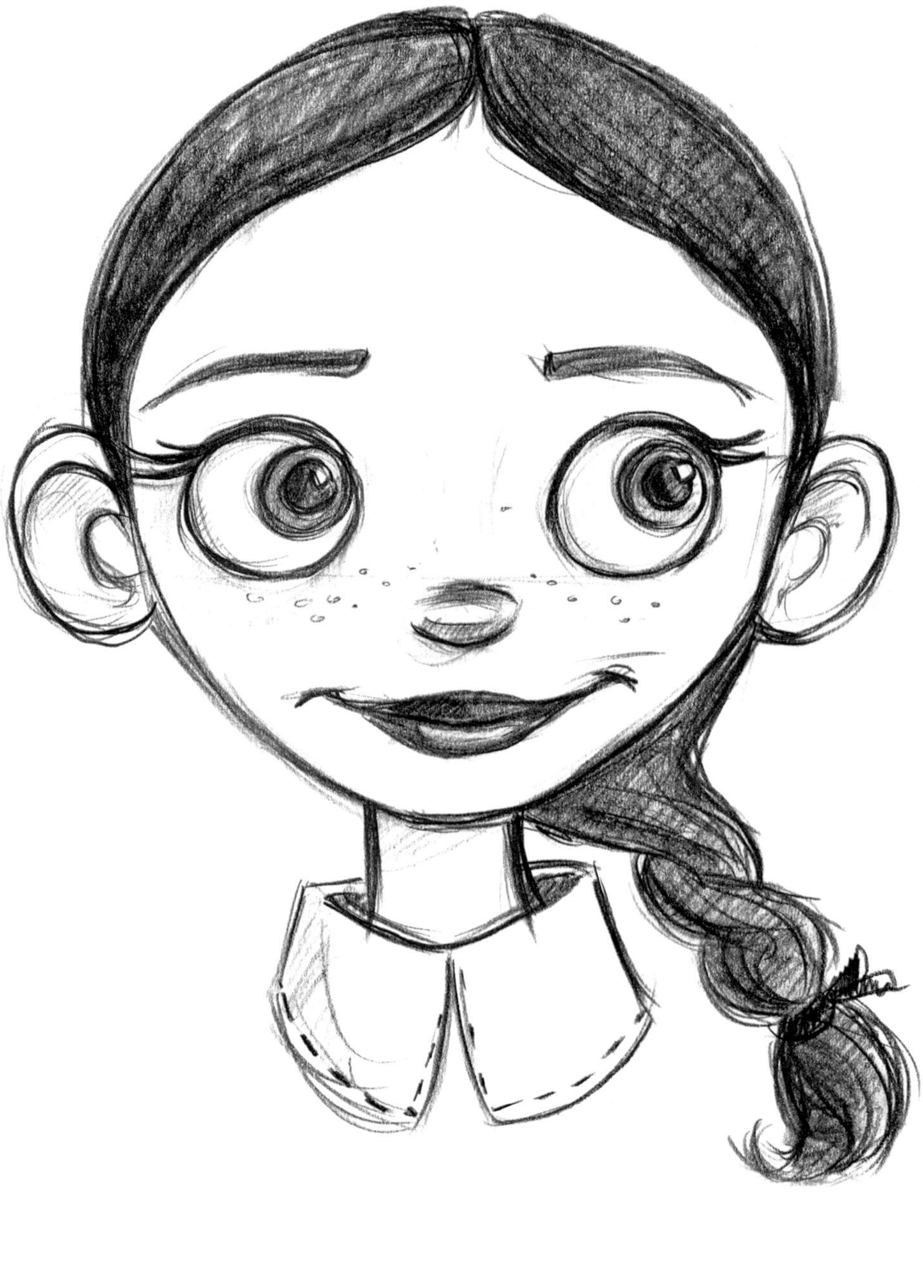

Jill Culton
Jessie
TOY STORY 2
Pencil
11 x 8½

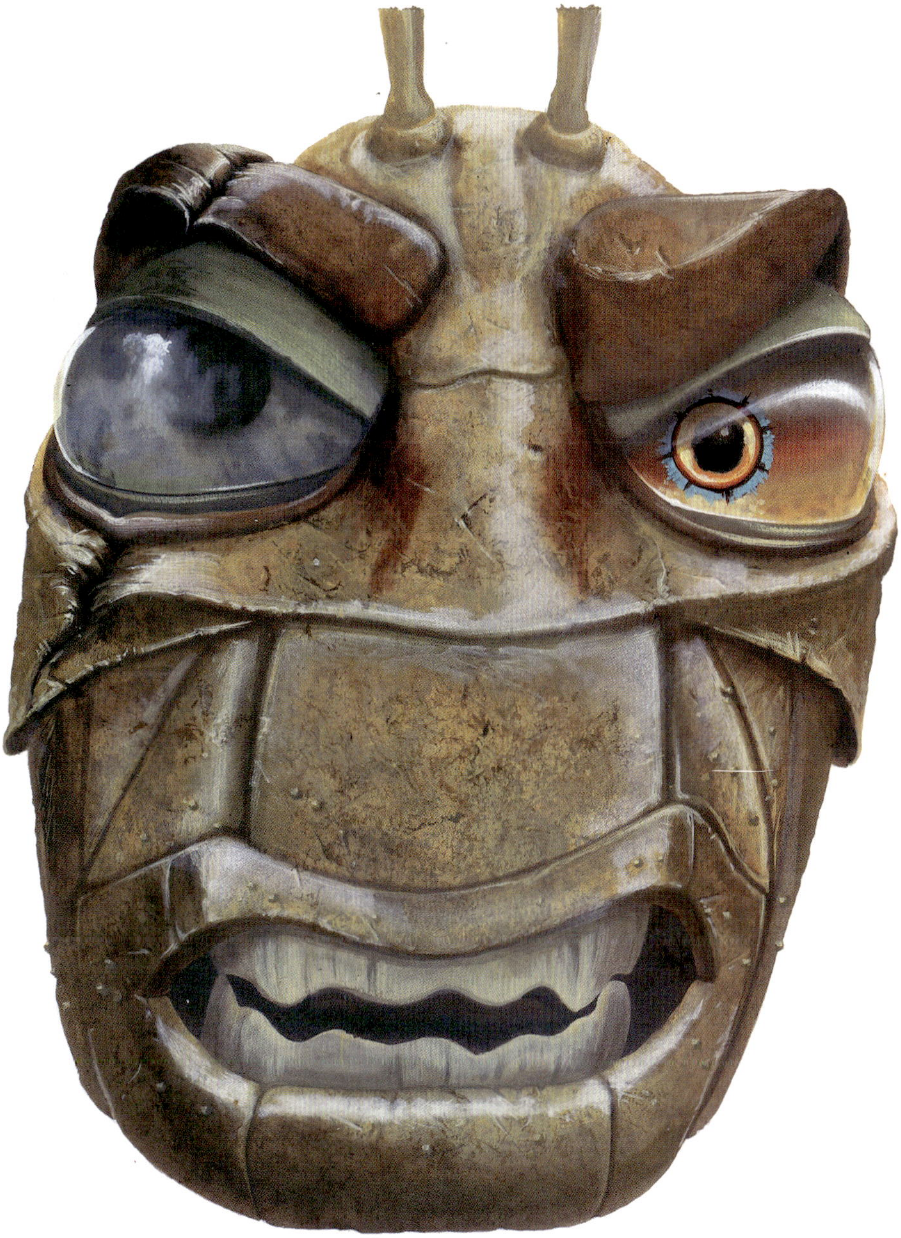

Tia Kratter
Hopper
Layout by Bob Pauley
A BUG'S LIFE
Acrylic
11 x 8½

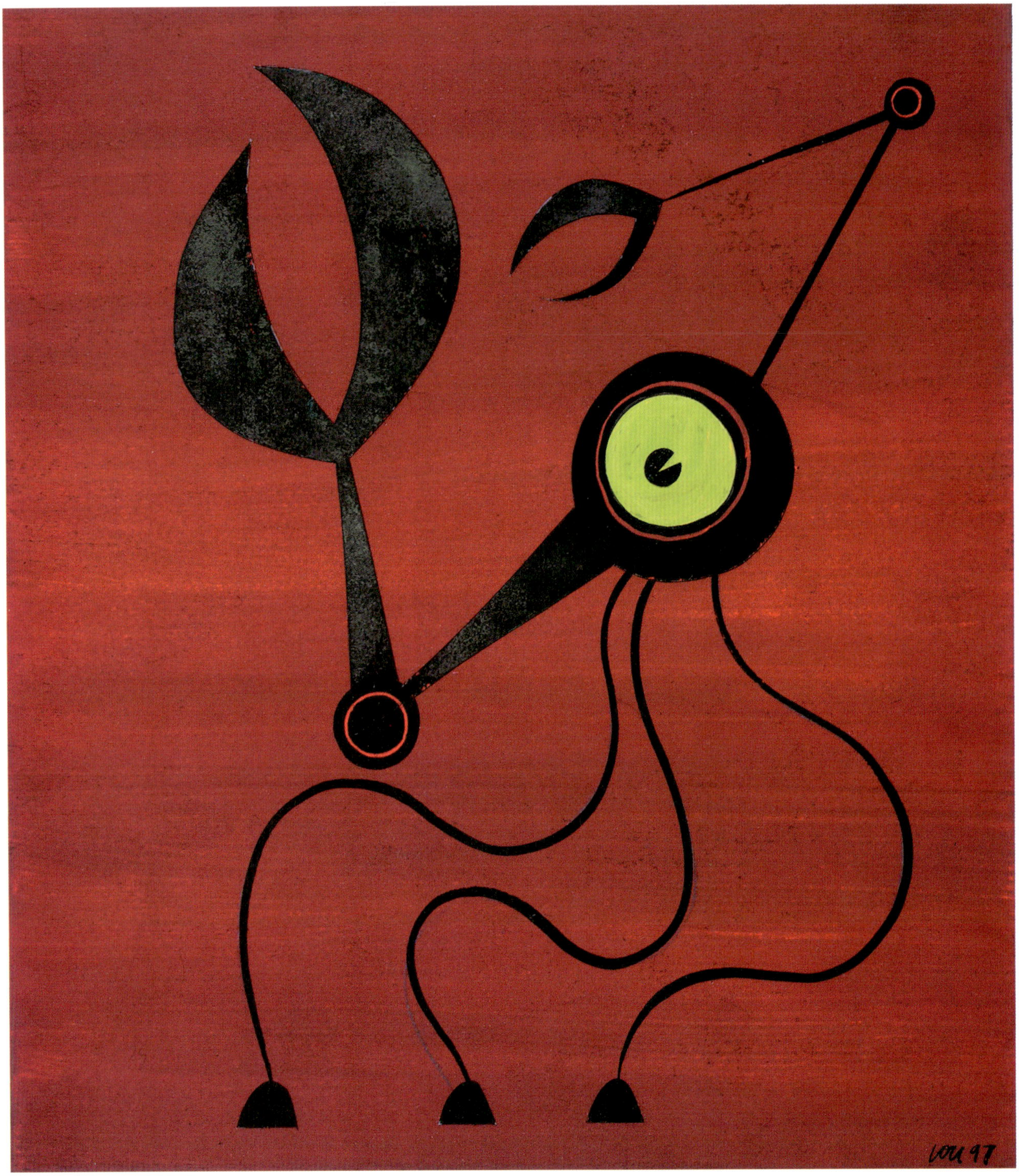

Lou Romano
Miscellaneous monster
MONSTERS, INC.
Gouache
9½ x 8⅝

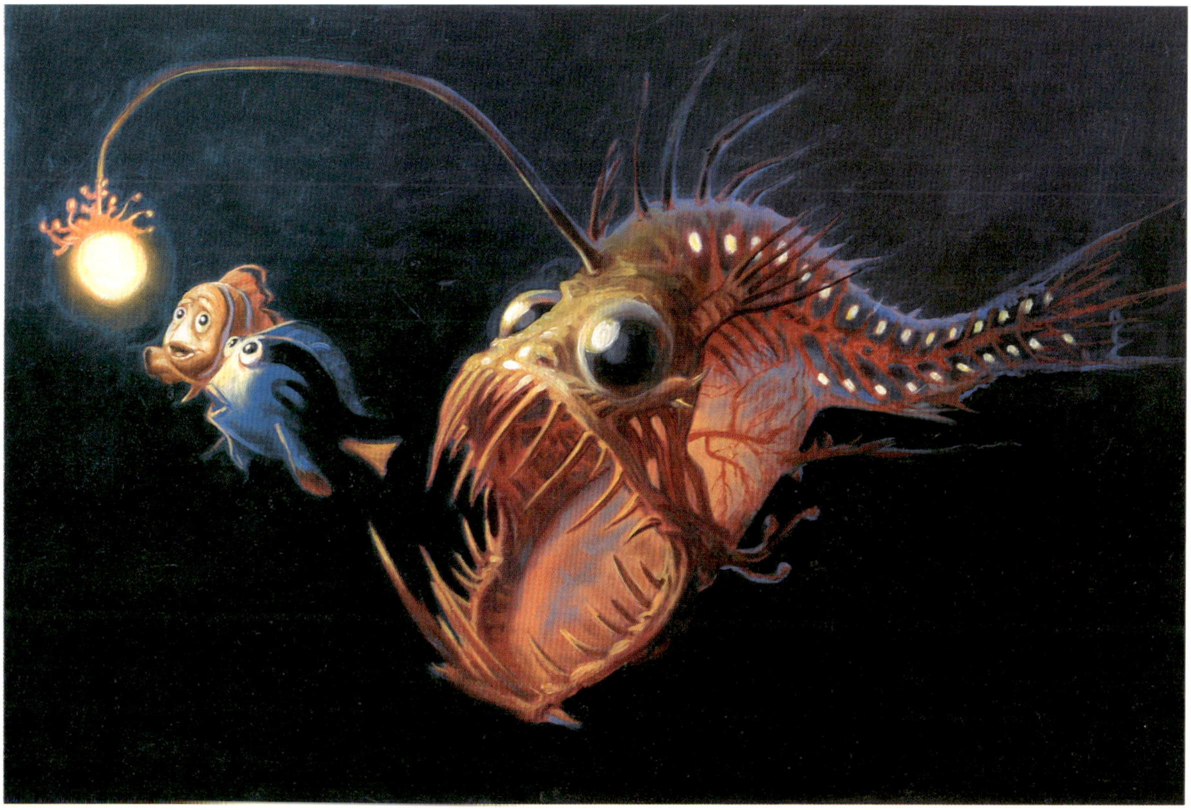

Randy Berrett
Anglerfish
FINDING NEMO
Oil
13 x 18½

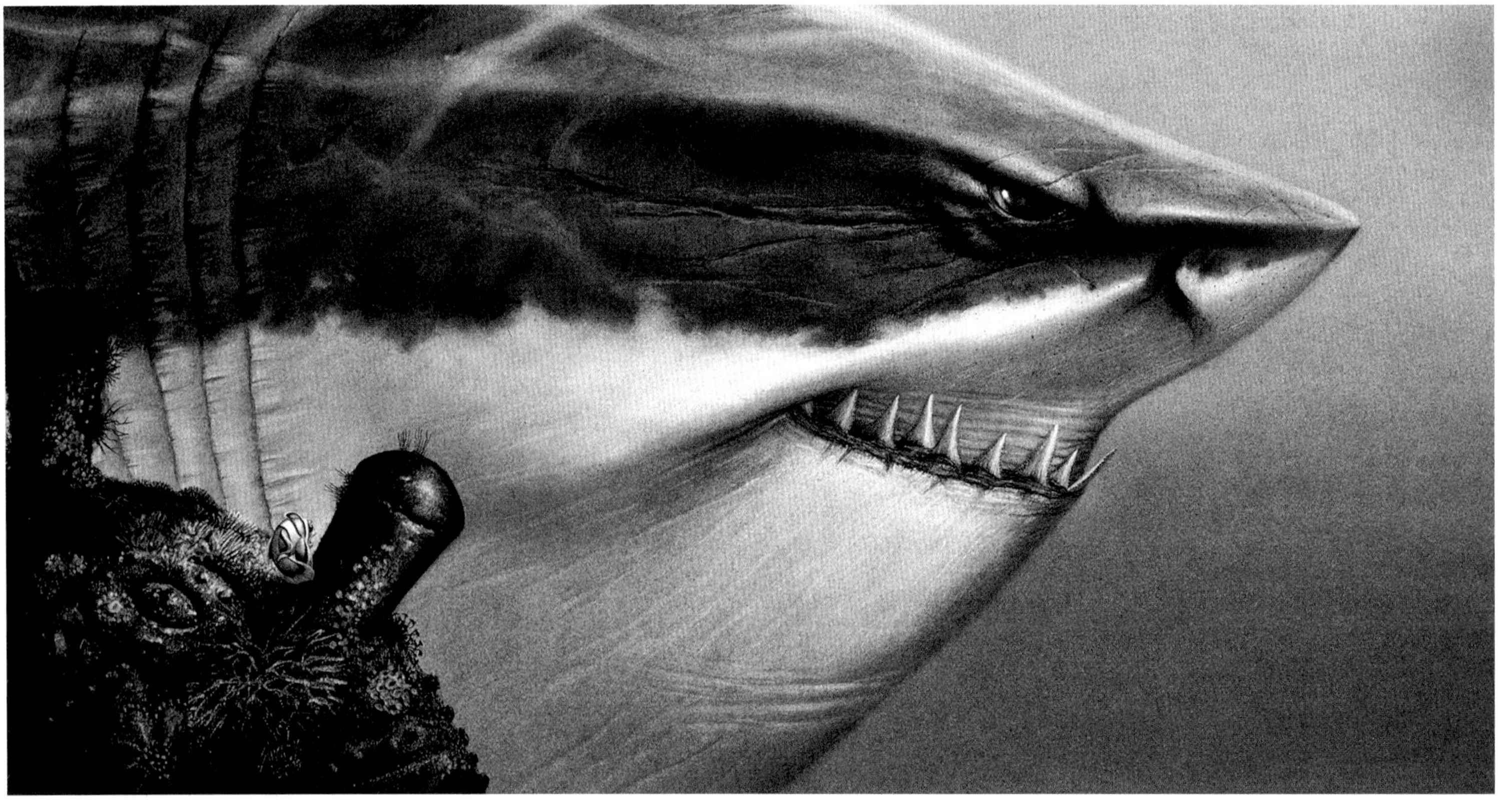

Simón Varela
Sharks
FINDING NEMO
Charcoal
17 x 29

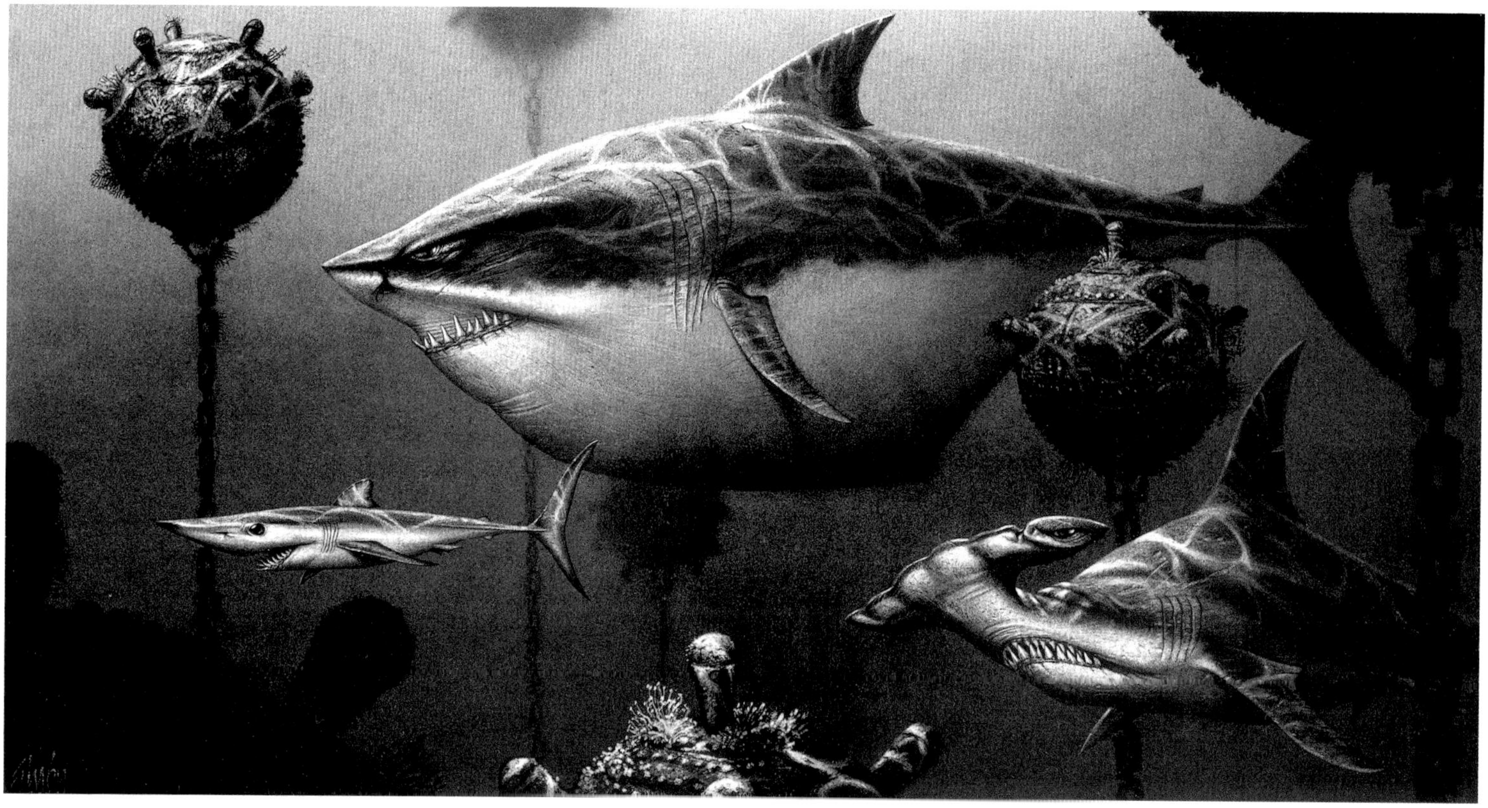

Simón Varela
Sharks
FINDING NEMO
Charcoal
17 x 29

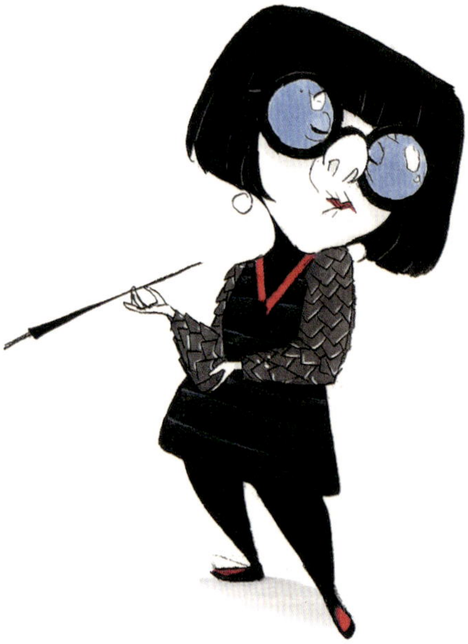

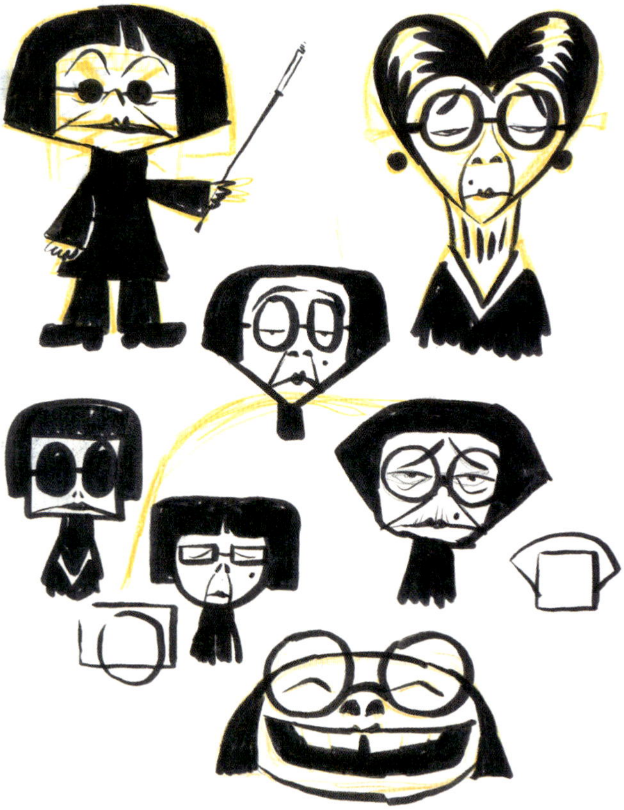

above, left:
Tony Fucile
Edna Mode (aka "E")
THE INCREDIBLES
Marker and pencil
11 x 8½

above, right:
Lou Romano
Edna Mode (aka "E")
THE INCREDIBLES
Marker
9½ x 8

opposite:
Teddy Newton
Edna Mode (aka "E")
THE INCREDIBLES
Collage
11 x 8½

E

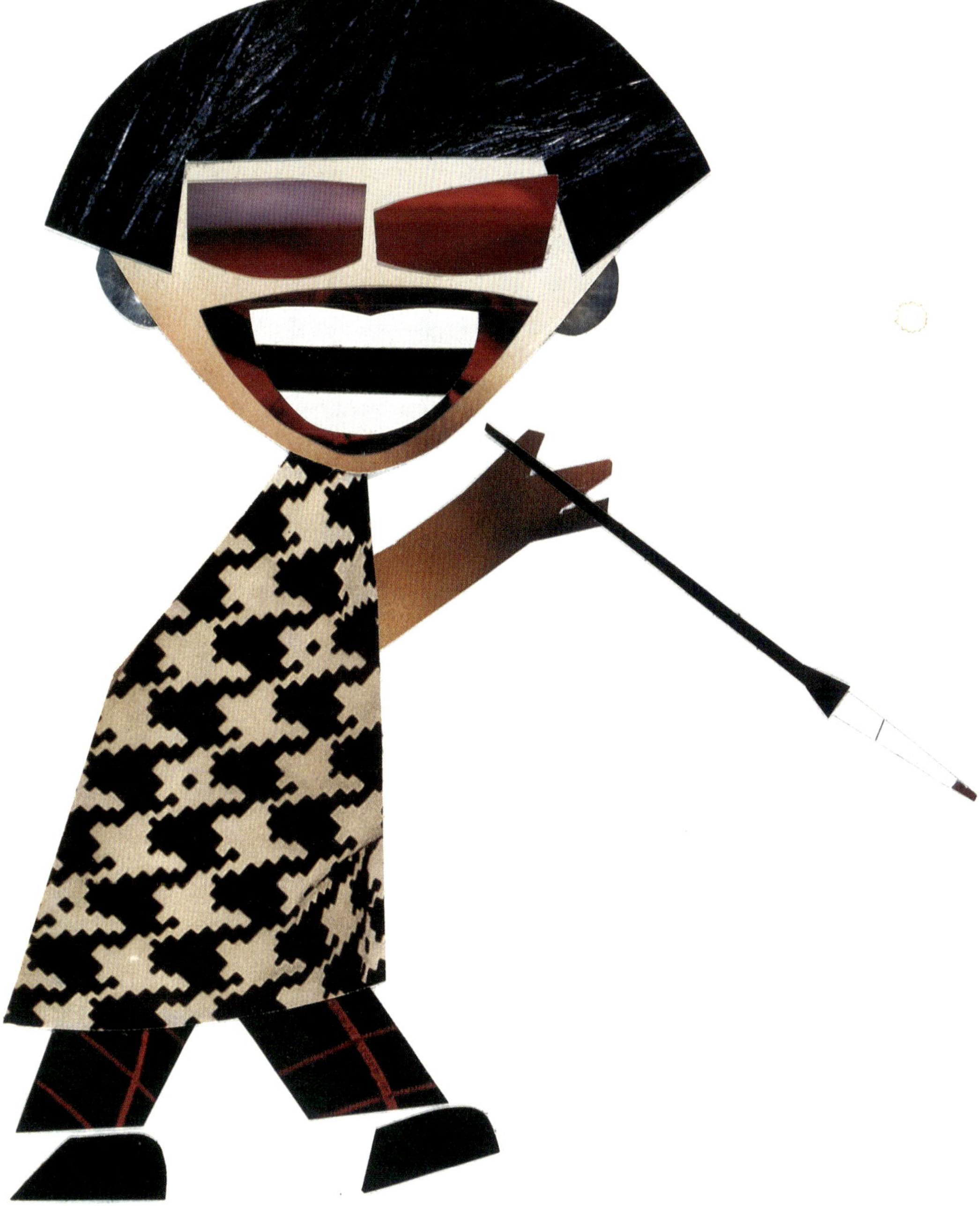

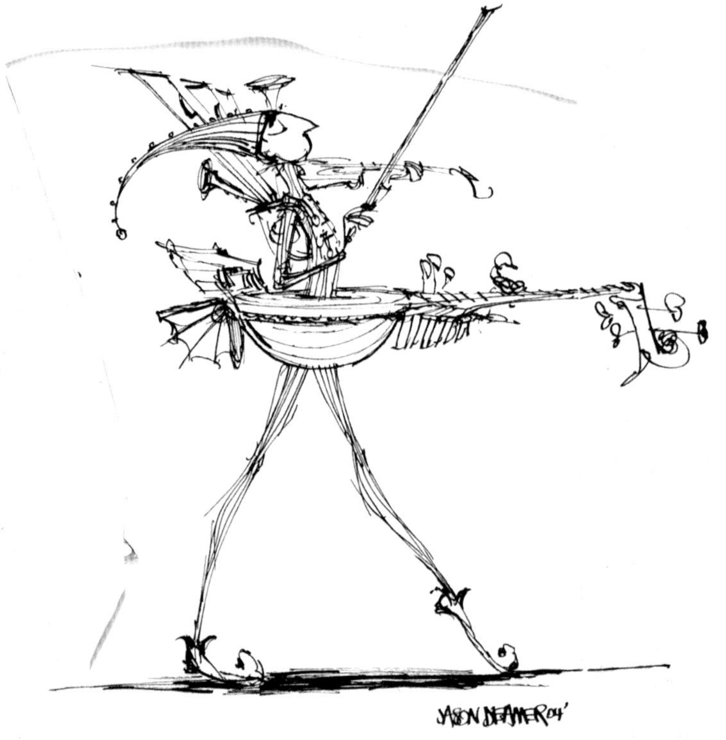

Jason Deamer
Treble
ONE MAN BAND
Mixed media
17 x 12½

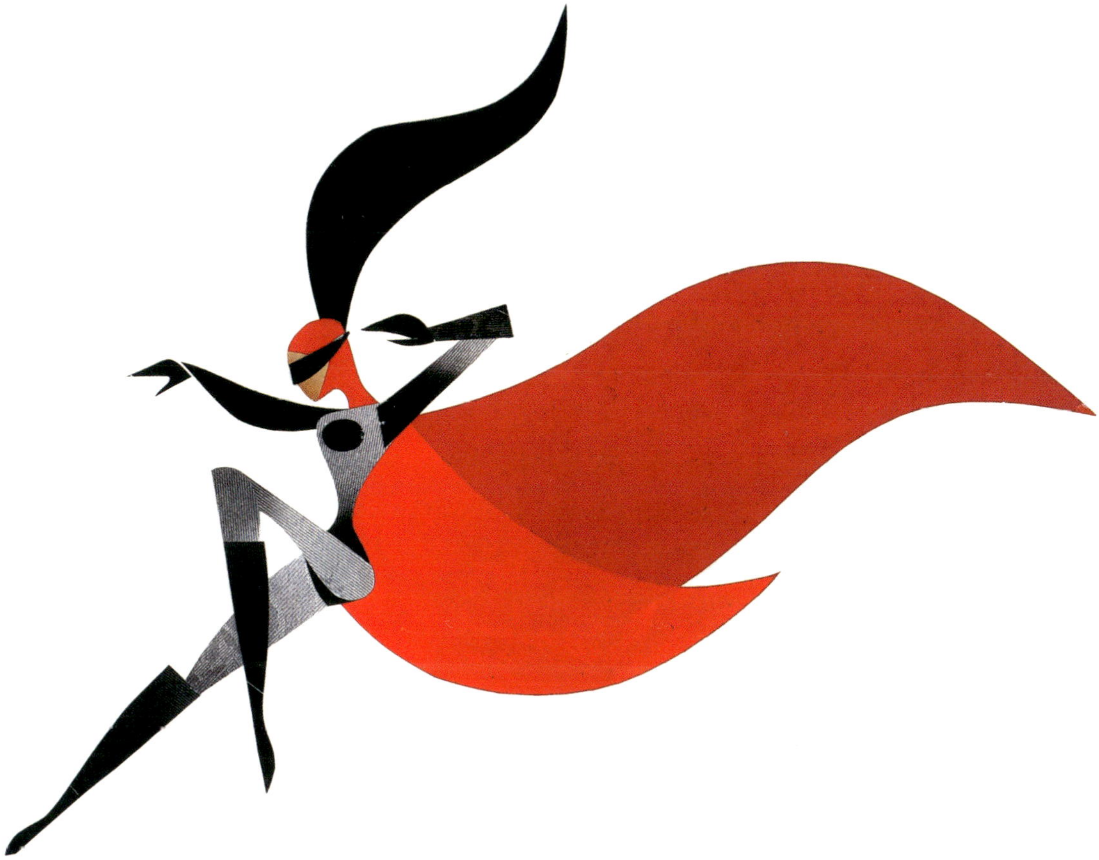

Teddy Newton
Miscellaneous superhero
THE INCREDIBLES
Collage
15 x 20

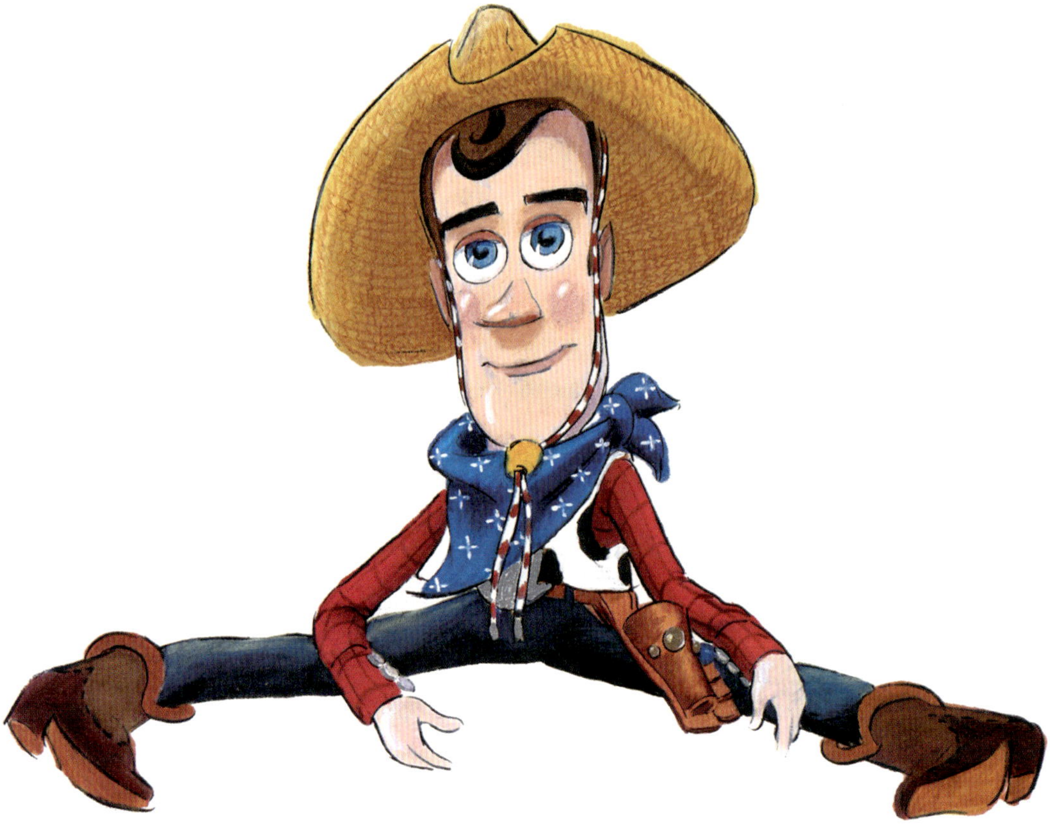

Bud Luckey
Woody
Color by Ralph Eggleston
TOY STORY
Mixed media
8½ x 11

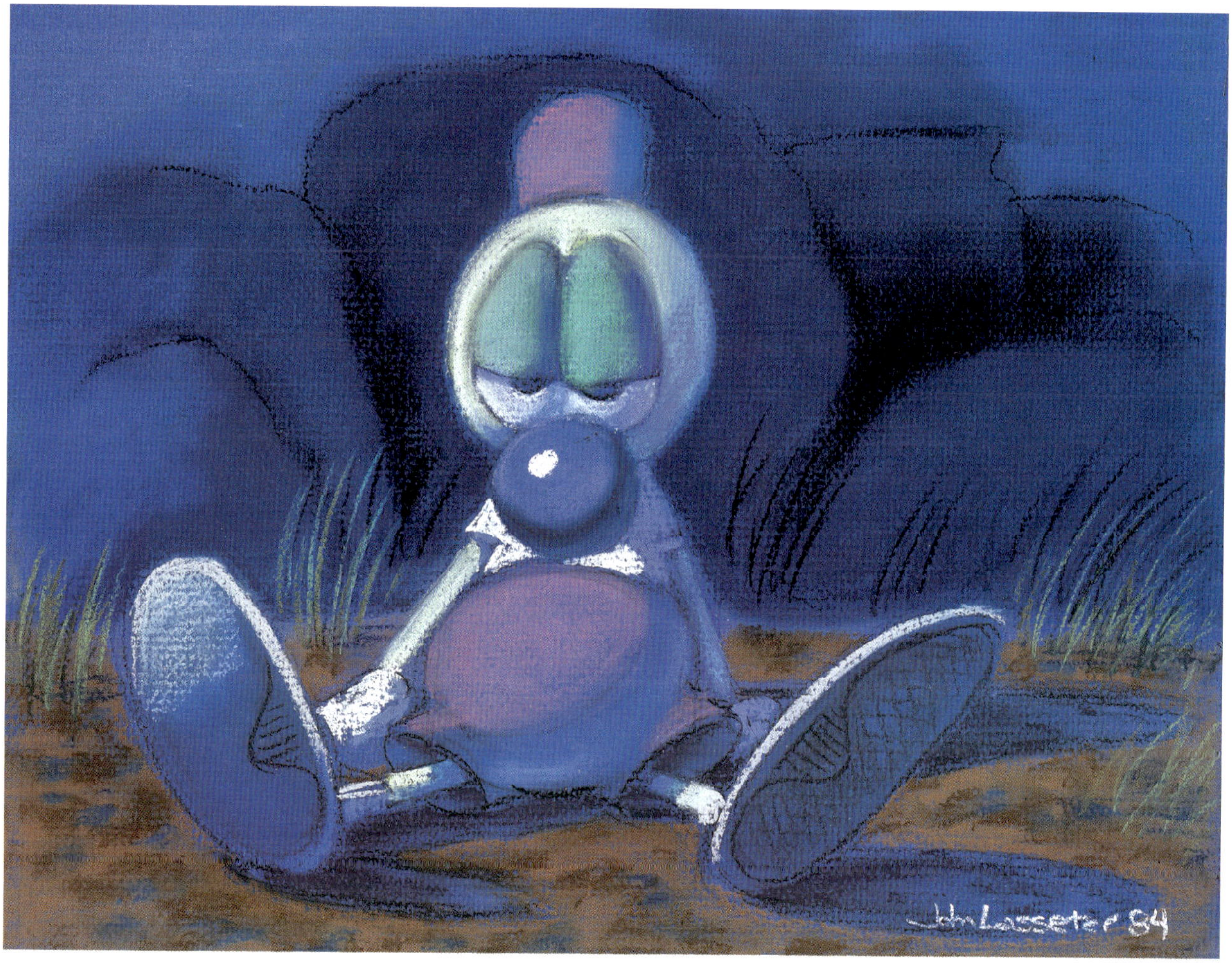

John Lasseter
André
THE ADVENTURES OF ANDRÉ & WALLY B.
Pastel
10 x 13

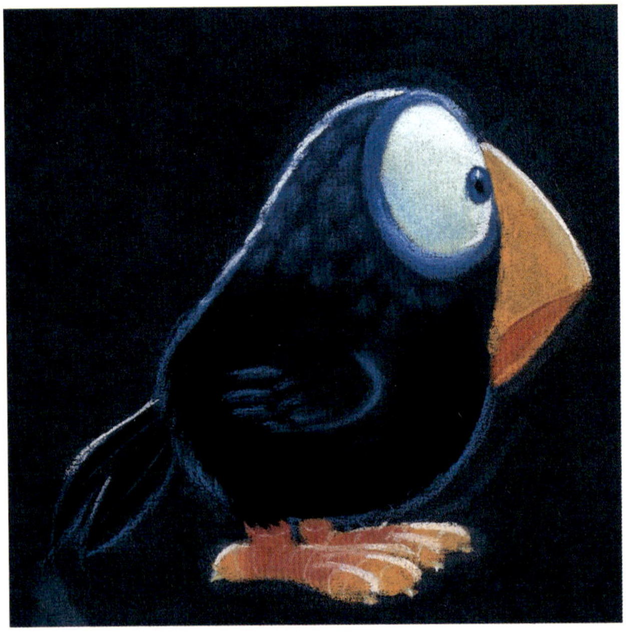

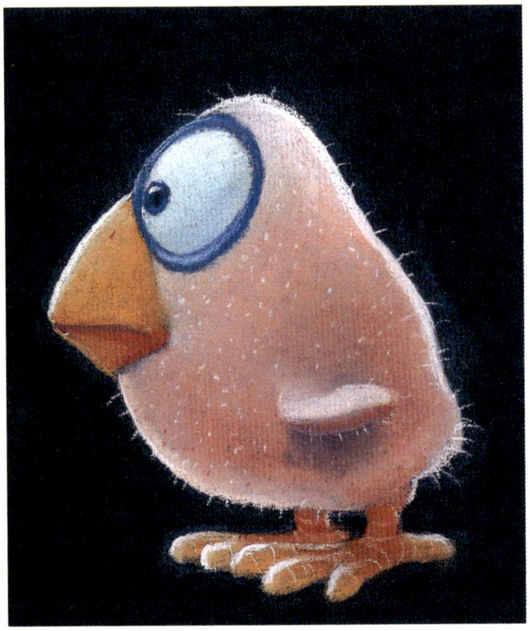

Ralph Eggleston
Preproduction sketch
FOR THE BIRDS
Pastel
11 x 17

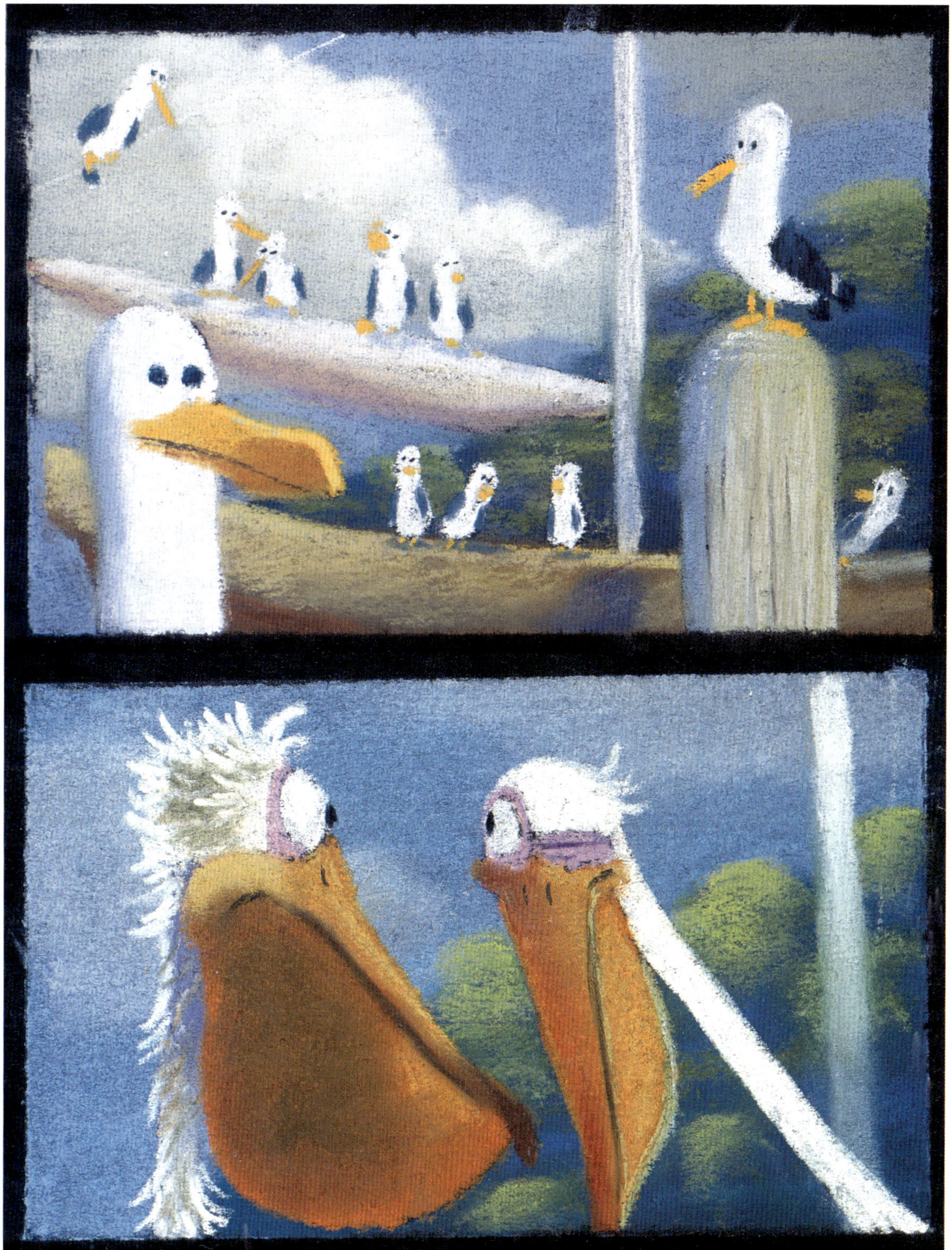

Ralph Eggleston
Sequence pastel: Pelicans
FINDING NEMO
Pastel
4⅝ x 6 (each)

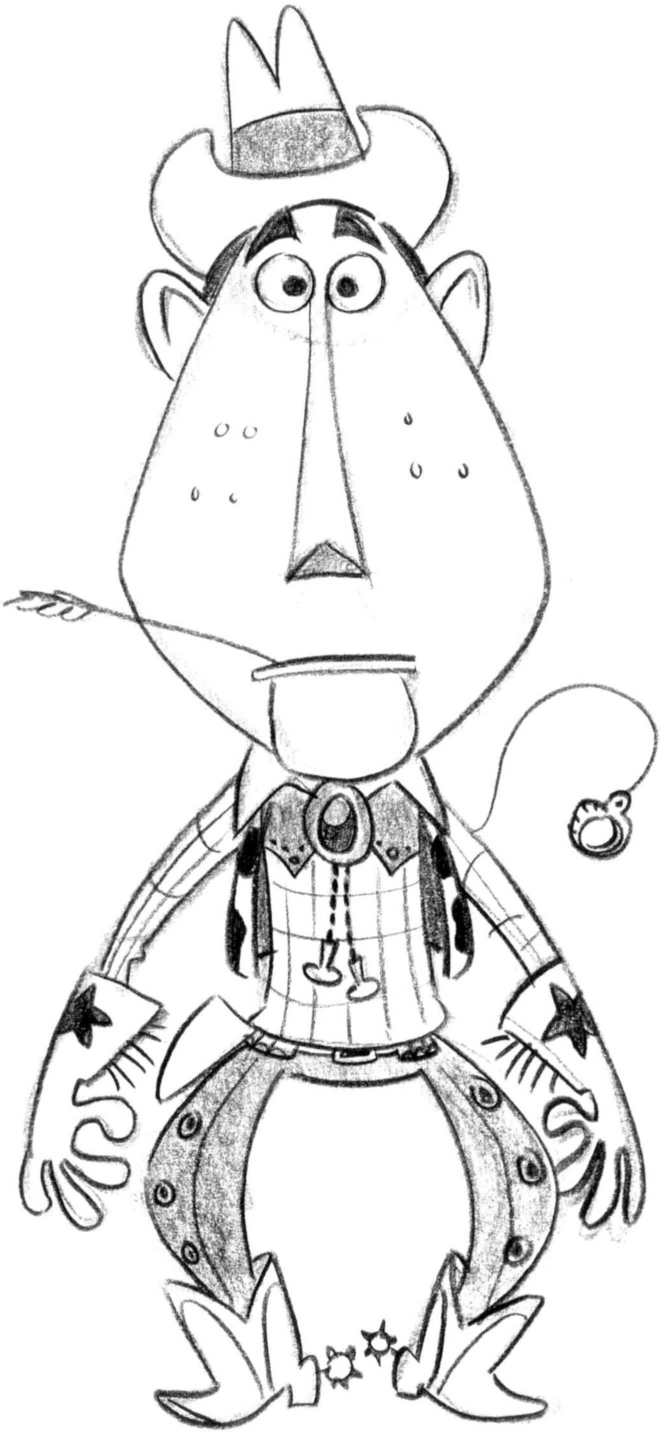

Jeff Pidgeon
Woody
TOY STORY
Pencil
10½ x 5⅝

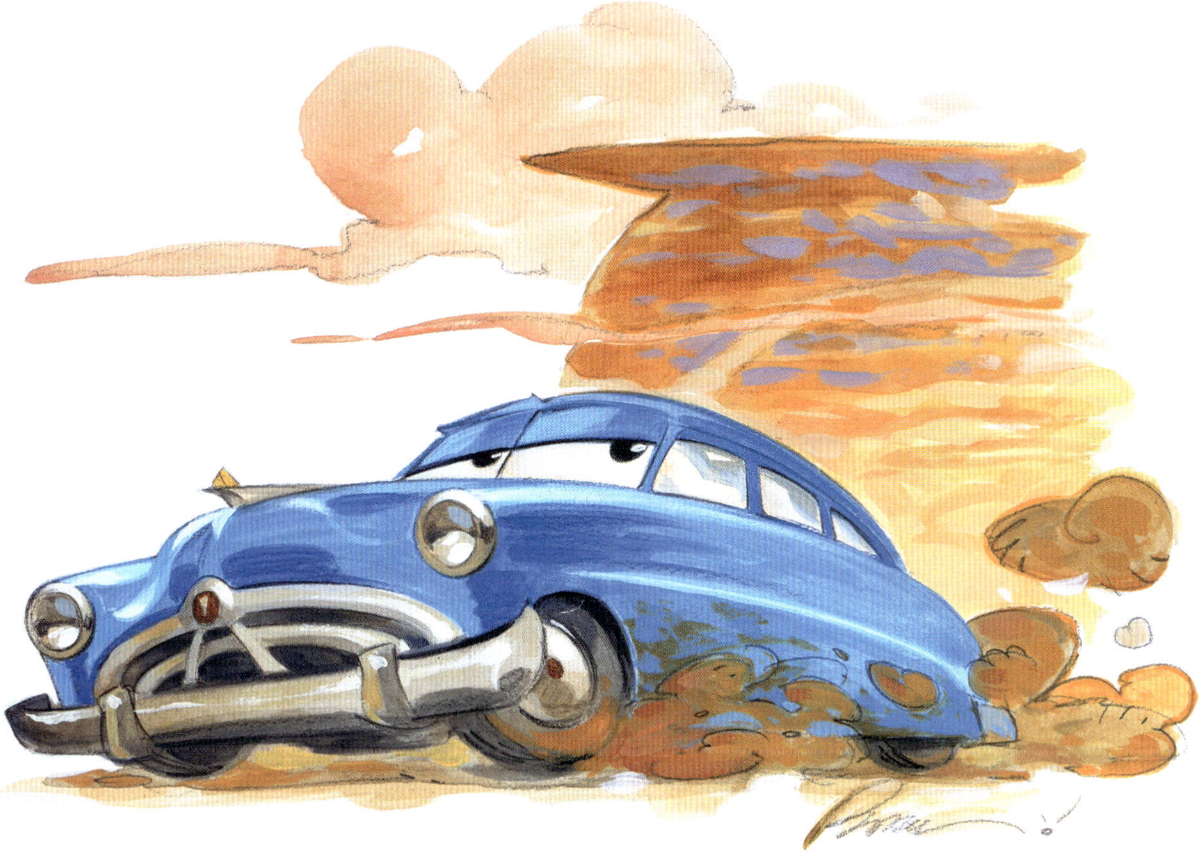

Steve Purcell
Doc Hudson
CARS
Acrylic
8½ x 11

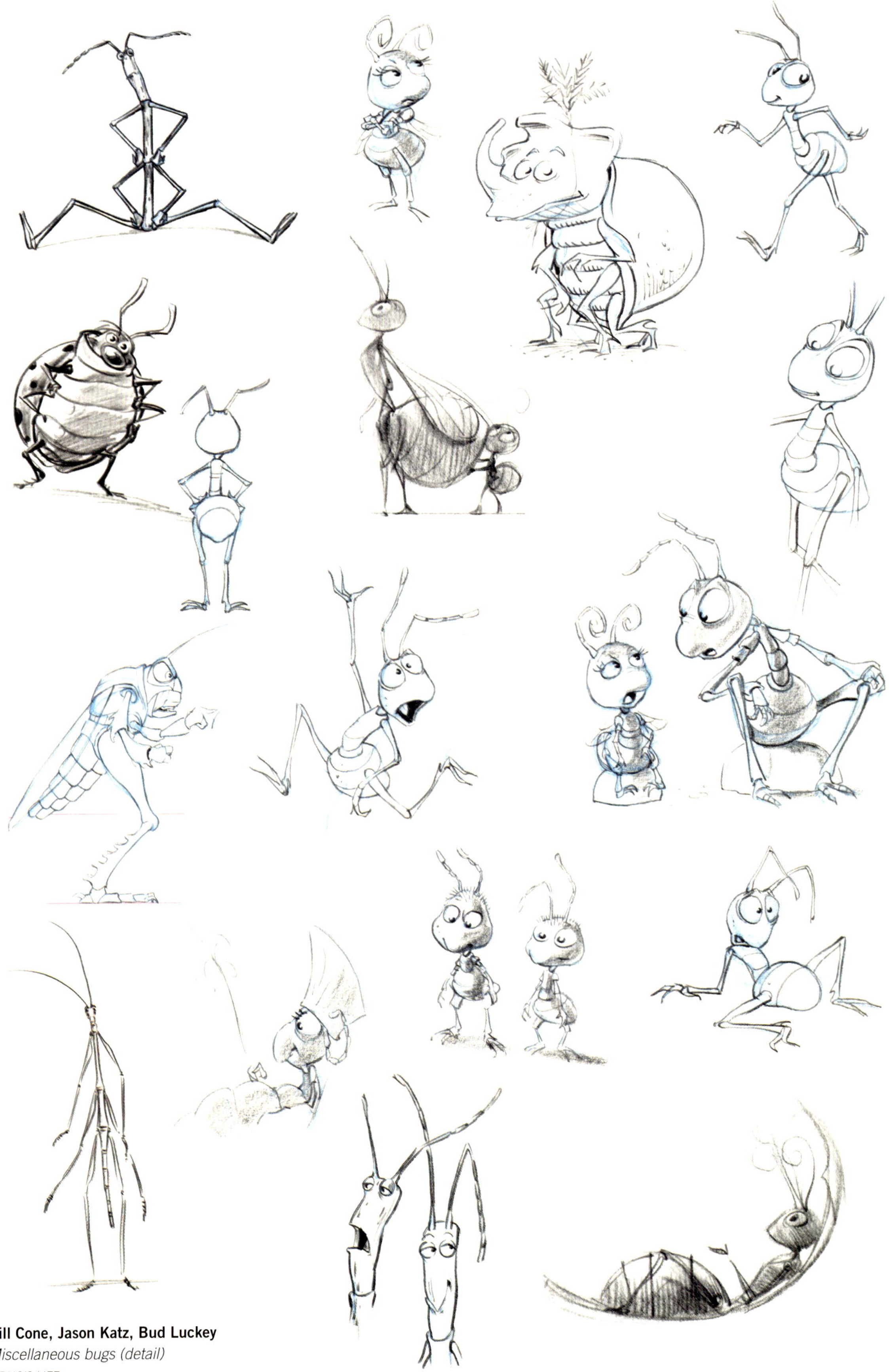

Bill Cone, Jason Katz, Bud Luckey
Miscellaneous bugs (detail)
A BUG'S LIFE
Digital wall application. Originals, pencil and ink
Dimensions vary

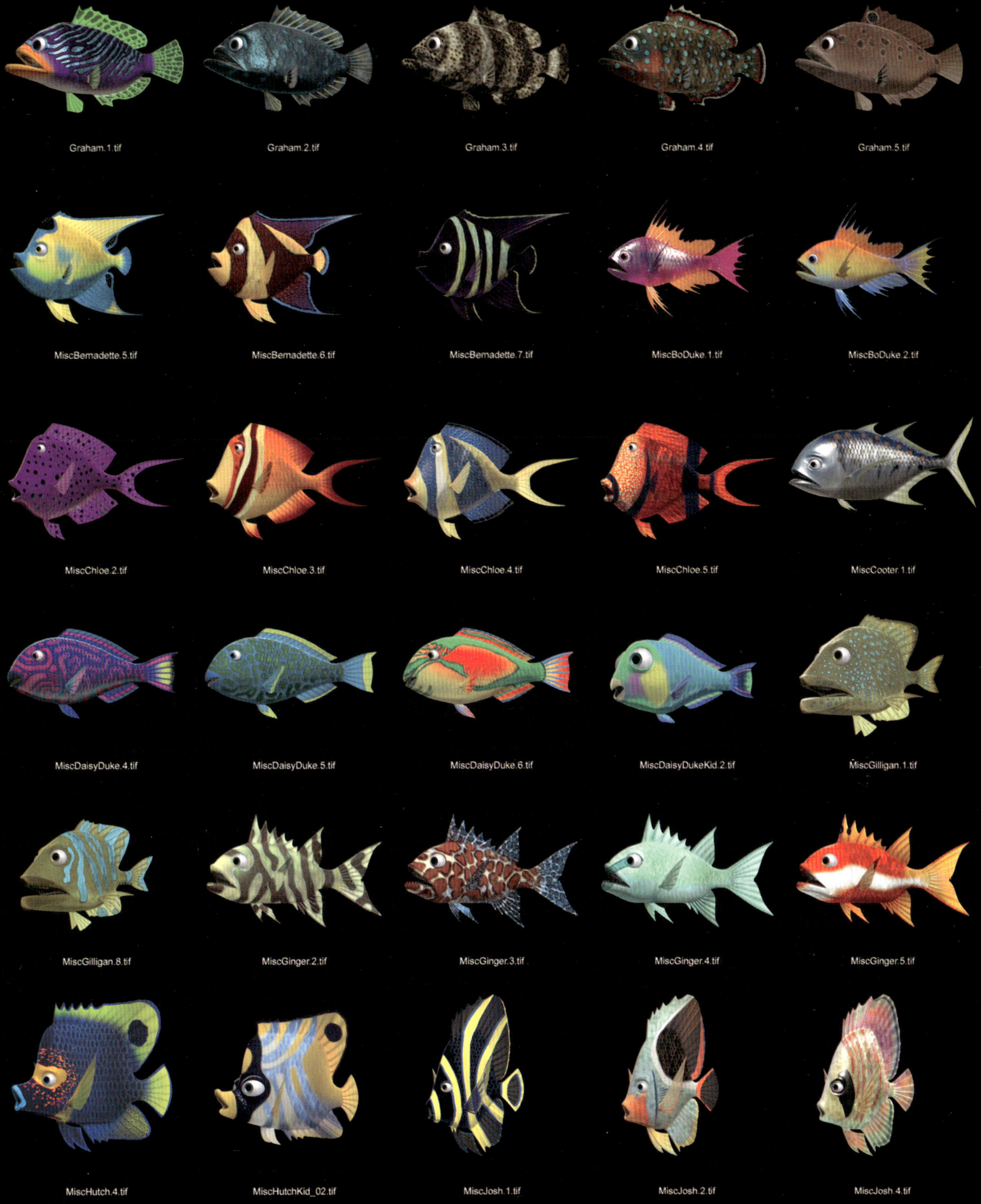

Chris Bernardi, Bert Berry,
Jamie Frye, Yvonne Herbst,
Laura Phillips, Belinda van Valkenburg
Miscellaneous fish (detail)
FINDING NEMO
Digital wall application

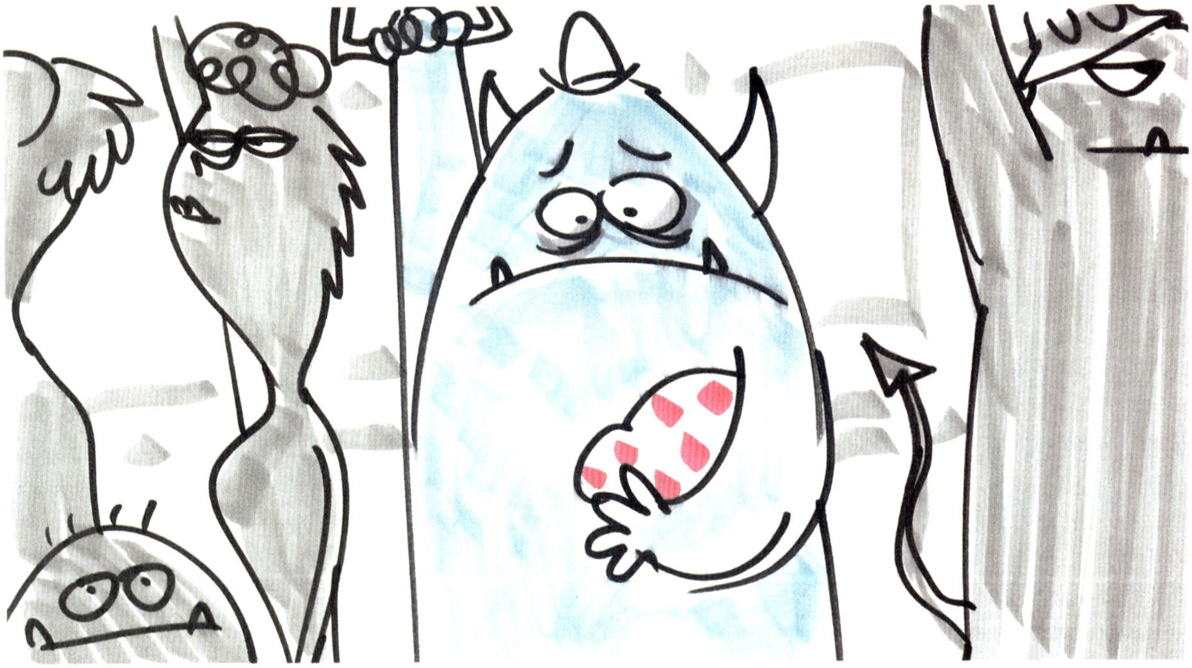

Ricky Nierva
Story sketch: Sullivan and Boo
MONSTERS, INC.
Marker
5½ x 10

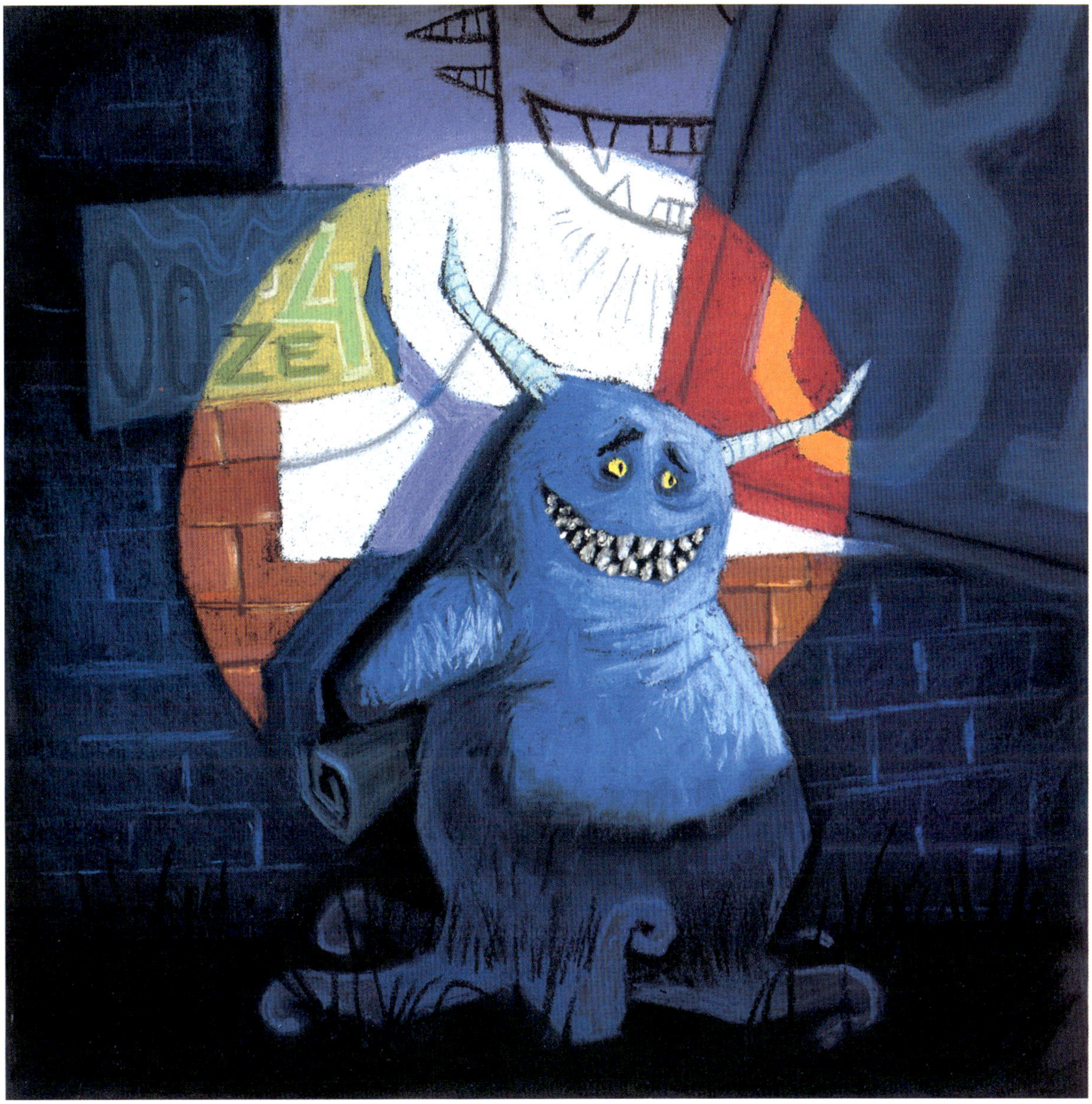

Geefwee Boedoe
Sullivan
MONSTERS, INC.
Pastel
10½ x 10⅝

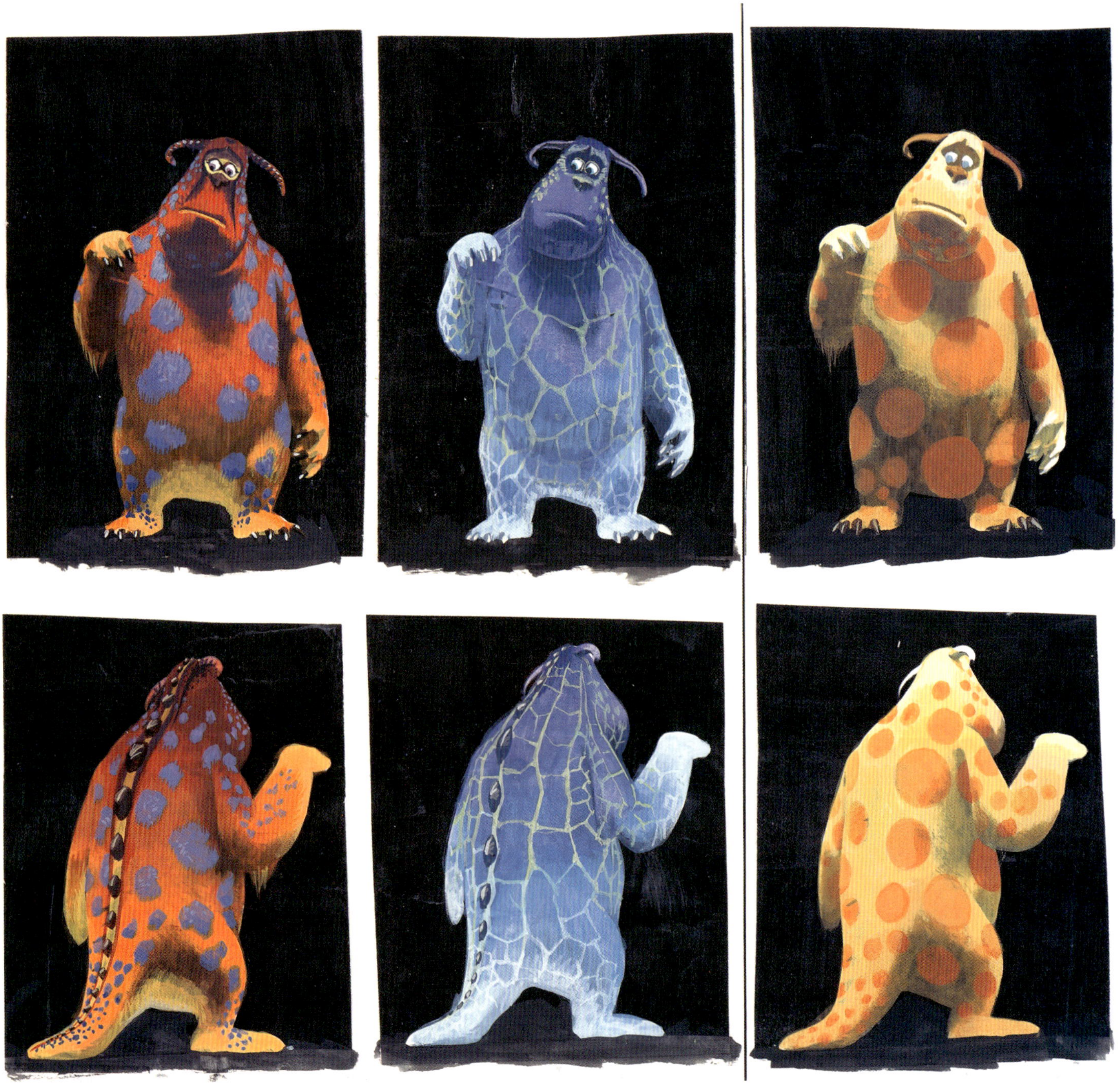

Tia Kratter
Sullivan fur pattern studies
Maquette by Jerome Ranft
MONSTERS, INC.
Mixed media
10½ x 11⅛

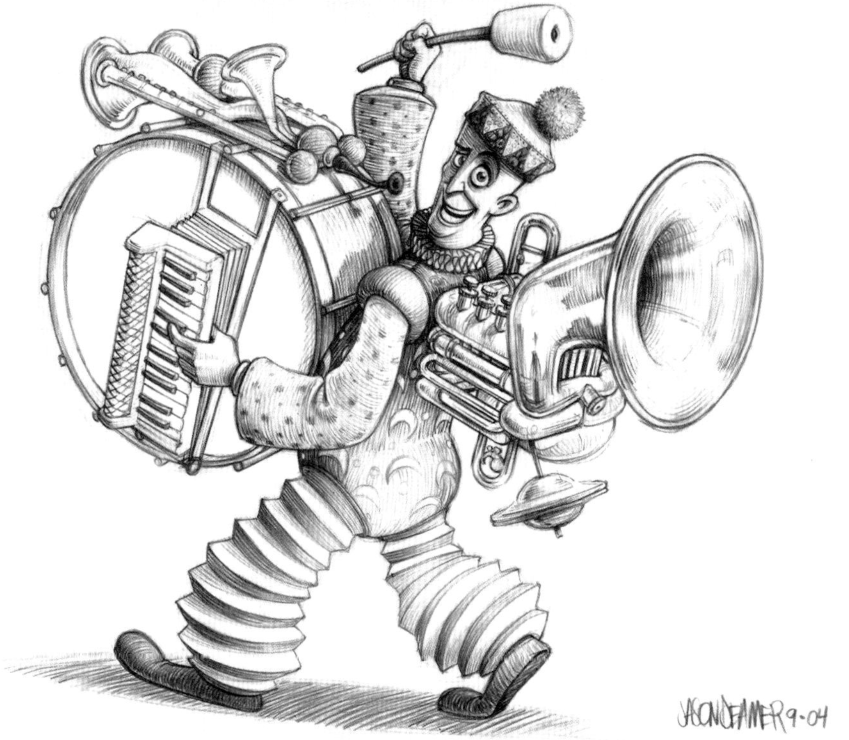

Jason Deamer
Bass
ONE MAN BAND
Pencil
13½ x 17

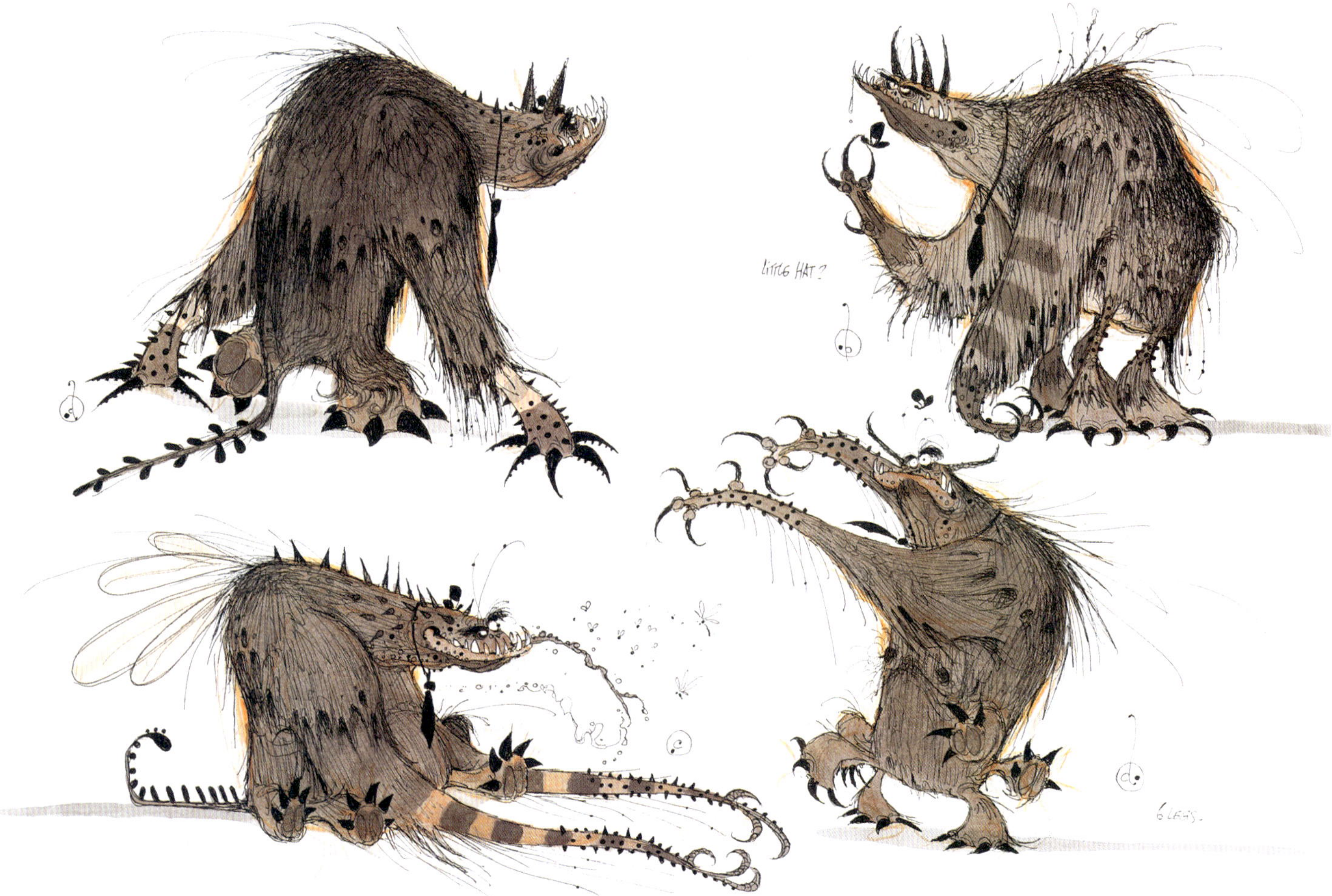

above:
Nicolas Marlet
Sullivan
MONSTERS, INC.
Pencil and ink
10½ x 10⅝

opposite:
Dominique R. Louis
Sullivan
MONSTERS, INC.
Pastel
24½ x 20

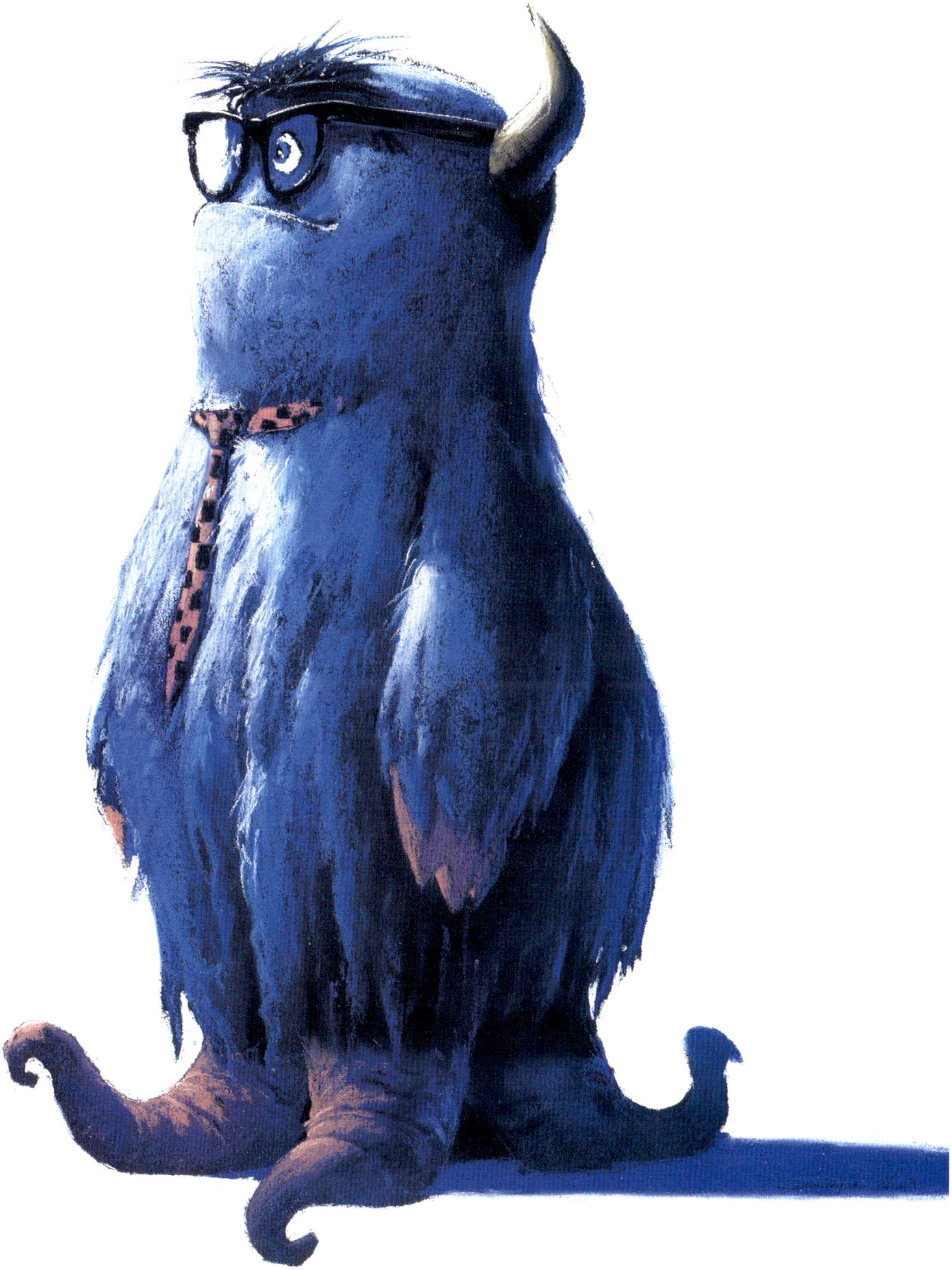

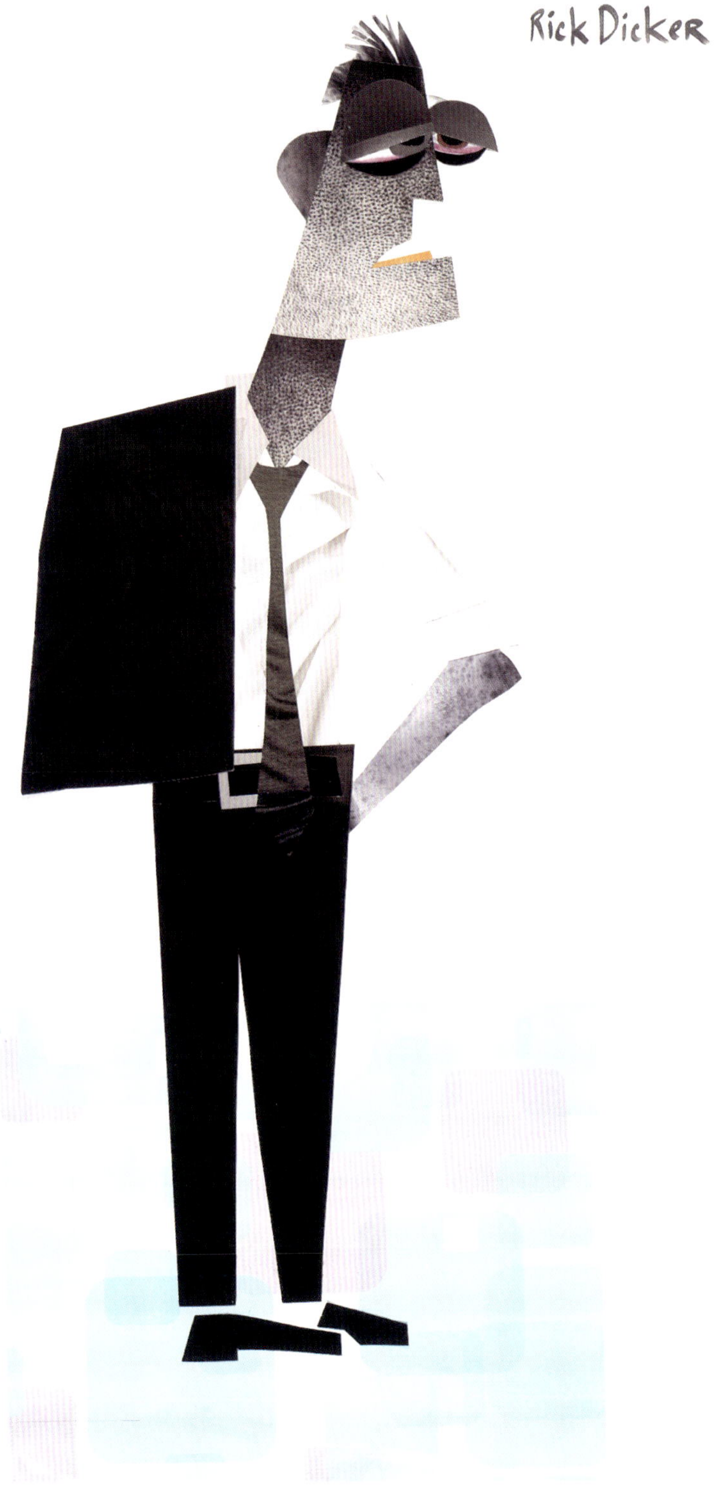

Teddy Newton
Rick Dicker
THE INCREDIBLES
Collage
20⅝ x 11

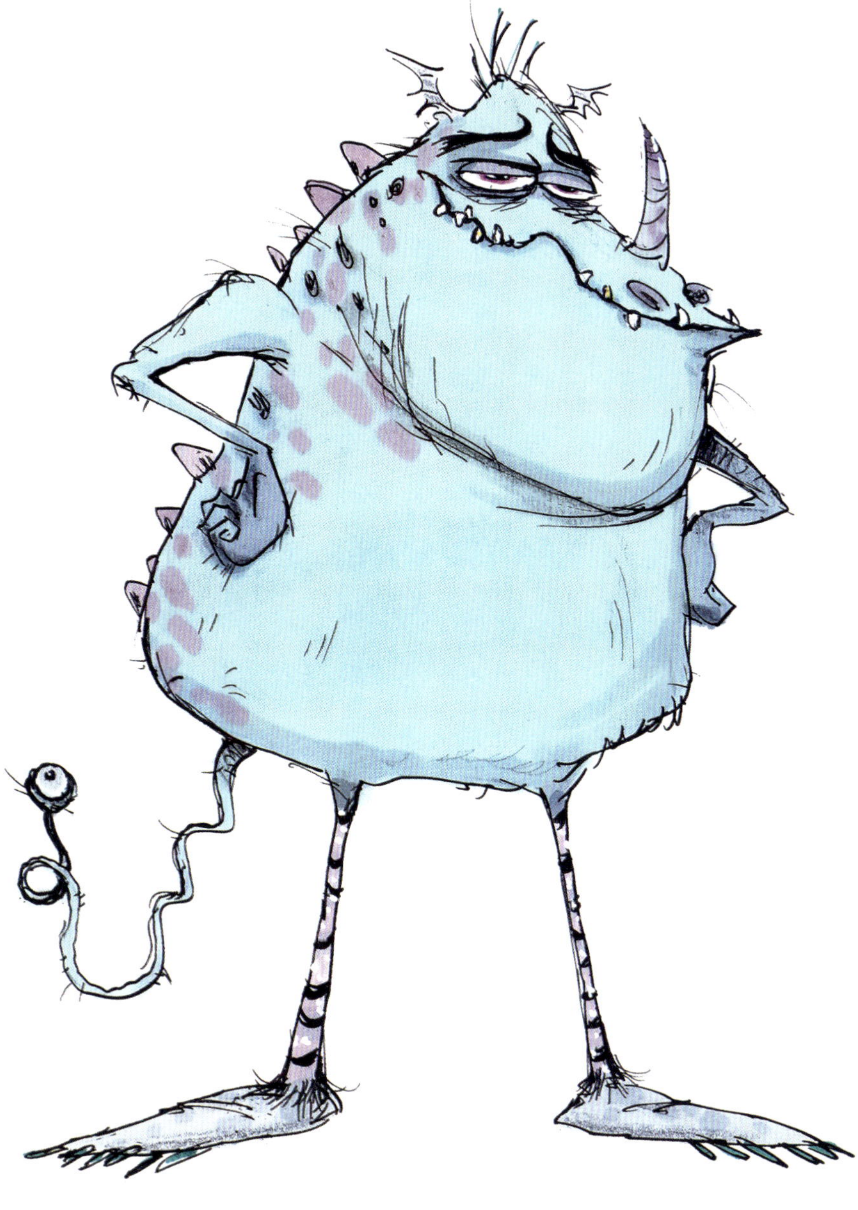

Ricky Nierva
Monster visual development
MONSTERS, INC.
Marker and ink
11 x 8½

Teddy Newton
Frozone facial explorations (detail)
THE INCREDIBLES
Digital. Original, marker

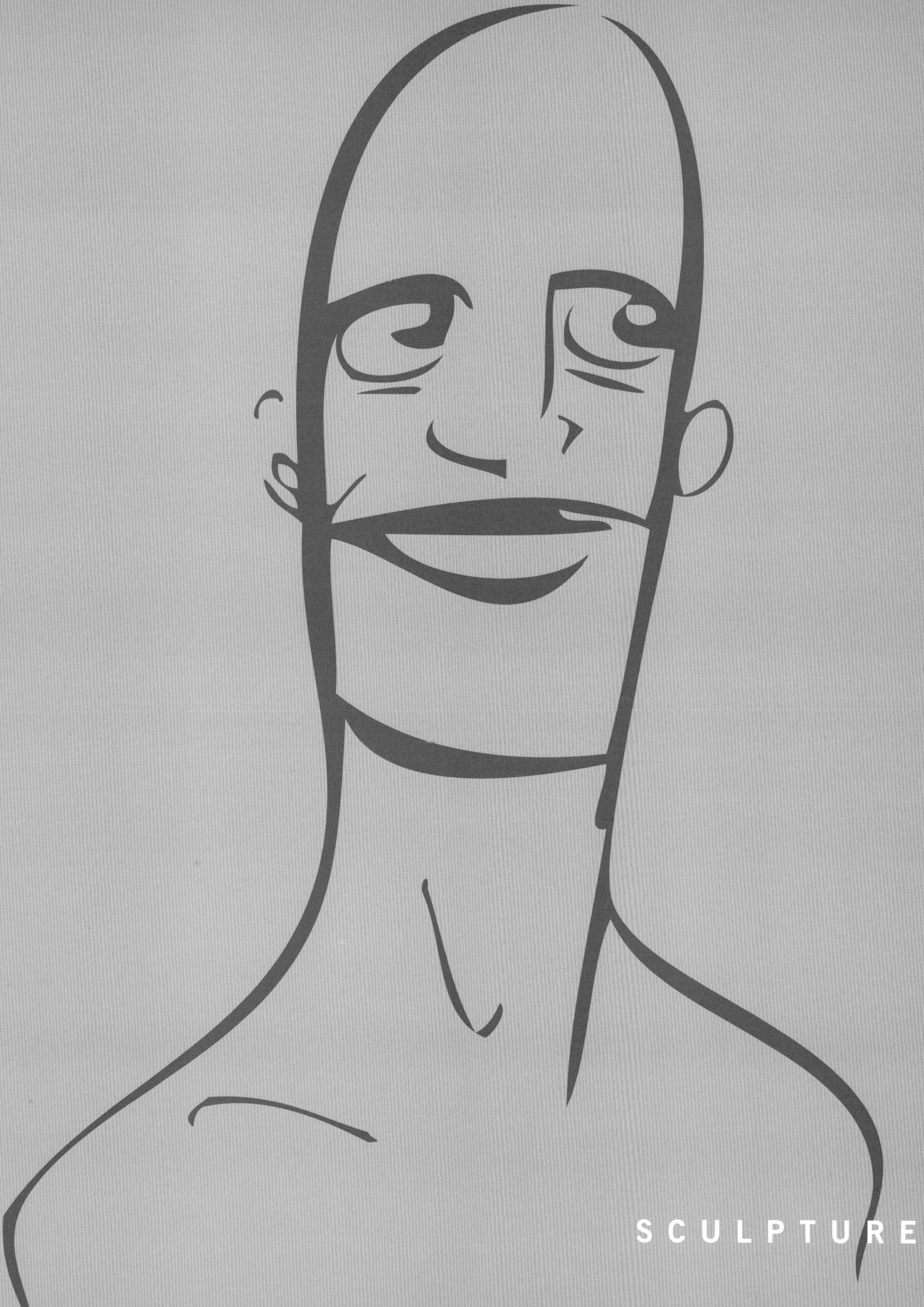

SCULPTURE

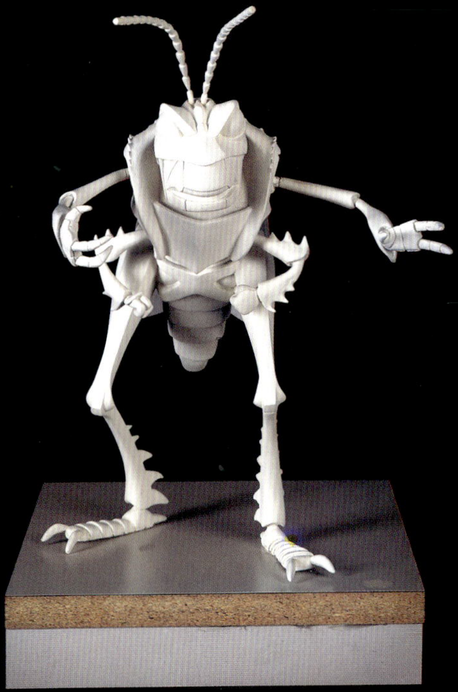

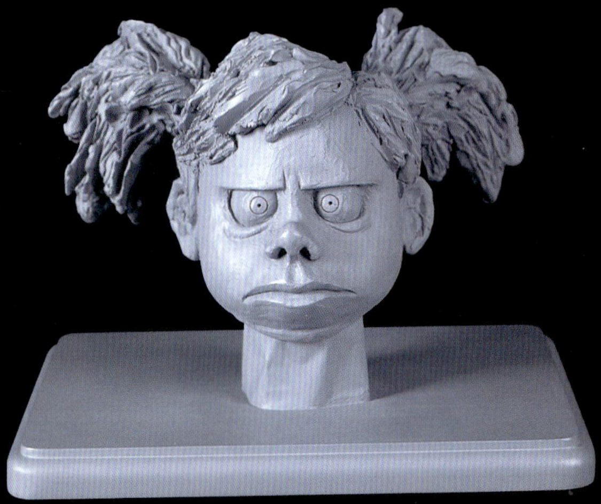

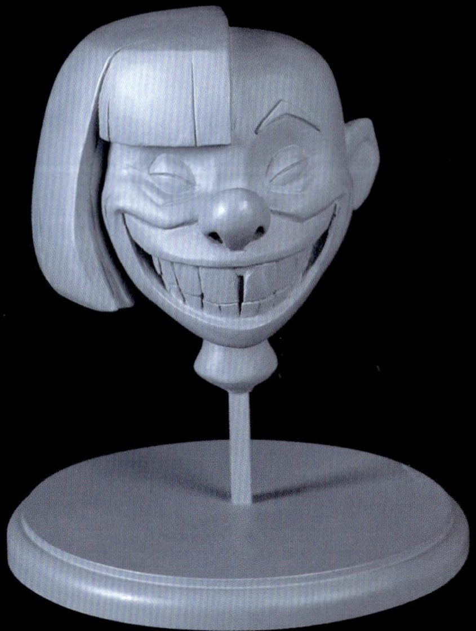

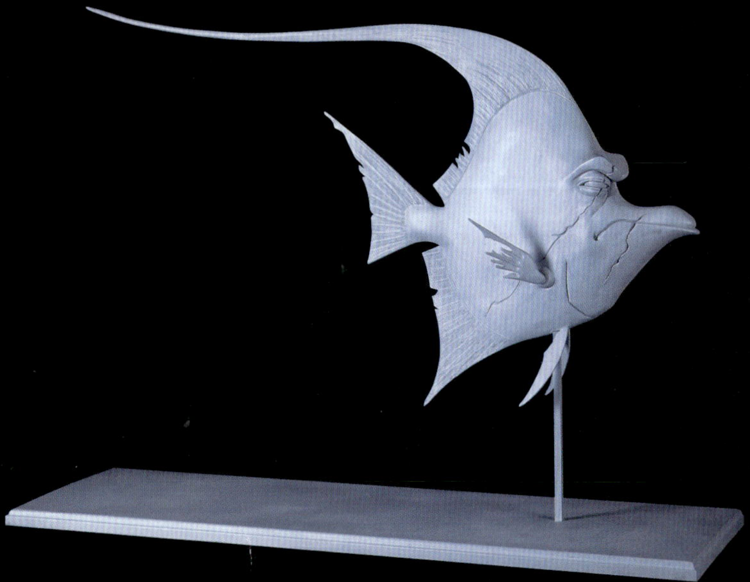

top left:
Norm DeCarlo
Hopper
A BUG'S LIFE
Cast urethane resin
16¼ x 11 x 13¼

bottom left:
Greg Dykstra
Edna Mode (aka "E") "grin"
THE INCREDIBLES
Cast urethane resin
7¼ x 6½ x 6½

top right:
Peter Sohn
Darla
FINDING NEMO
Cast urethane resin
7 x 9 x 7

bottom right:
Jerome Ranft
Gill
FINDING NEMO
Cast urethane resin
22 x 32 x 10

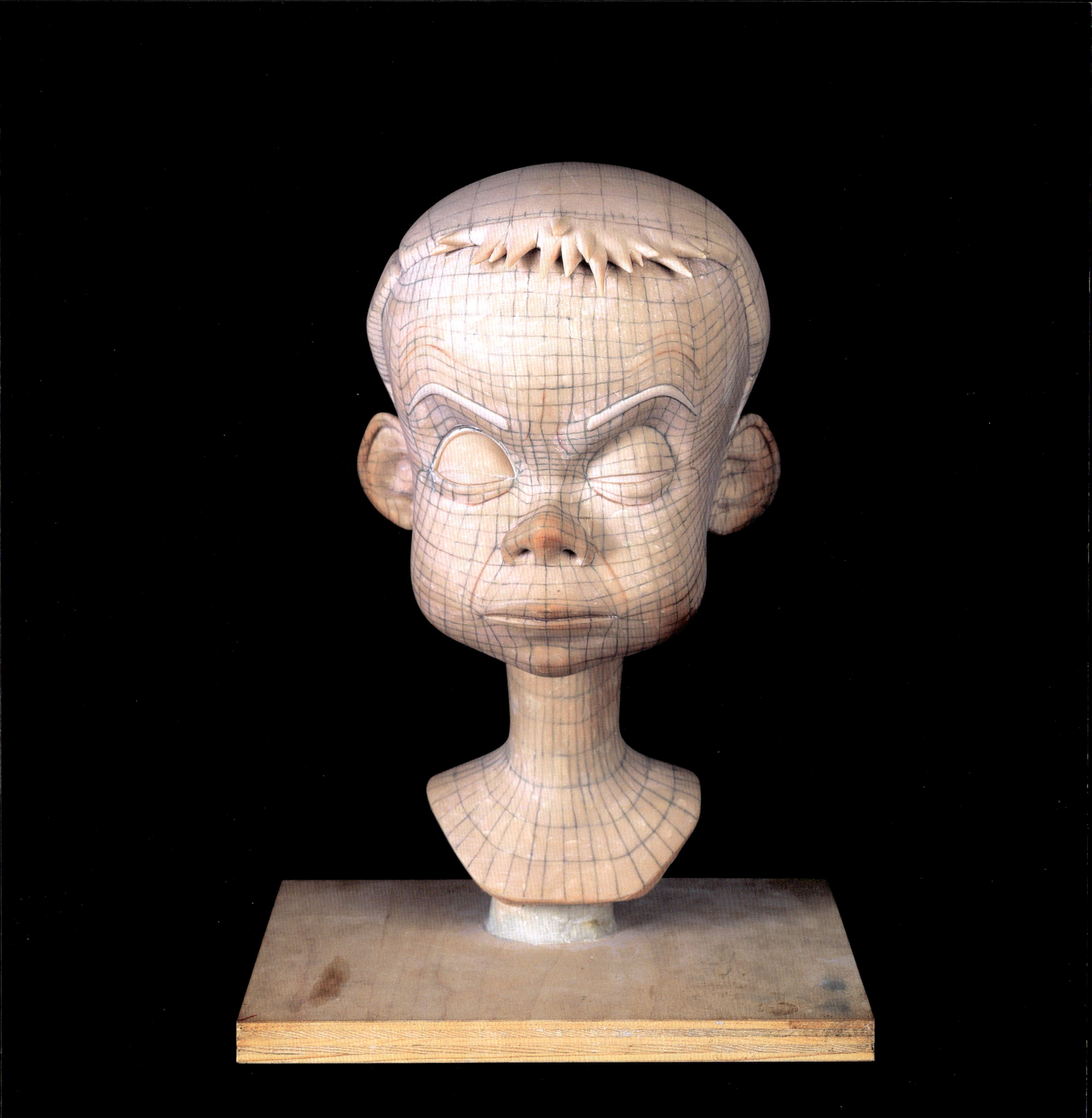

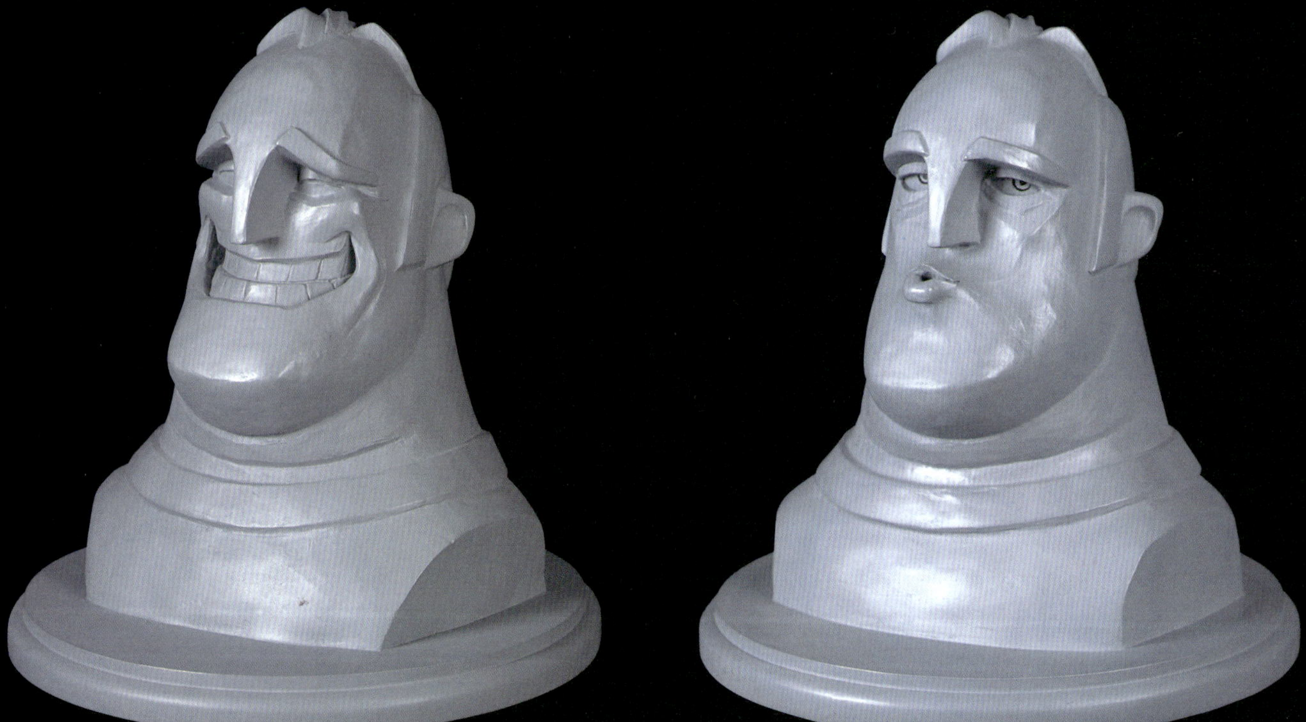

Greg Dykstra
Bob "grin"
THE INCREDIBLES
Cast urethane resin
9 x 8½ x 8½

Greg Dykstra
Bob "oo"
THE INCREDIBLES
Cast urethane resin
9 x 8½ x 8½

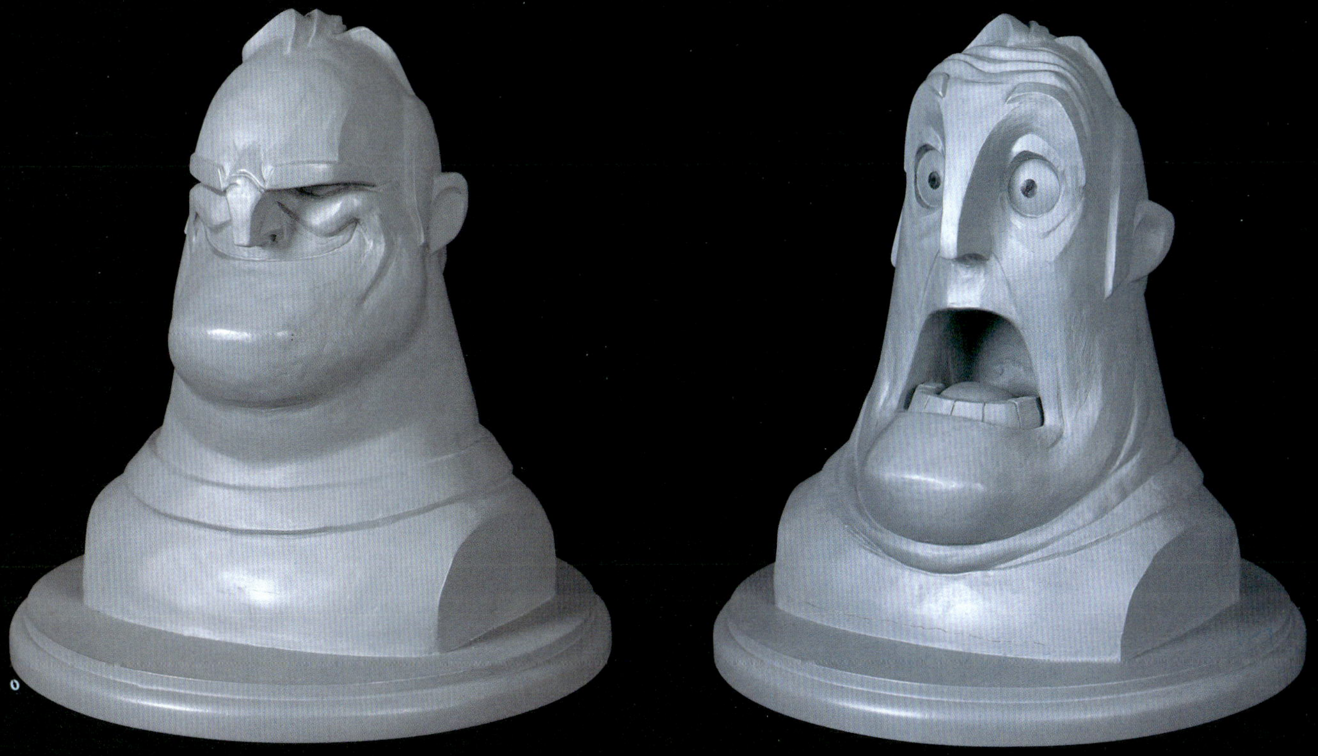

Greg Dykstra
Bob "squash"
THE INCREDIBLES
Cast urethane resin
9 x 8½ x 8½

Greg Dykstra
Bob "stretch"
THE INCREDIBLES
Cast urethane resin
9 x 8½ x 8½

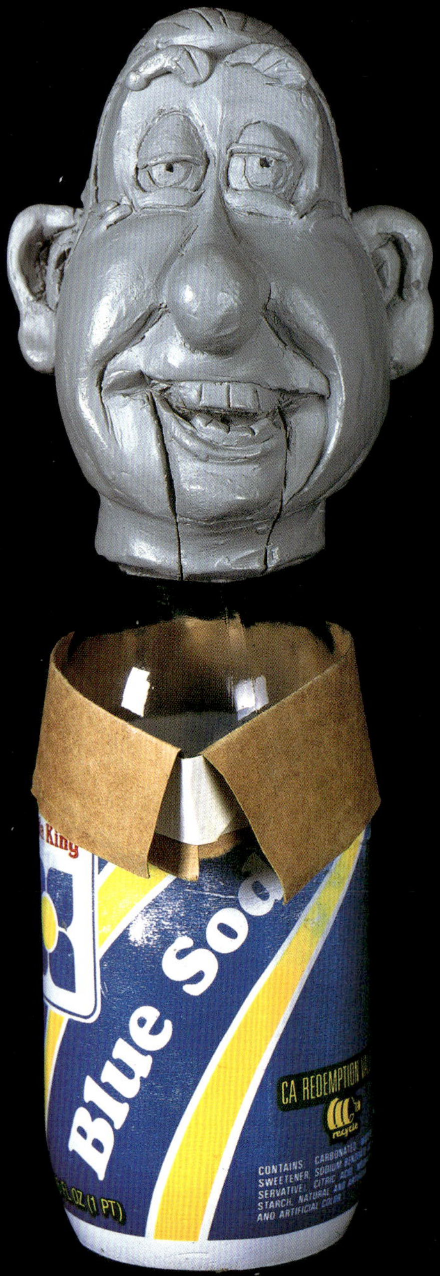

Bud Luckey
Woody
TOY STORY
Cast urethane resin
11 x 5 x 5

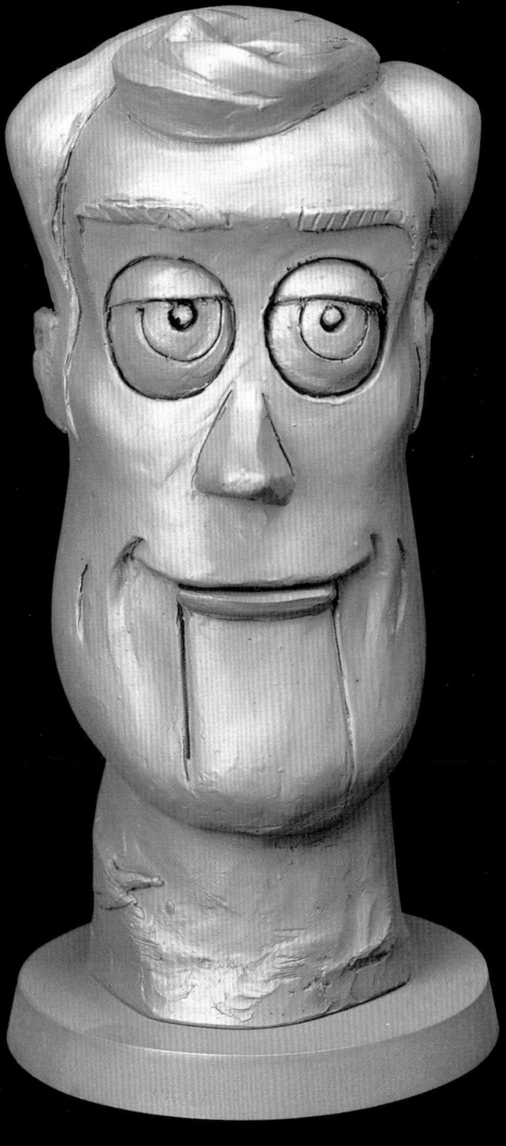

Bud Luckey
Woody
TOY STORY
Cast urethane resin
9½ x 5 x 5½

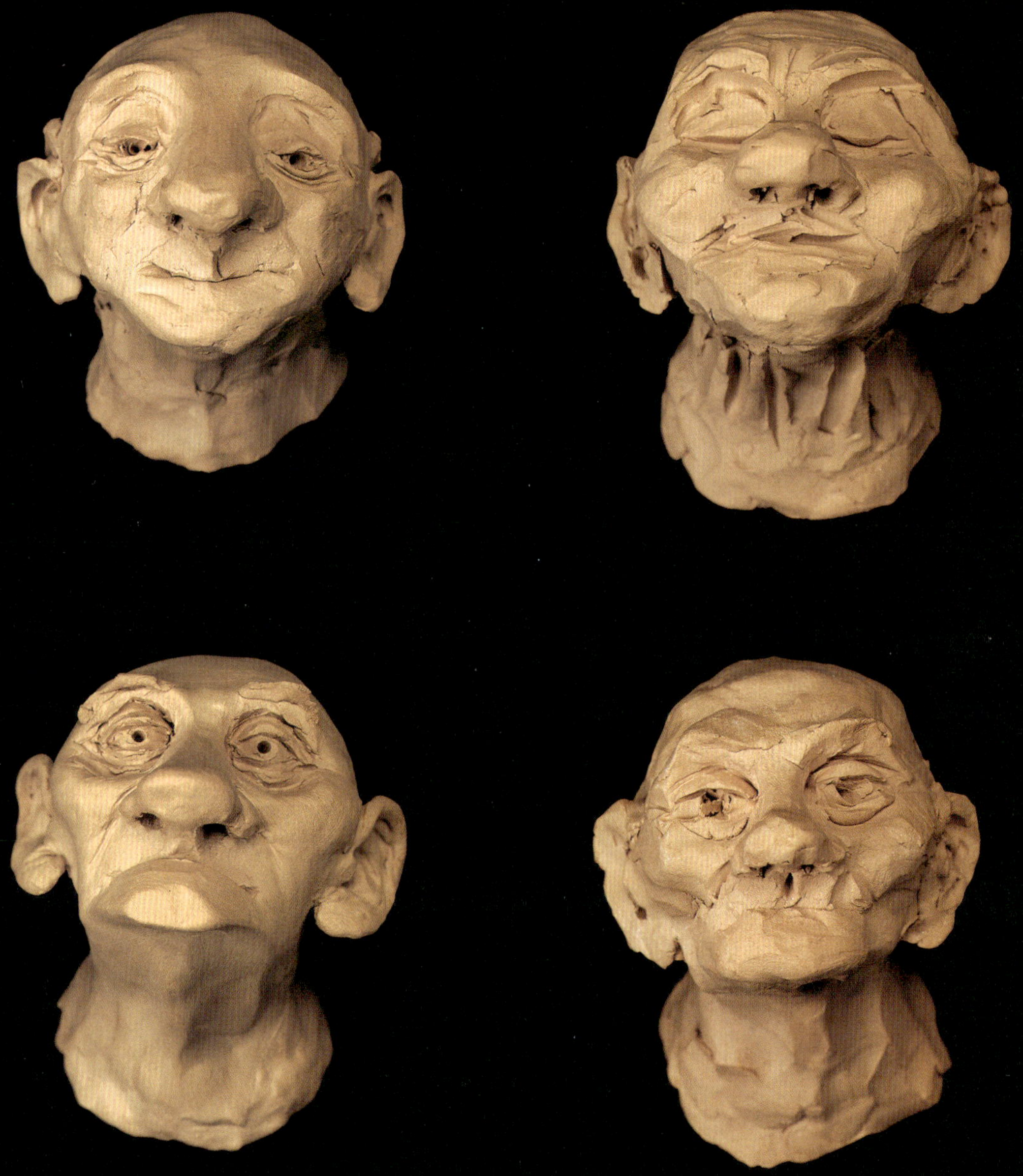

Jan Pinkava
Geri
GERI'S GAME
Ceramic
$4\frac{5}{8} \times 3\frac{7}{8} \times 3\frac{7}{8}$

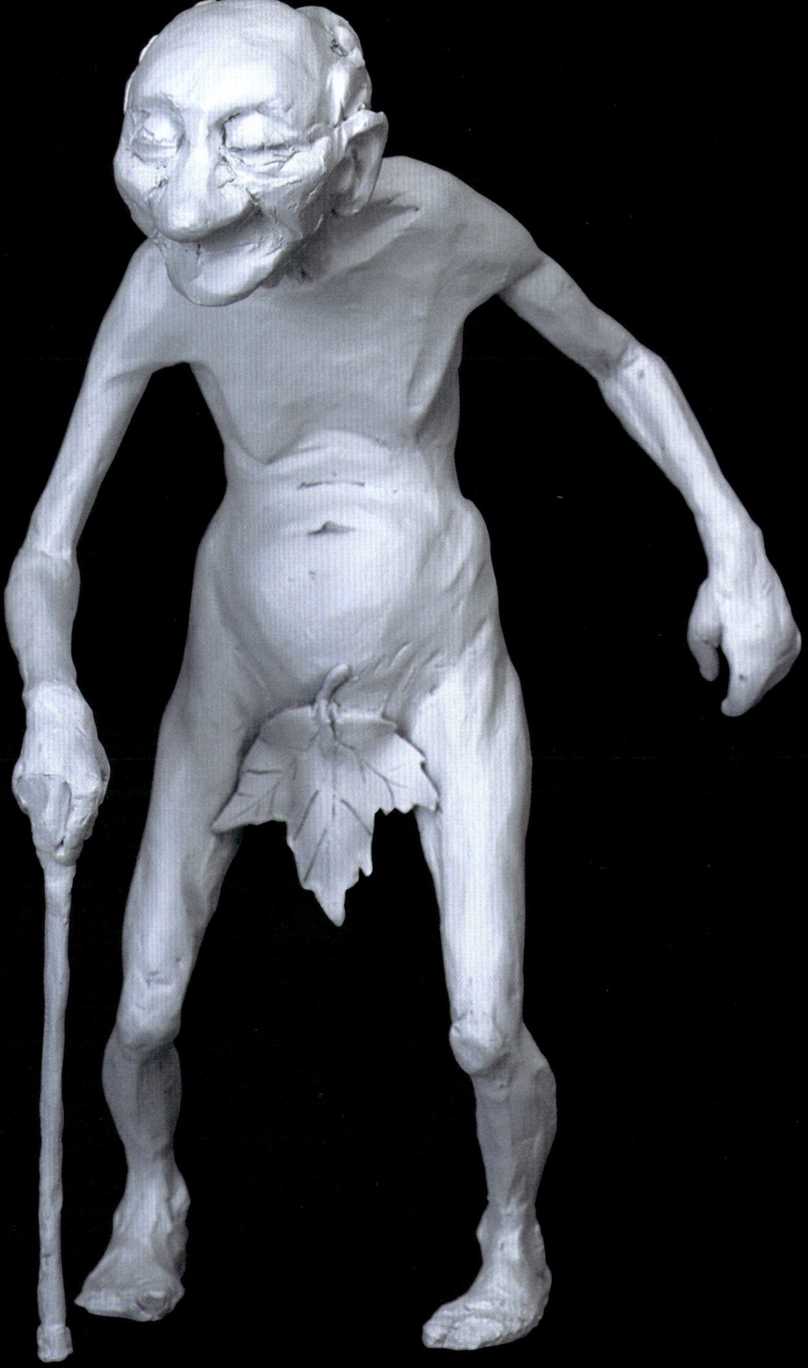

Jan Pinkava
Geri with fig leaf
GERI'S GAME
Cast urethane resin
11½ x 11 x 8

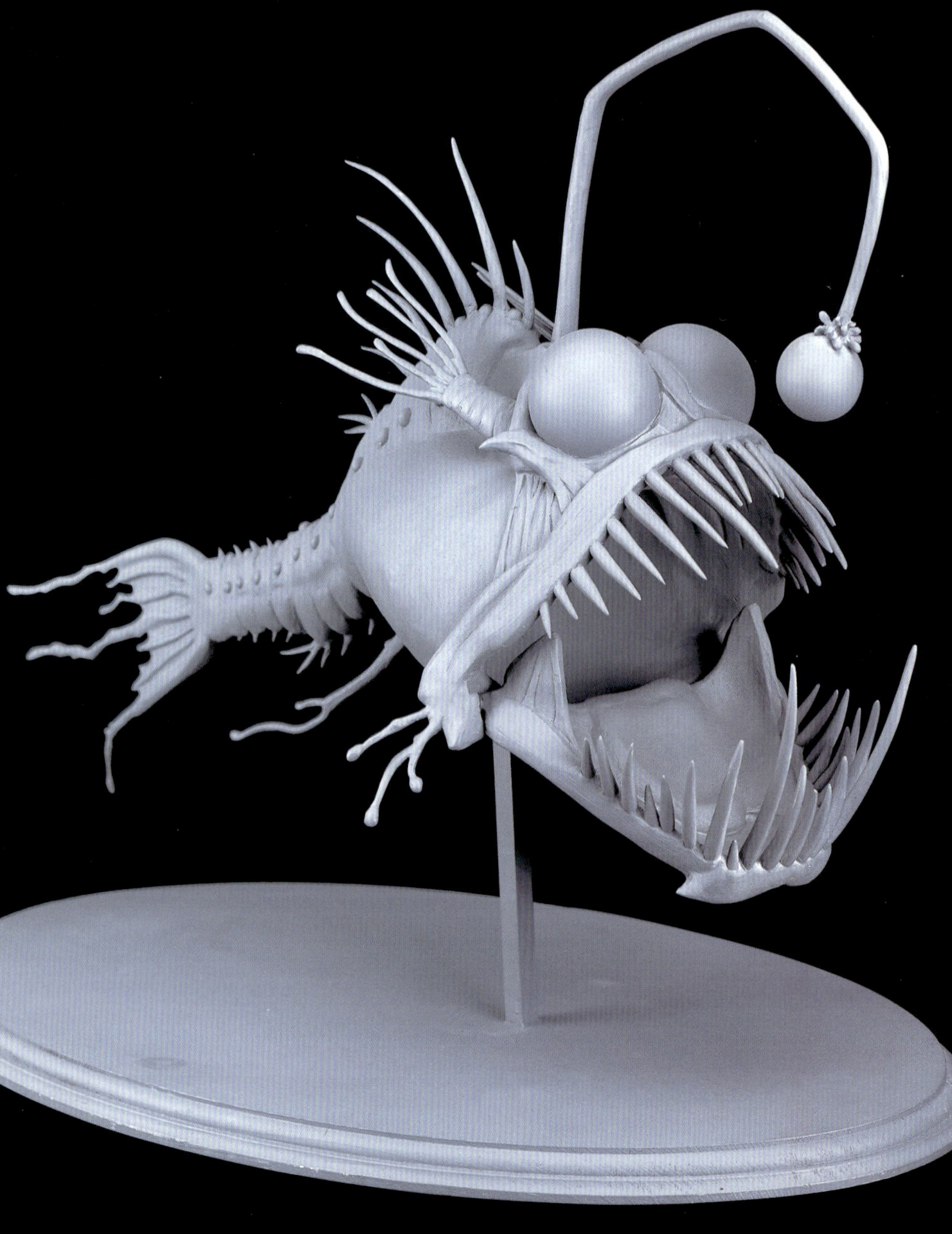

Greg Dykstra
Anglerfish
FINDING NEMO
Cast urethane resin
16½ x 8½ x 12½

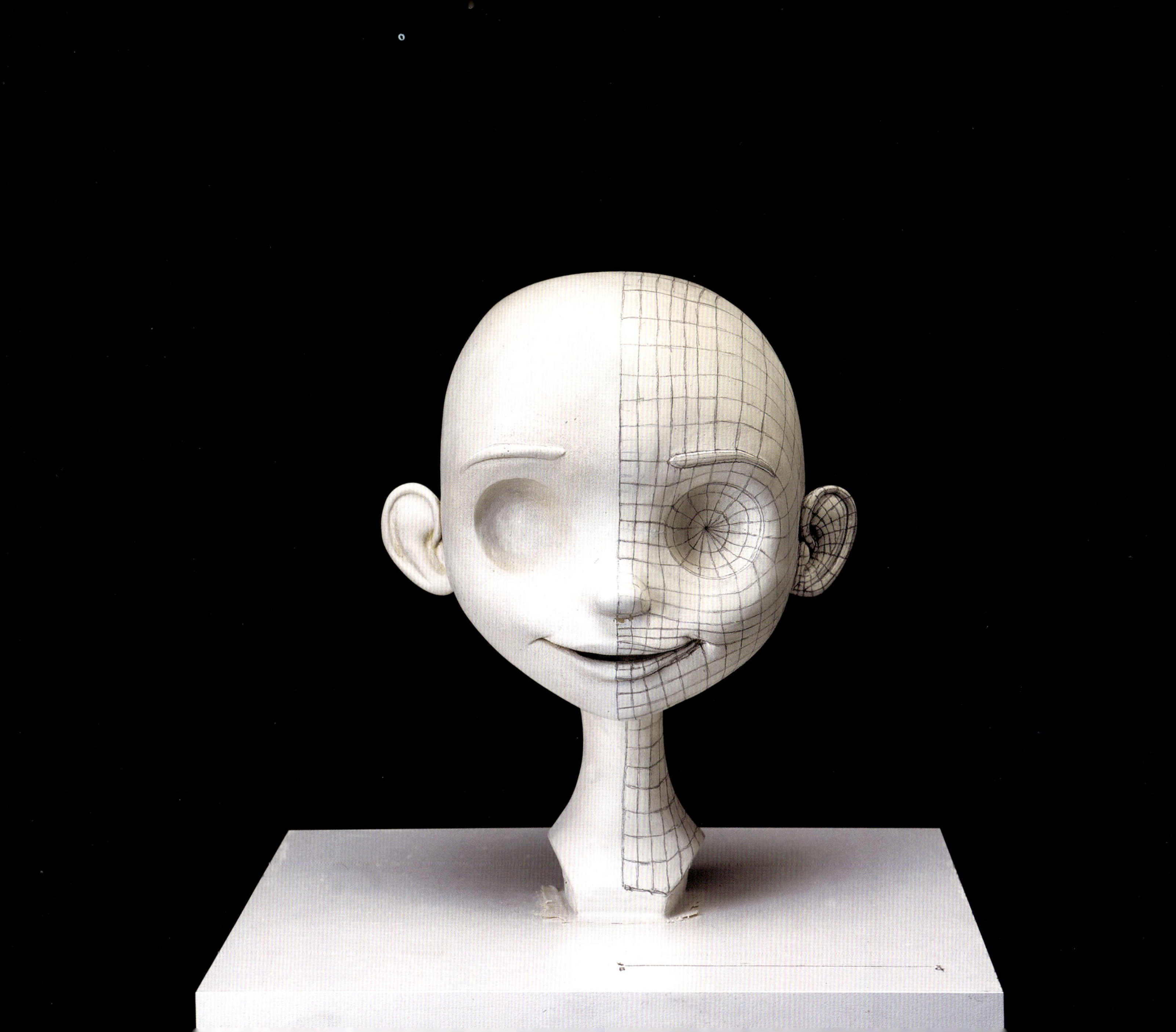

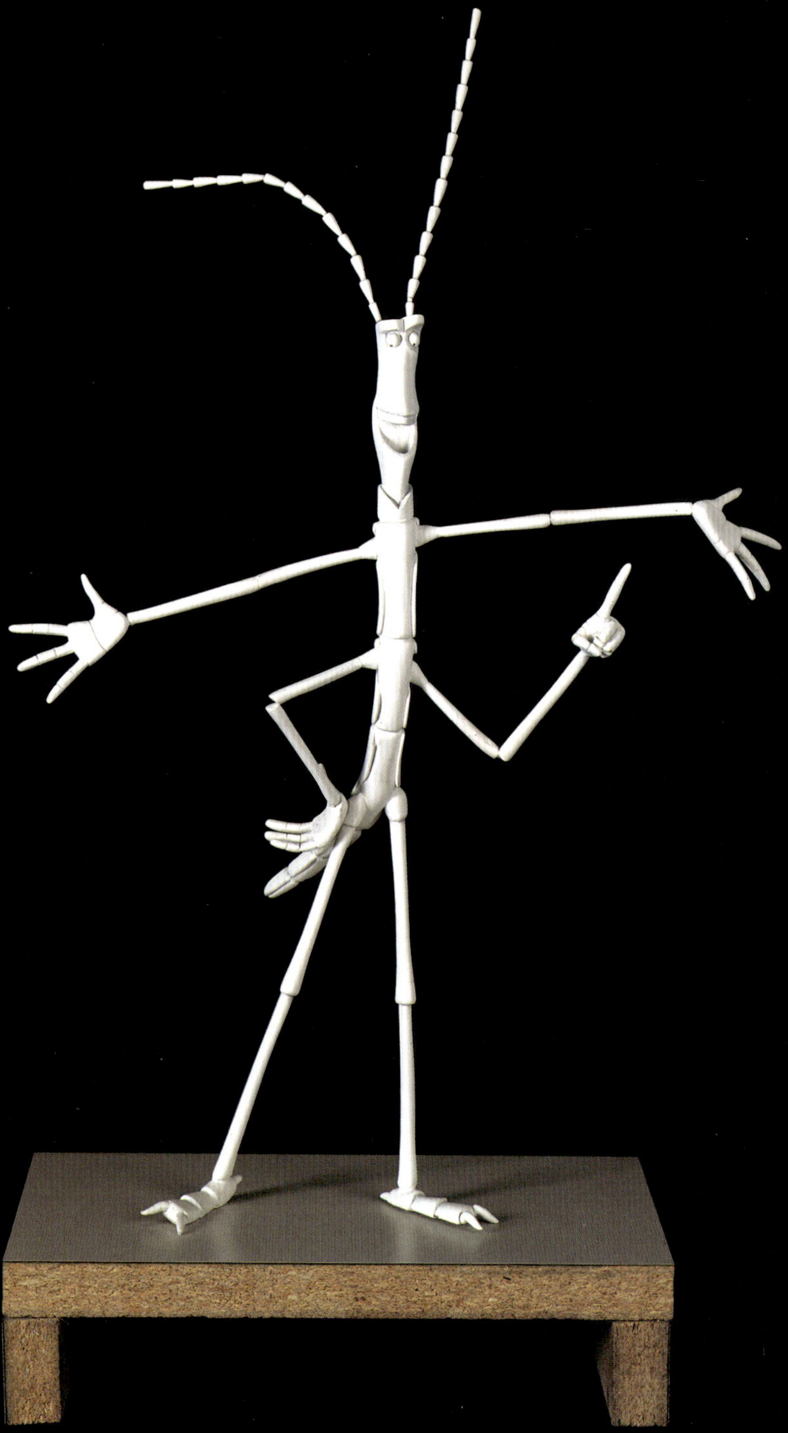

Norm DeCarlo
Slim
A BUG'S LIFE
Cast urethane resin
19¾ x 9½ x 5¾

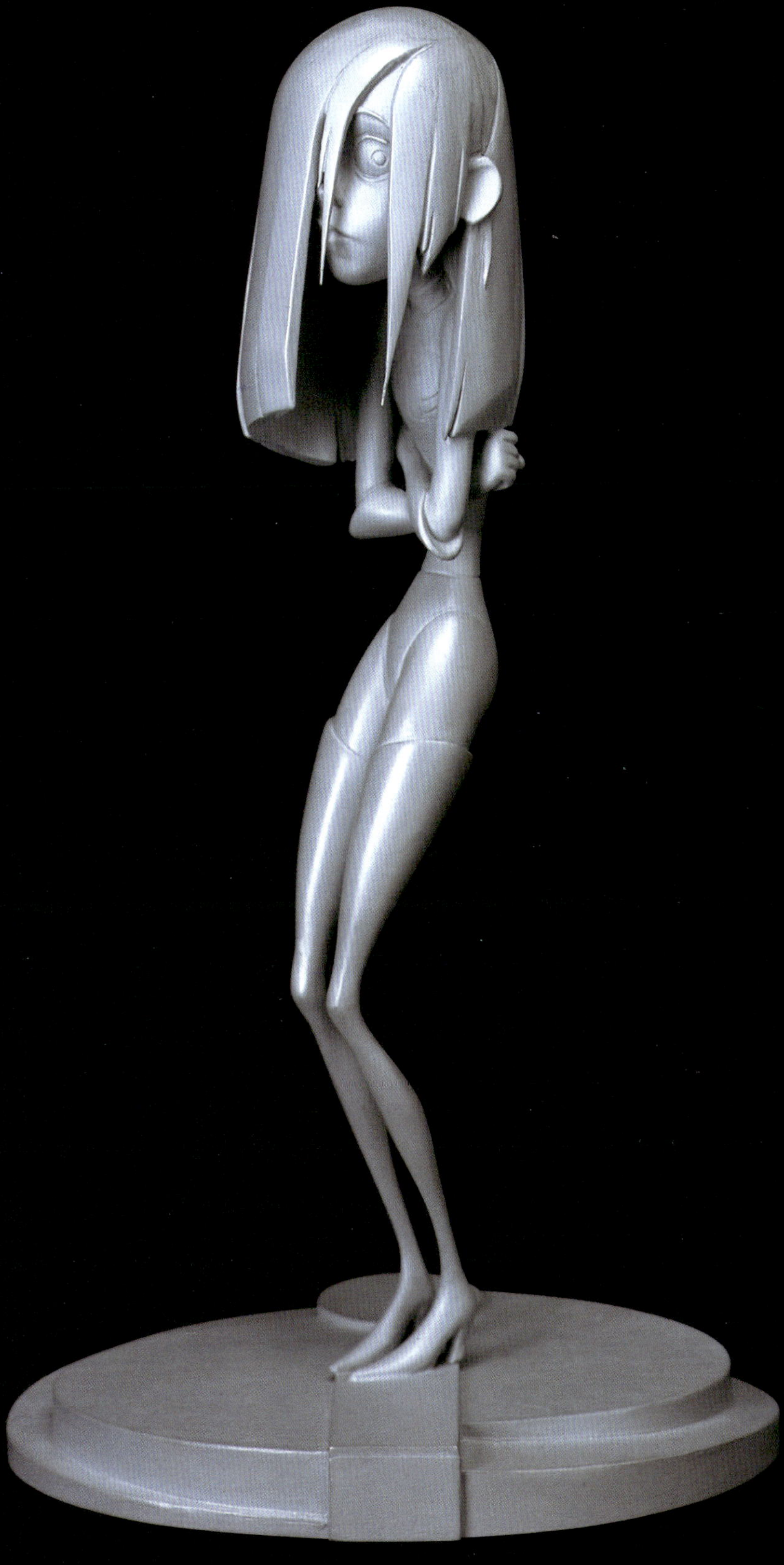

Kent Melton
Violet
THE INCREDIBLES
Cast urethane resin
13 x 7 x 5

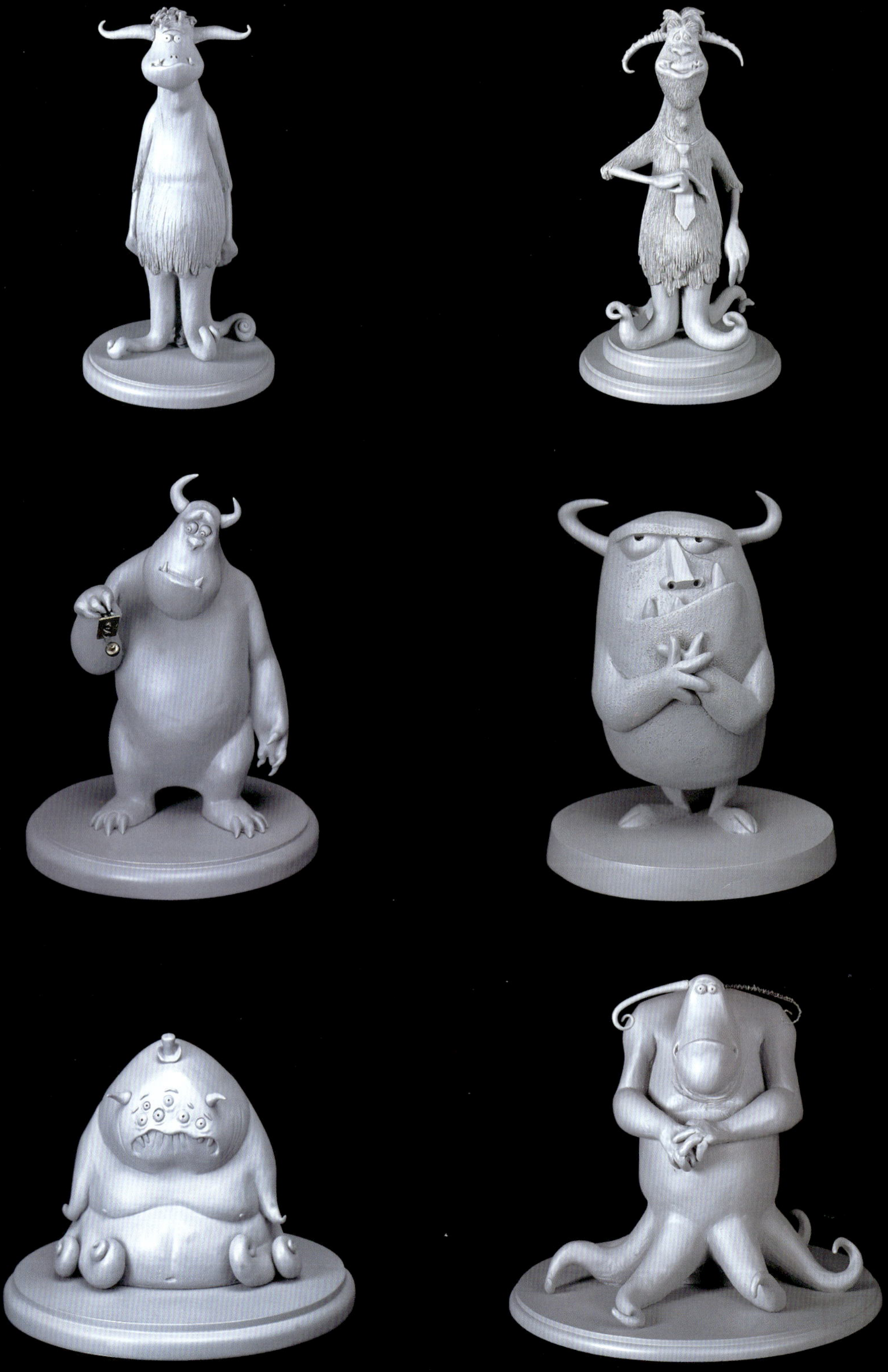

Jerome Ranft
Sullivan studies
MONSTERS, INC.
Cast urethane resin

top left: 12½ x 6 x 6½
middle left: 8¾ x 6½ x 7½
bottom left: 7 x 8½x 8½

top right: 15½ x 8¾ x 8¾
middle right: 9¼ x 8½ x 7¼
bottom right: 12½ x 13¾ x 13¾

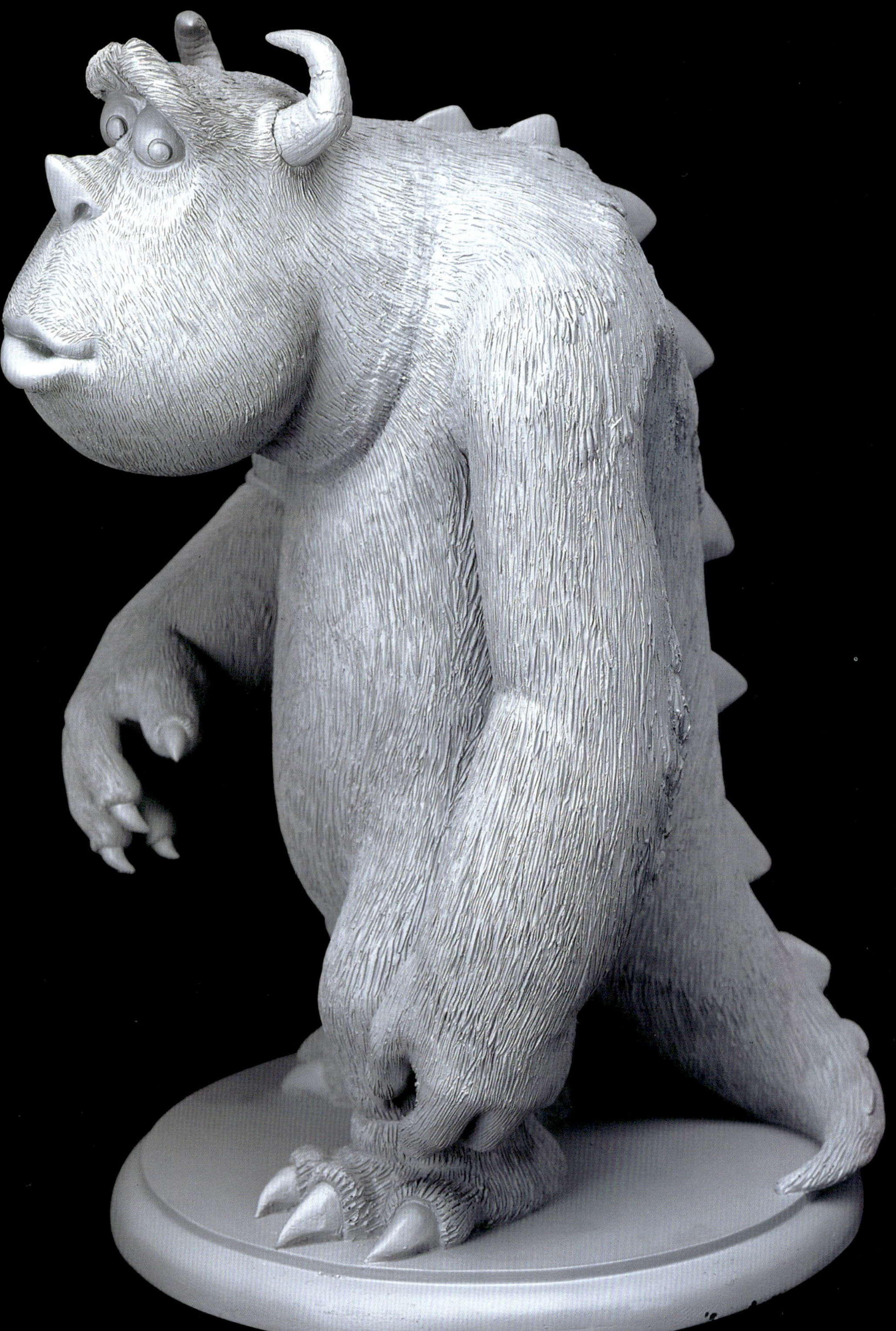

Jerome Ranft
Sullivan
MONSTERS, INC.
Cast urethane resin
14½ x 9½ x 9¼

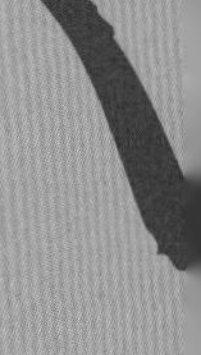

Andrew Stanton
Seagulls (detail)
FINDING NEMO
Digital. Original, marker

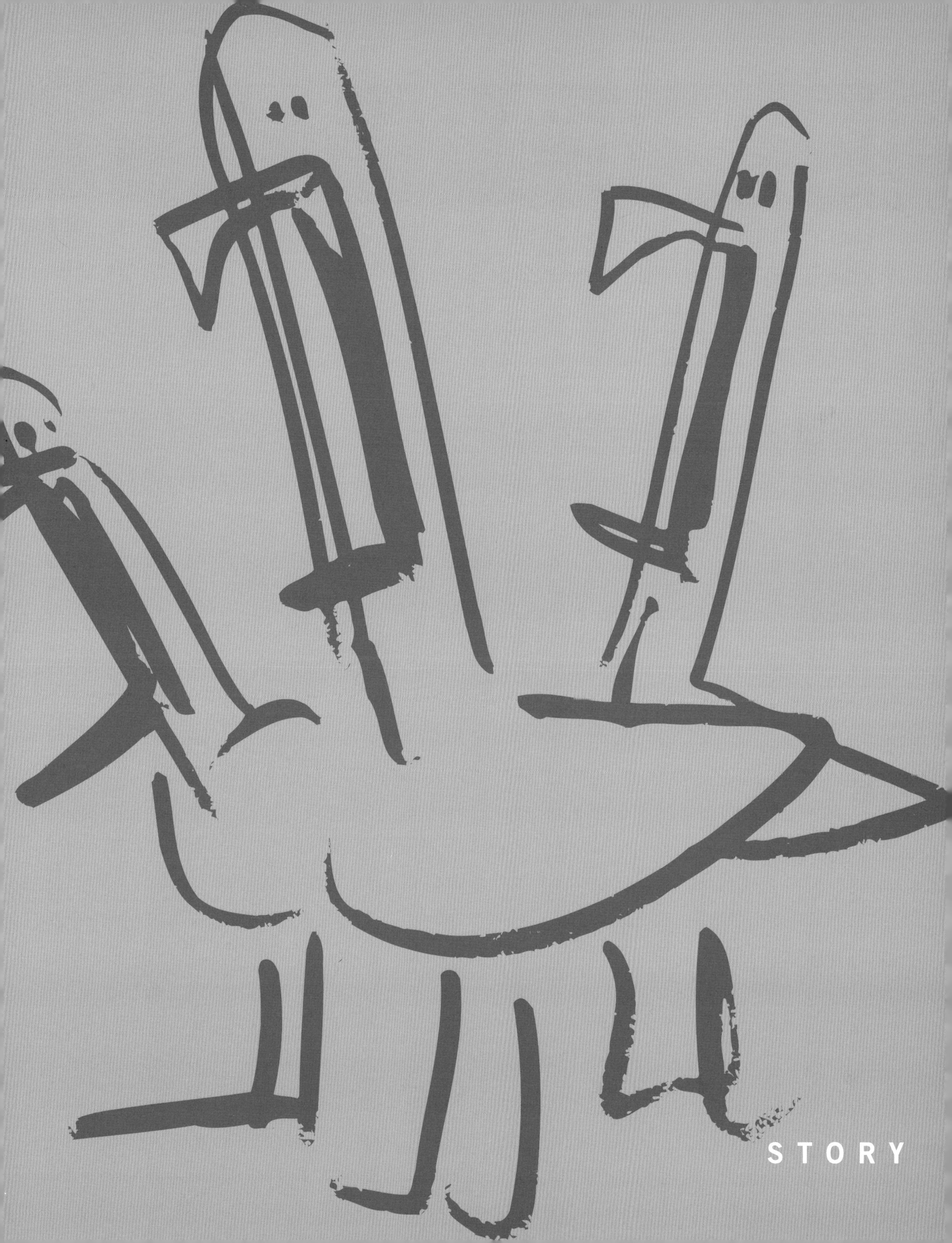

STORY

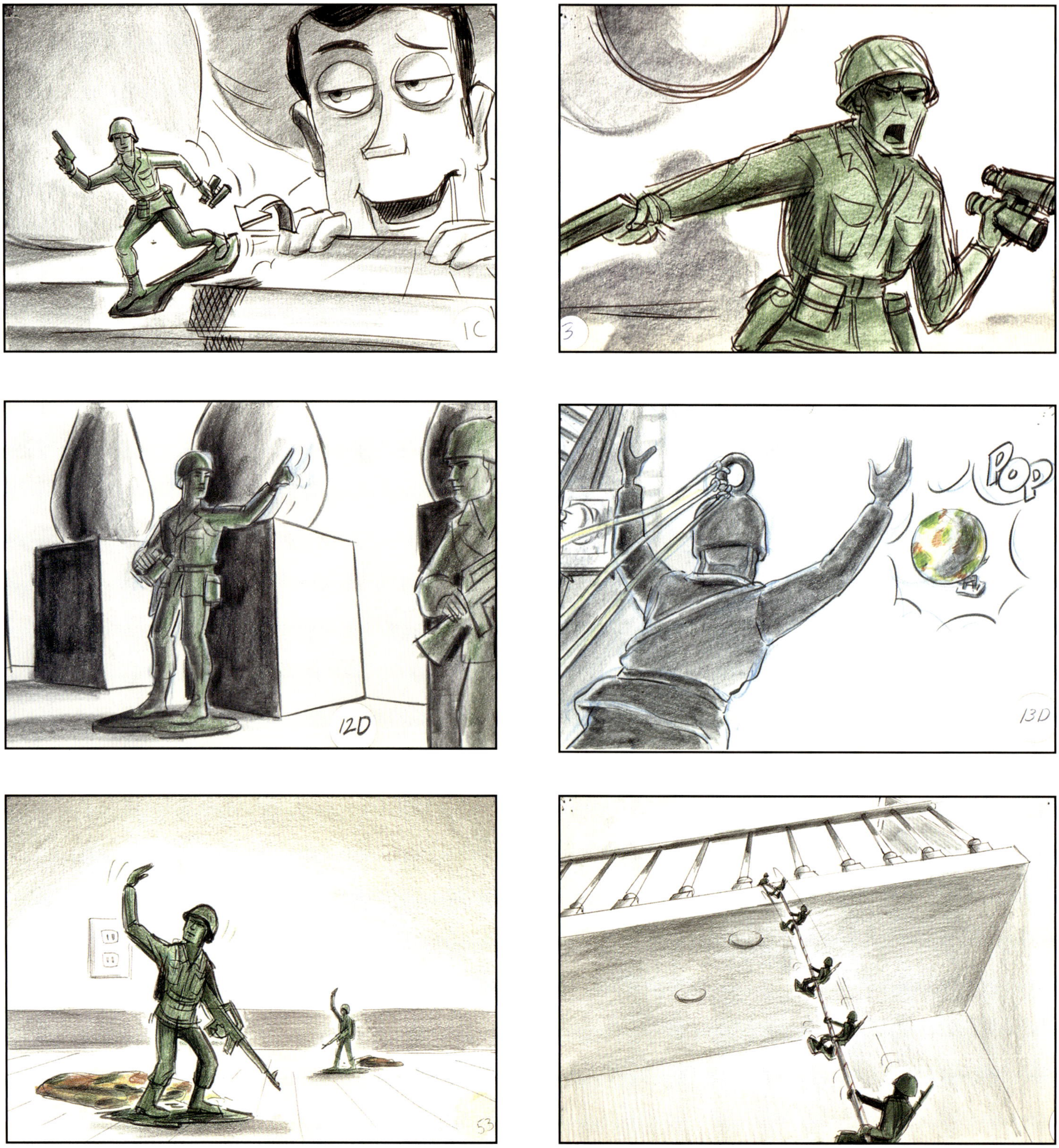

Joe Ranft
Storyboard
TOY STORY
Pencil and ink
5½ x 8½ (each)

Bud Luckey
Storyboard
(panel 12D and 13D)
TOY STORY
Pencil and ink
5½ x 8½ (each)

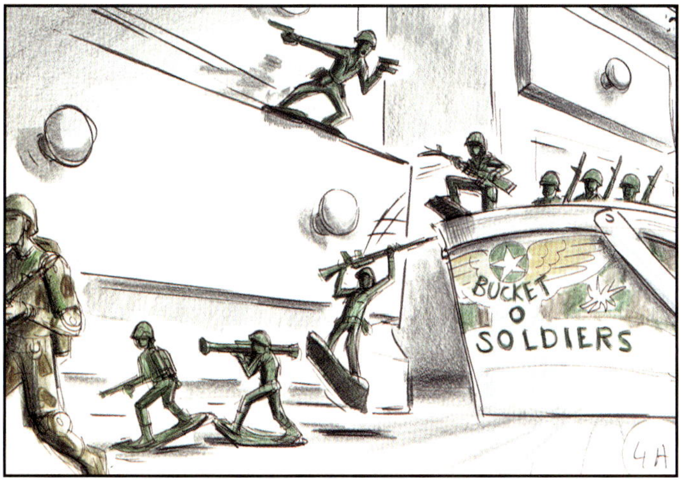
BUCKET
O
SOLDIERS
4A

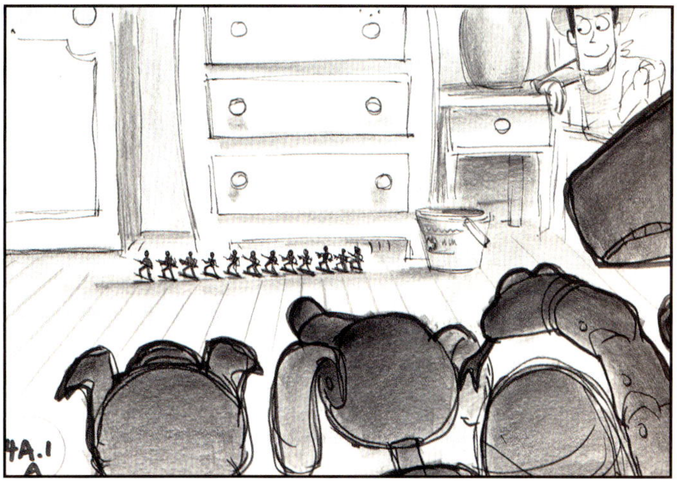
4A.1

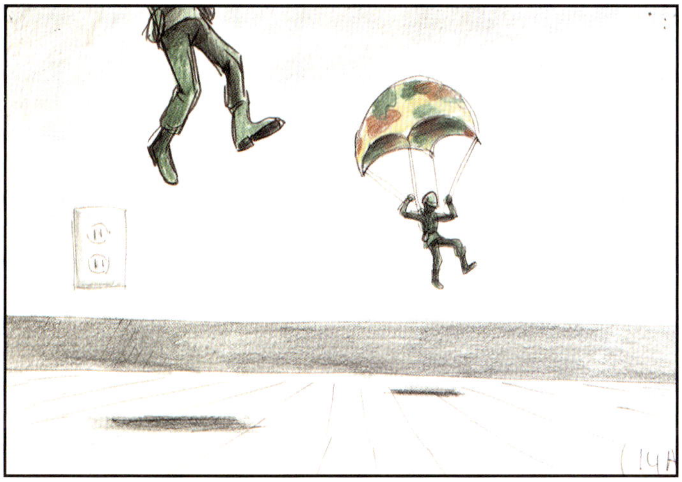
14A

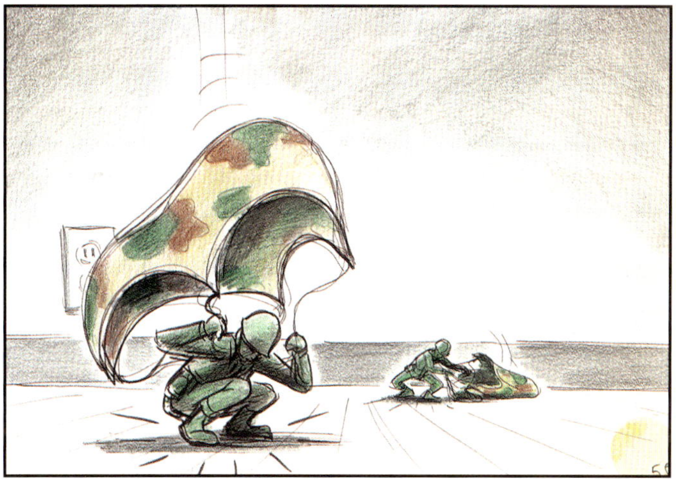

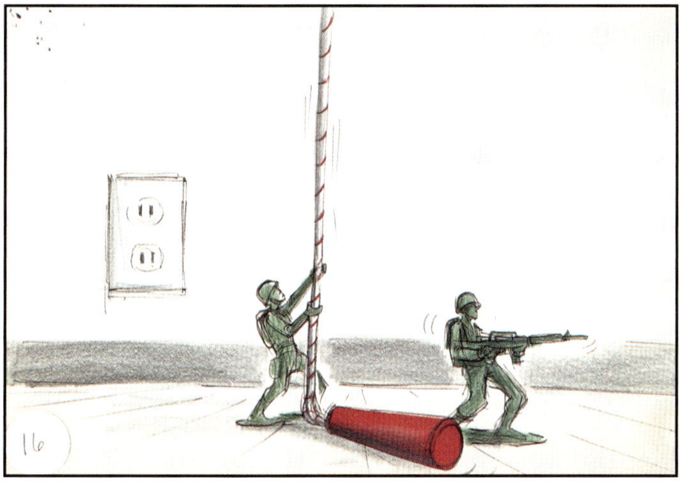
16

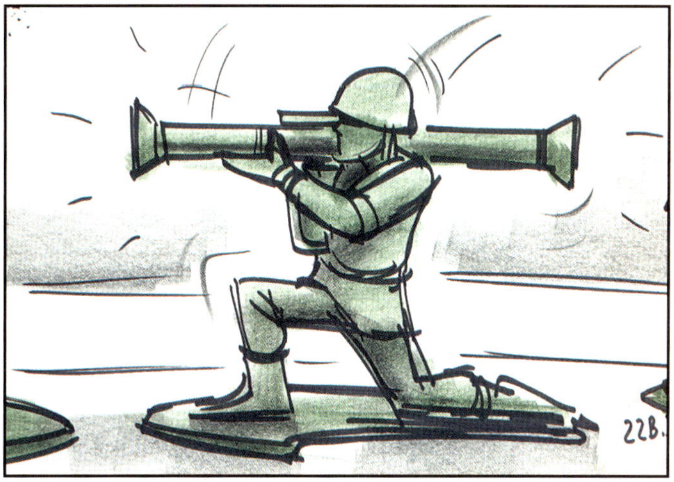
22B.

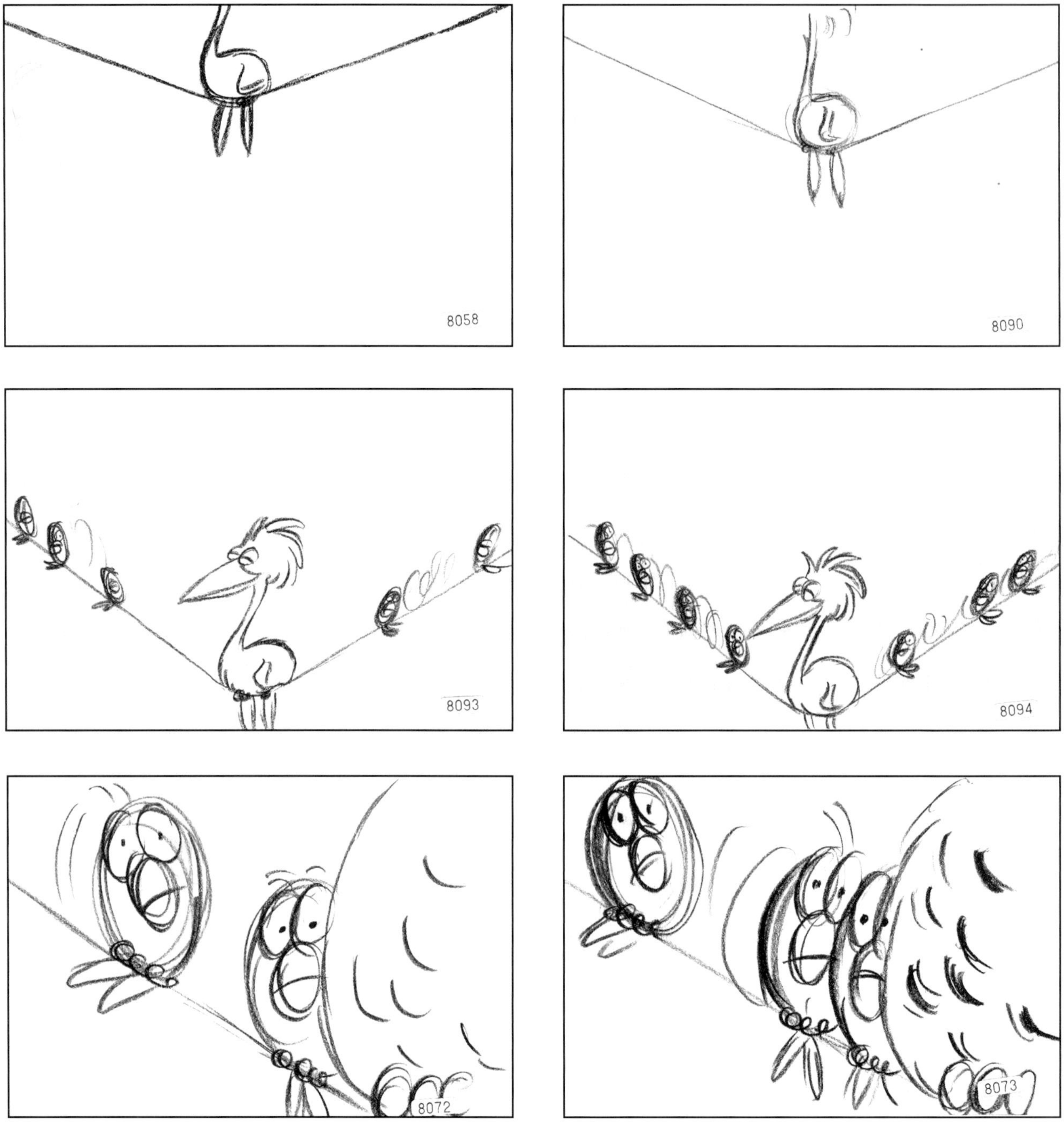

Ralph Eggleston
Storyboard
FOR THE BIRDS
China marker
5½ x 8½ (each)

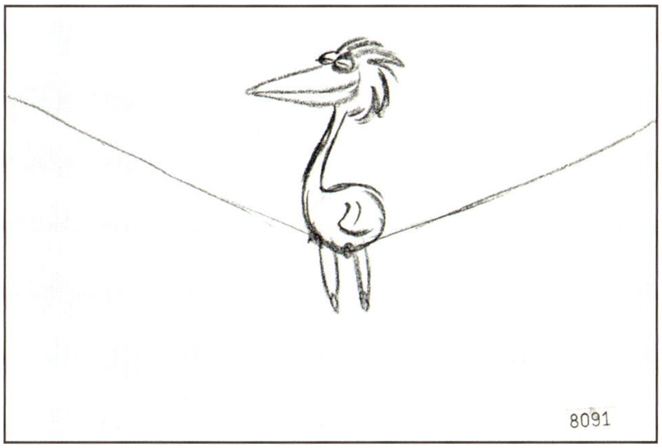
8091

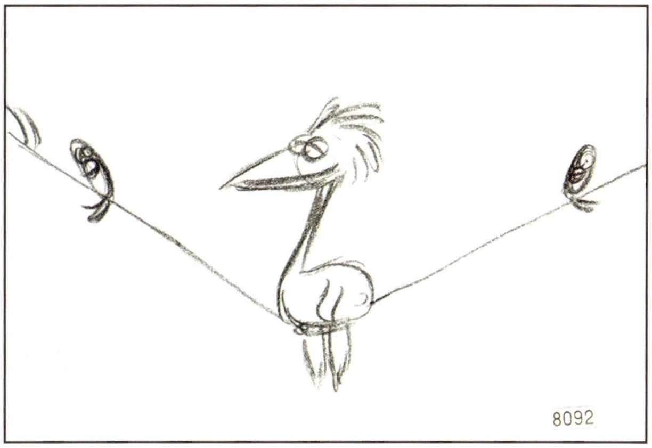
8092

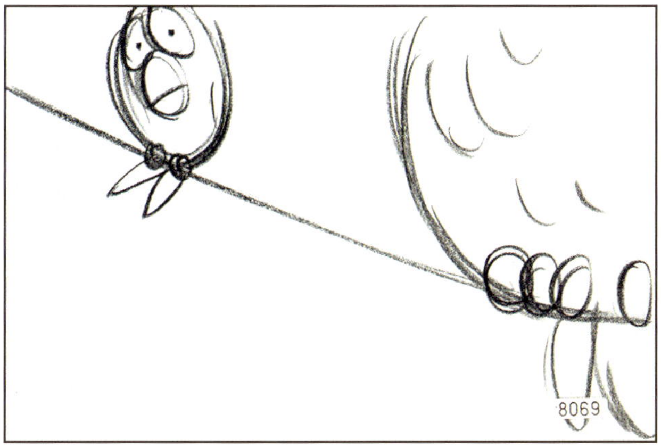
8069

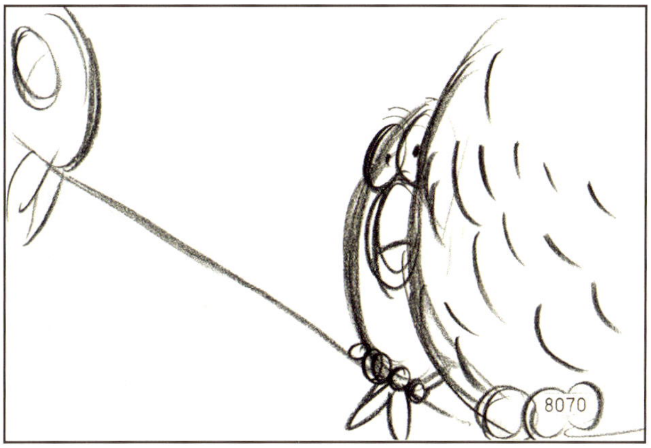
8070

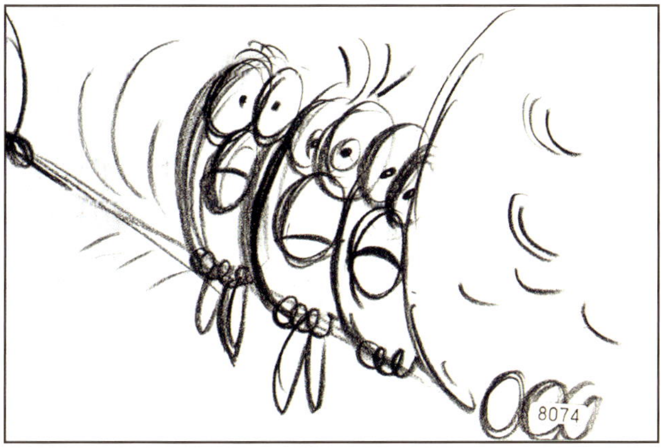
8074

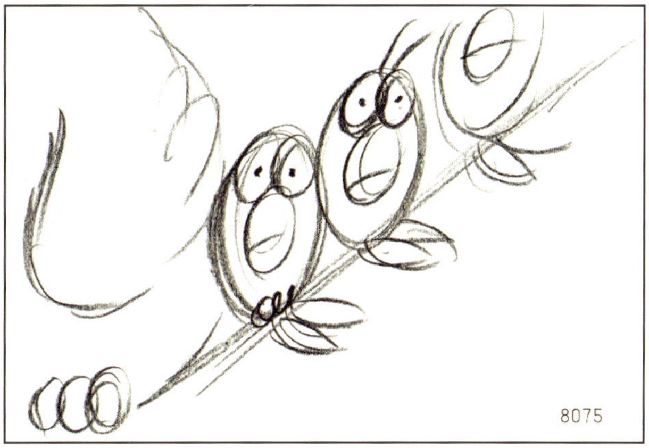
8075

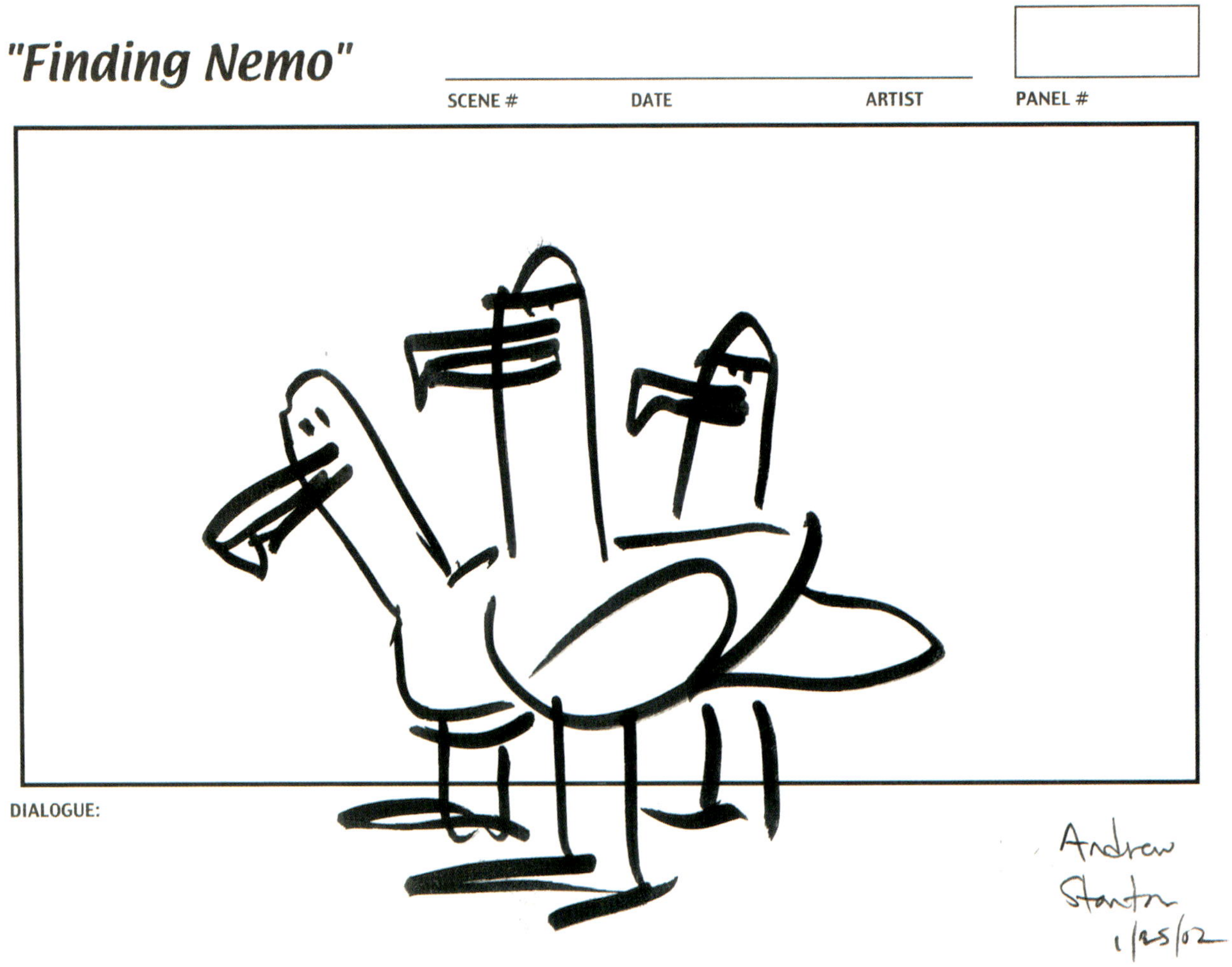

above and opposite:
Andrew Stanton
Seagulls
FINDING NEMO
Marker
6¼ x 8½

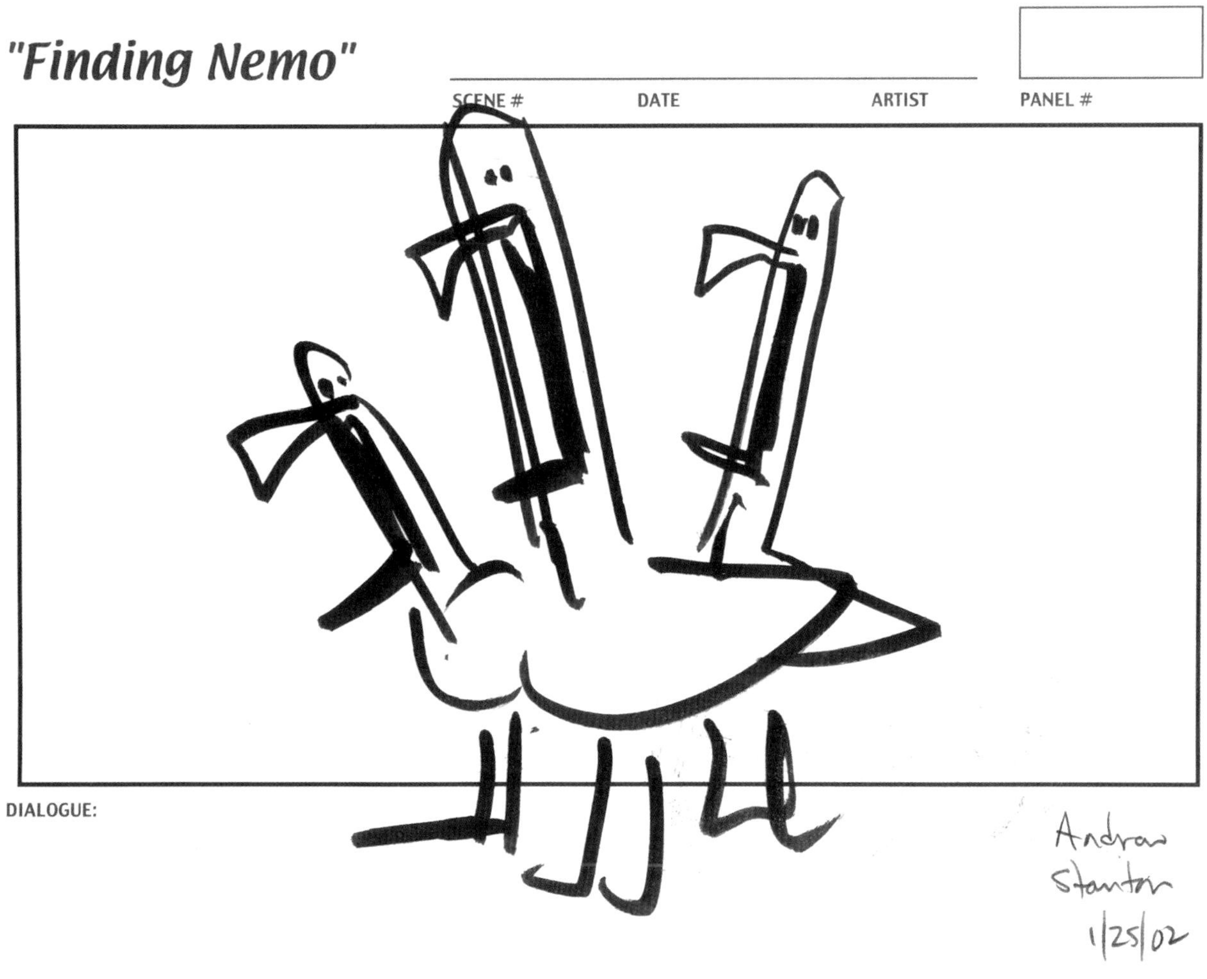
"Finding Nemo"
SCENE #
DATE
ARTIST
PANEL #
DIALOGUE:
Andrew
Stanton
1/25/02

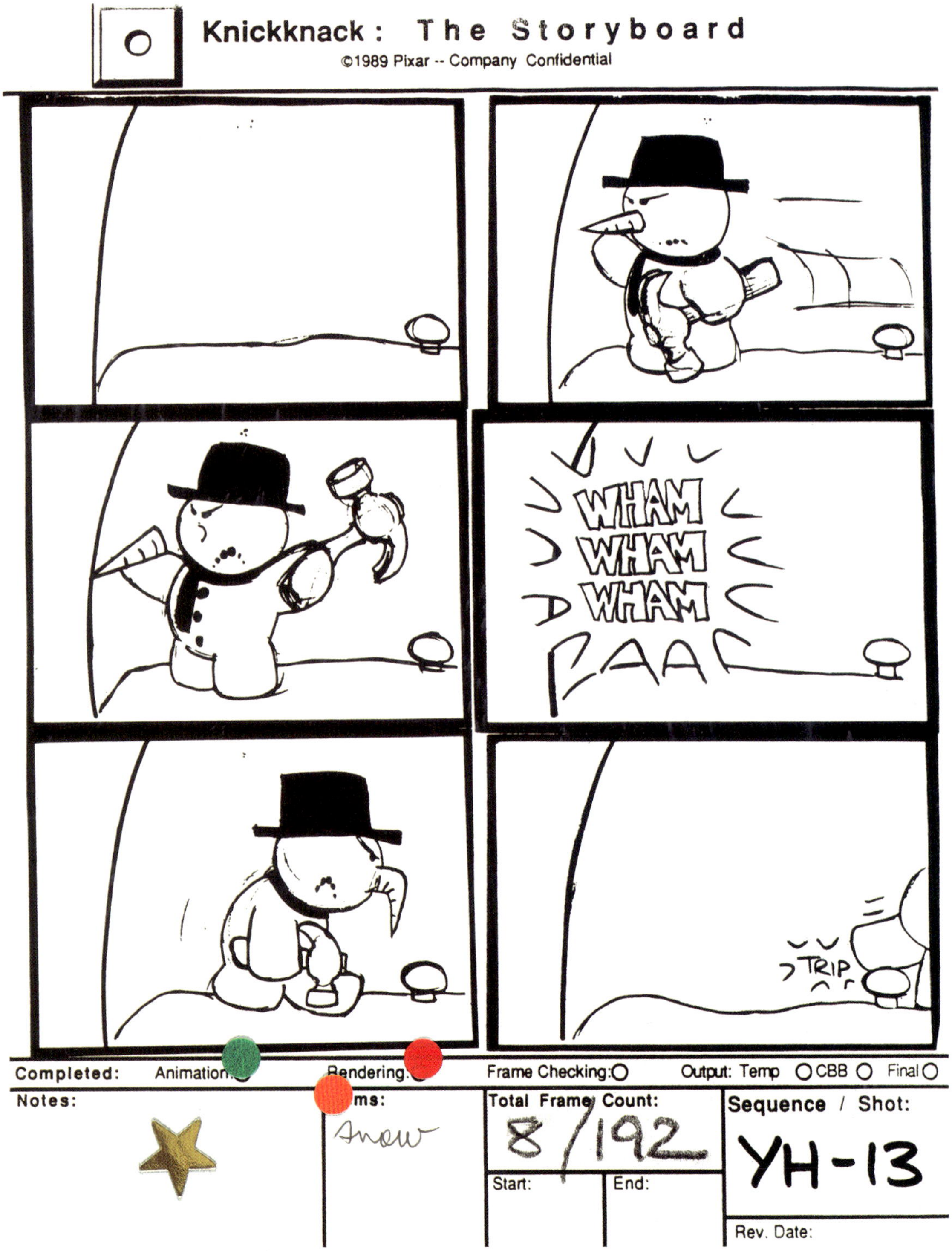

above and opposite:
John Lasseter
Storyboard
KNICK KNACK
Mixed media
8 x 6

Knickknack : The Storyboard

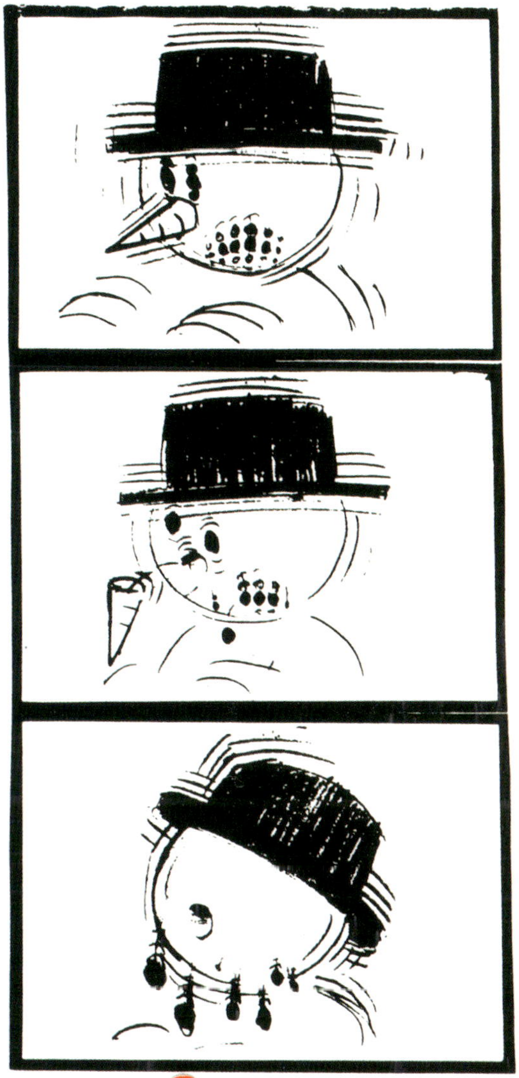

Completed: Animatio[n] ○ Rendering: ○ Frame Checking: ○ Output: Temp ○ CBB ○ Final ○

Notes:	Elems:	Total Frame Count:	Sequence / Shot:
	snow efx?	3/72	PG-15
		Start: End:	Rev. Date:

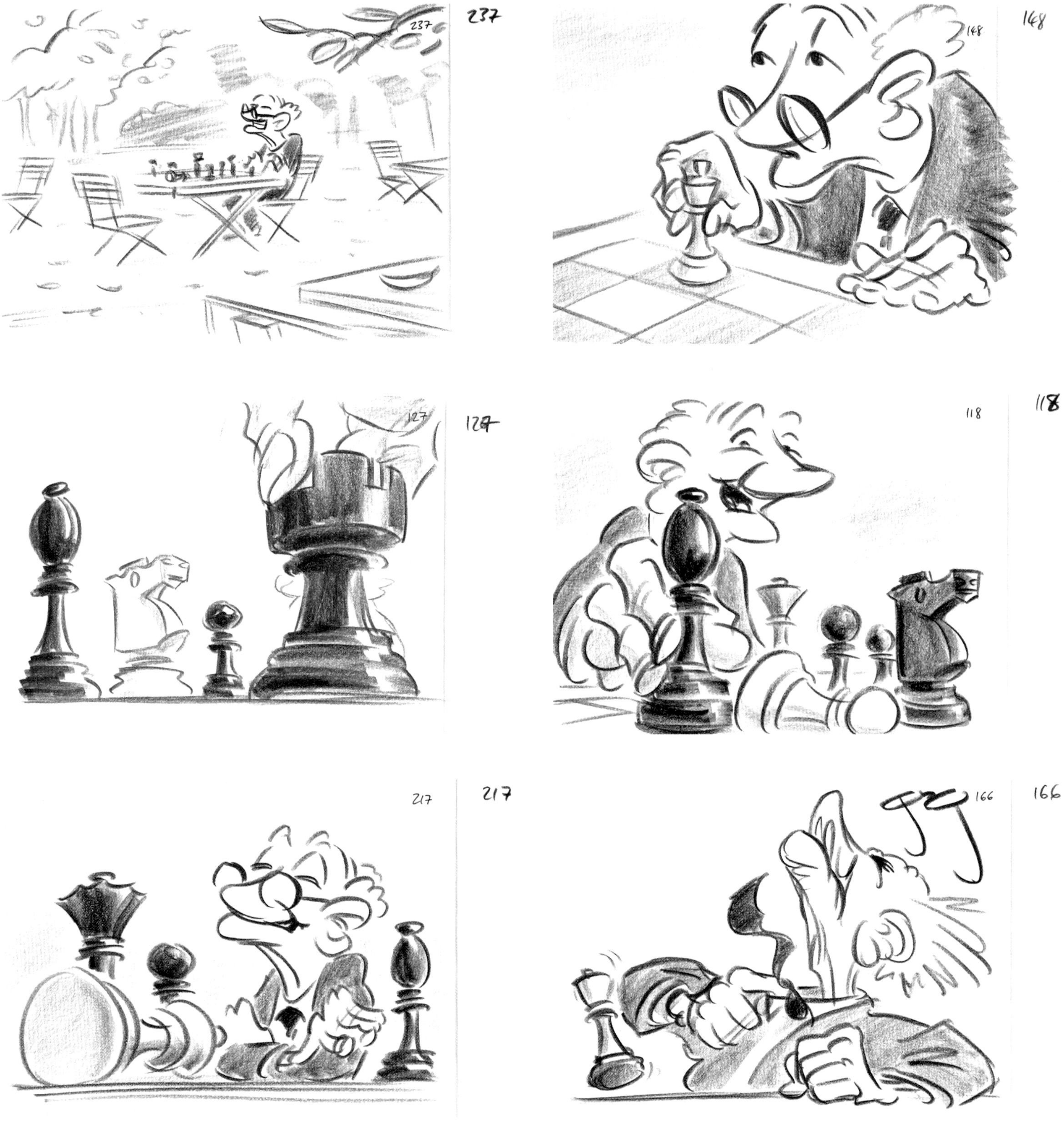

above and opposite:
Jan Pinkava
Storyboard
GERI'S GAME
Pencil
5½ x 8½ (each)

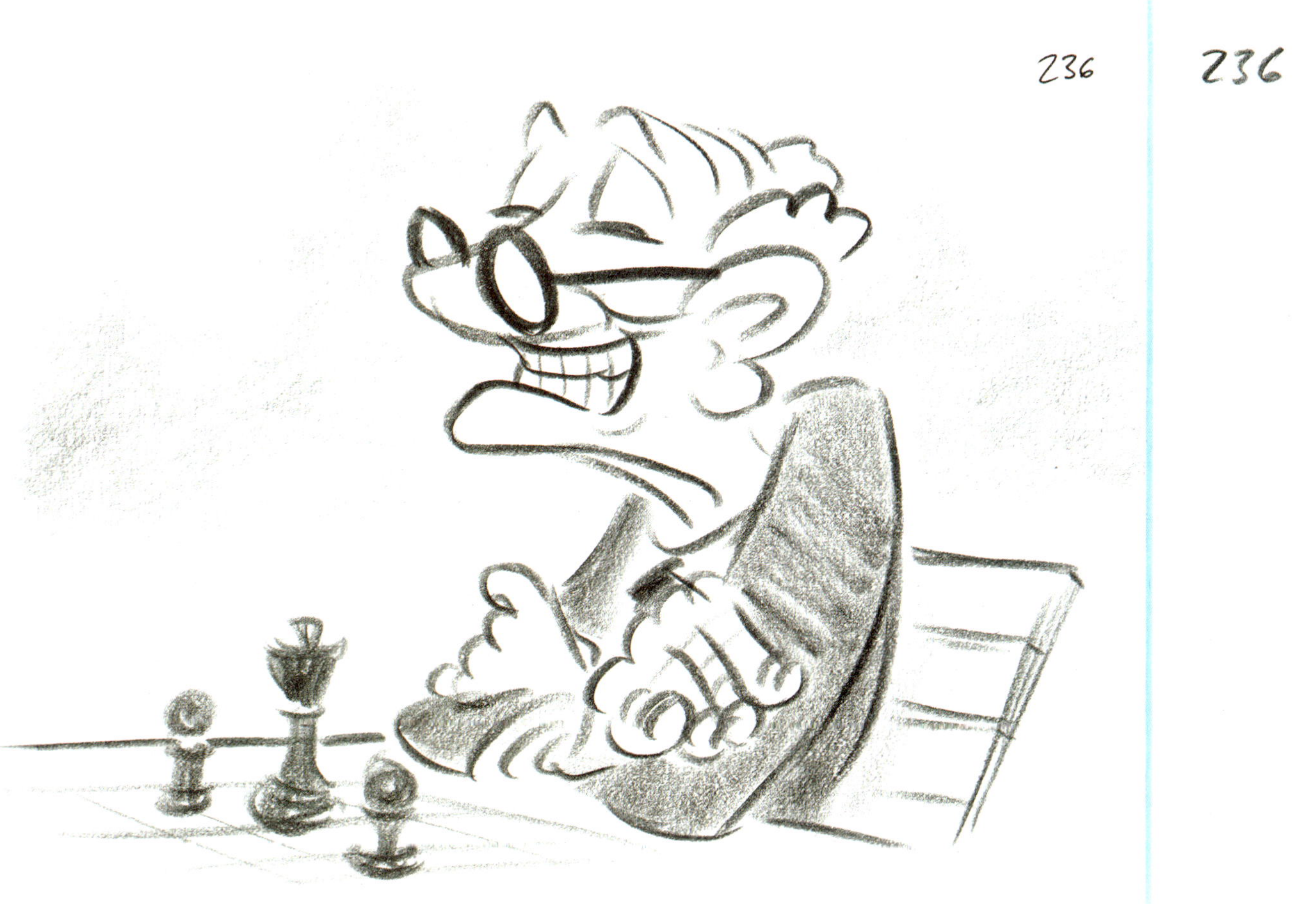
236
236

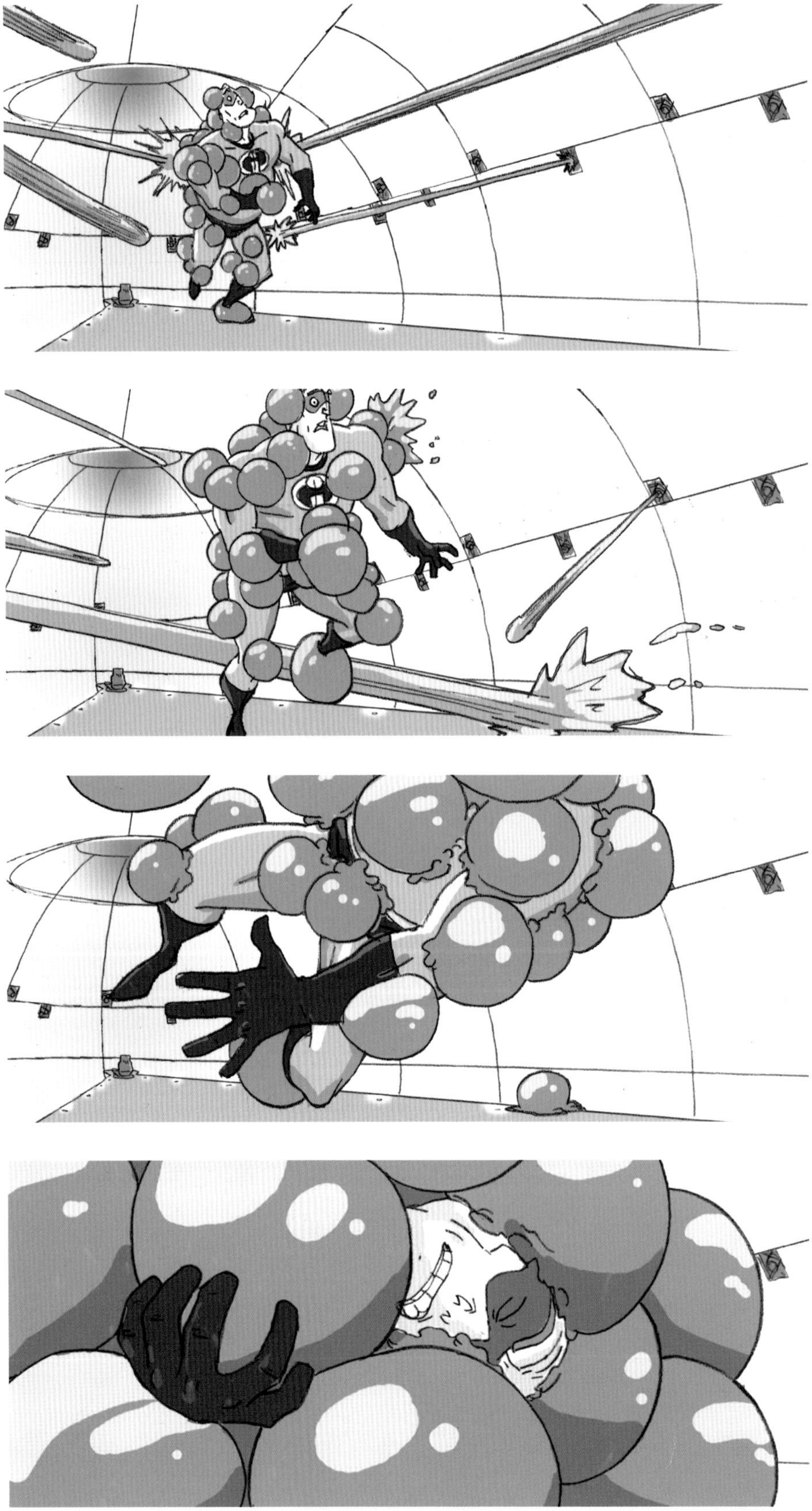

Ricardo Curtis
Storyboard
THE INCREDIBLES
Digital

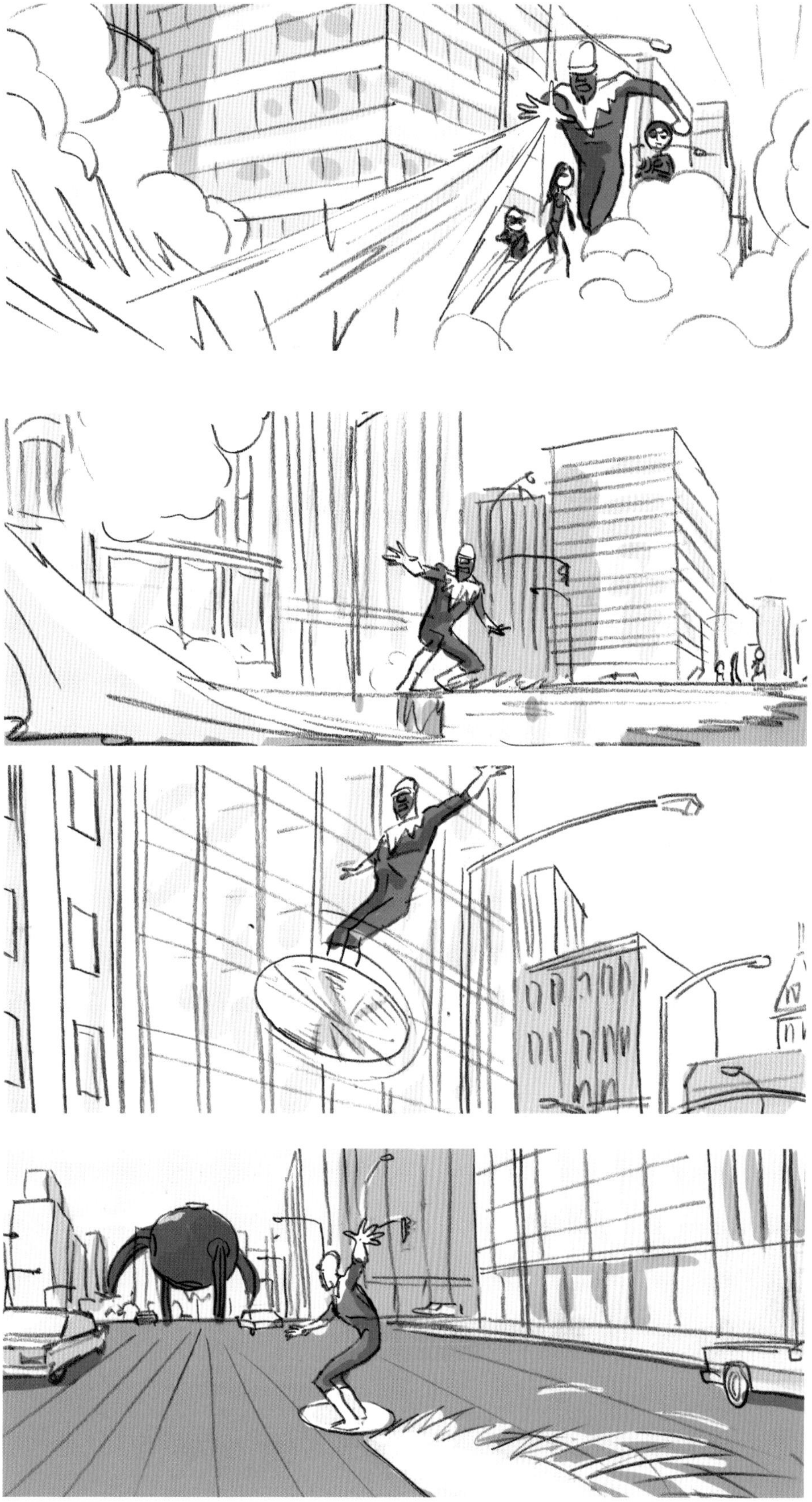

Mark Andrews
Storyboard
THE INCREDIBLES
Digital

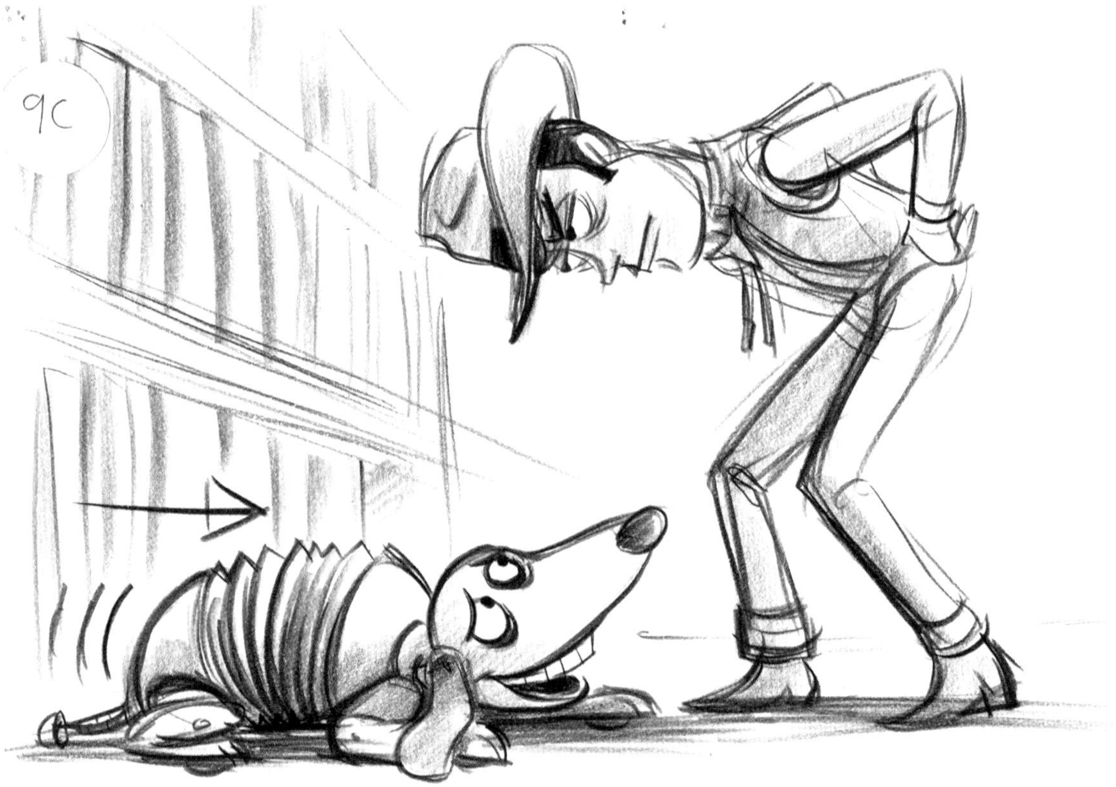

above and opposite:
Joe Ranft
Storyboard
TOY STORY
Pencil
5½ x 8½

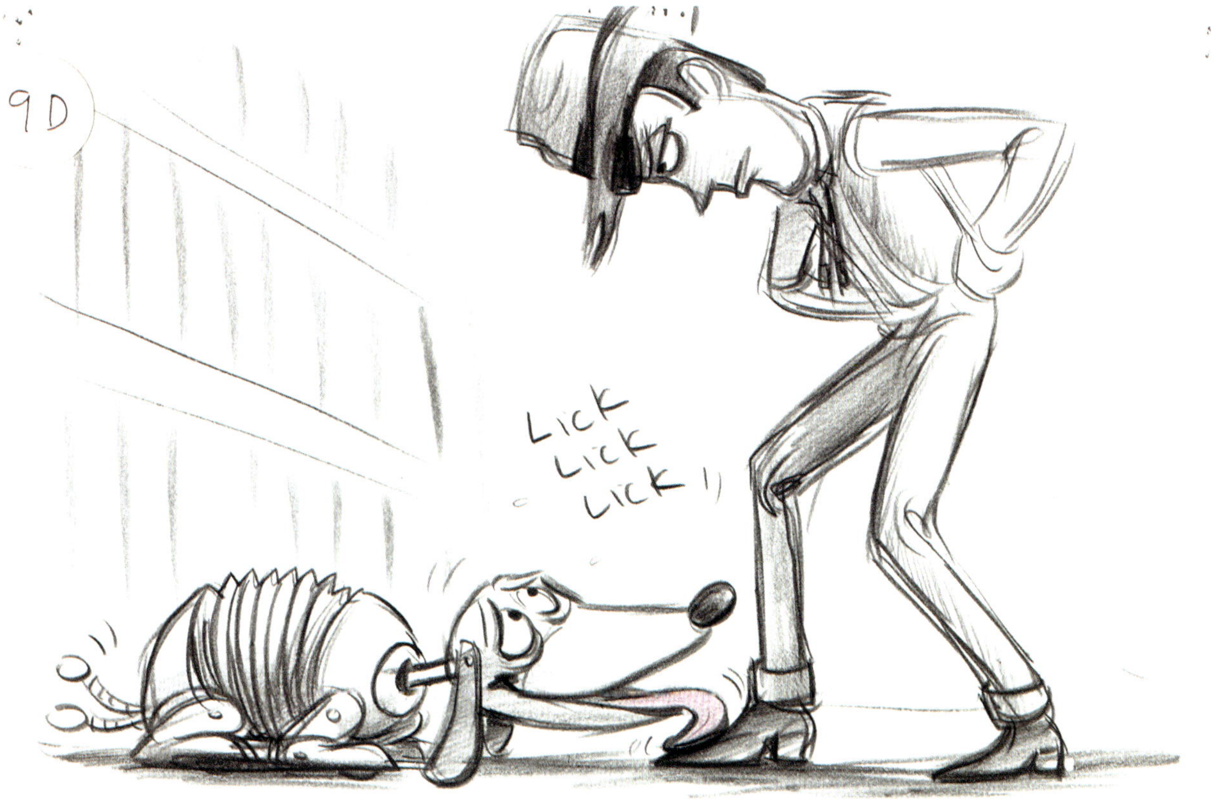
9D
Lick
Lick
Lick!!

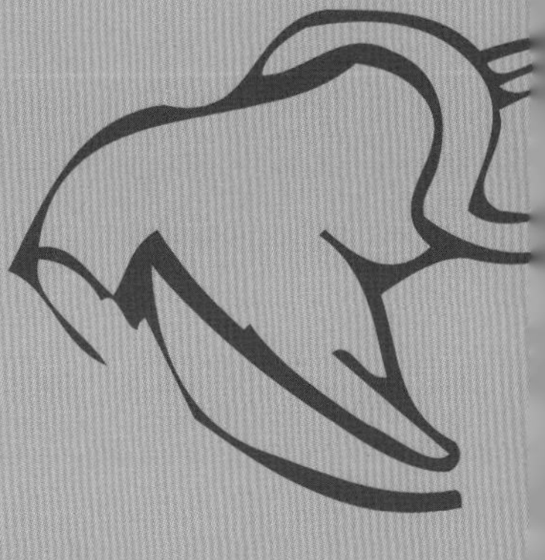

Bud Luckey
Woody (detail)
TOY STORY
Digital. Original, mixed media

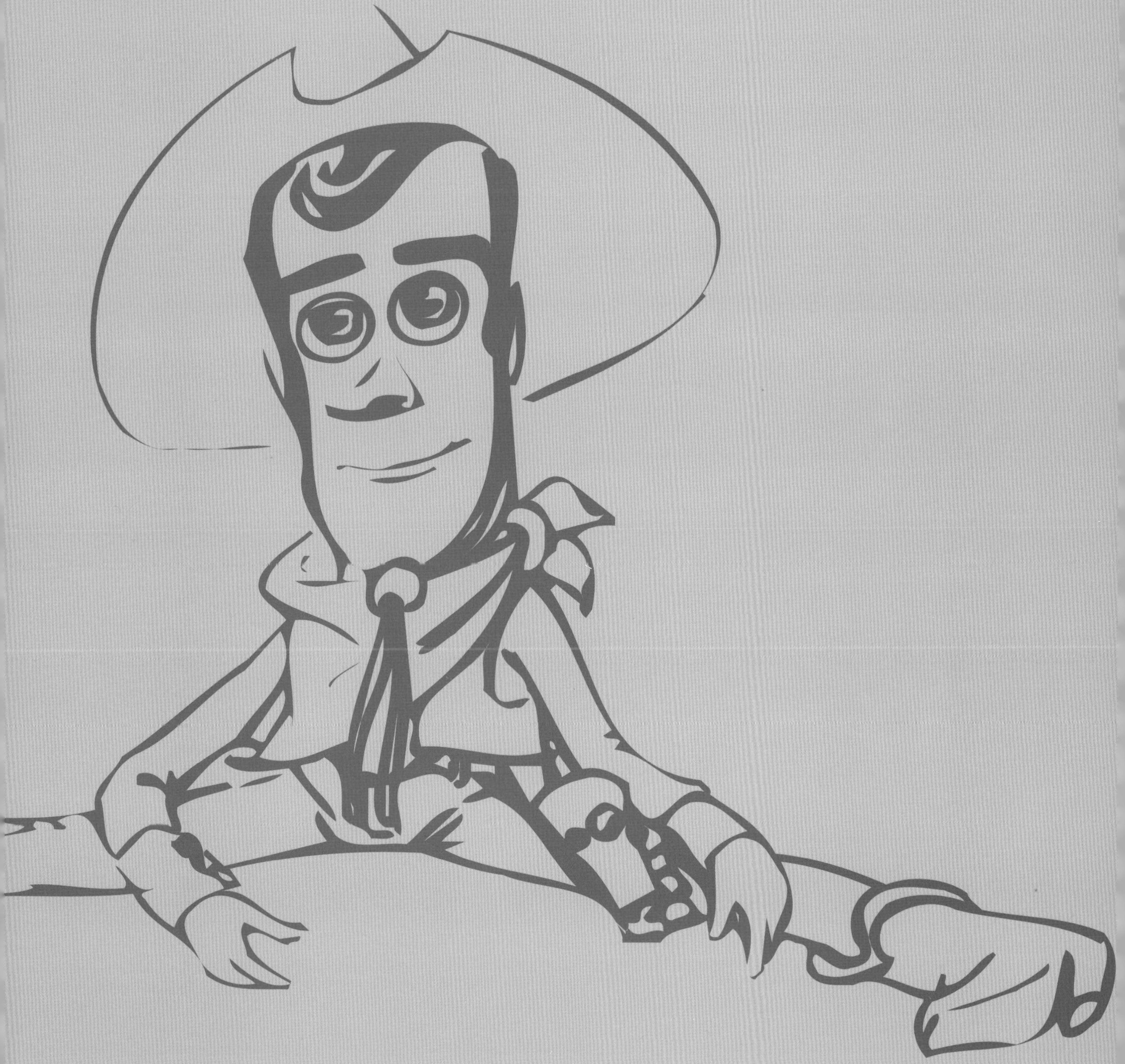

COLORSCRIPTS

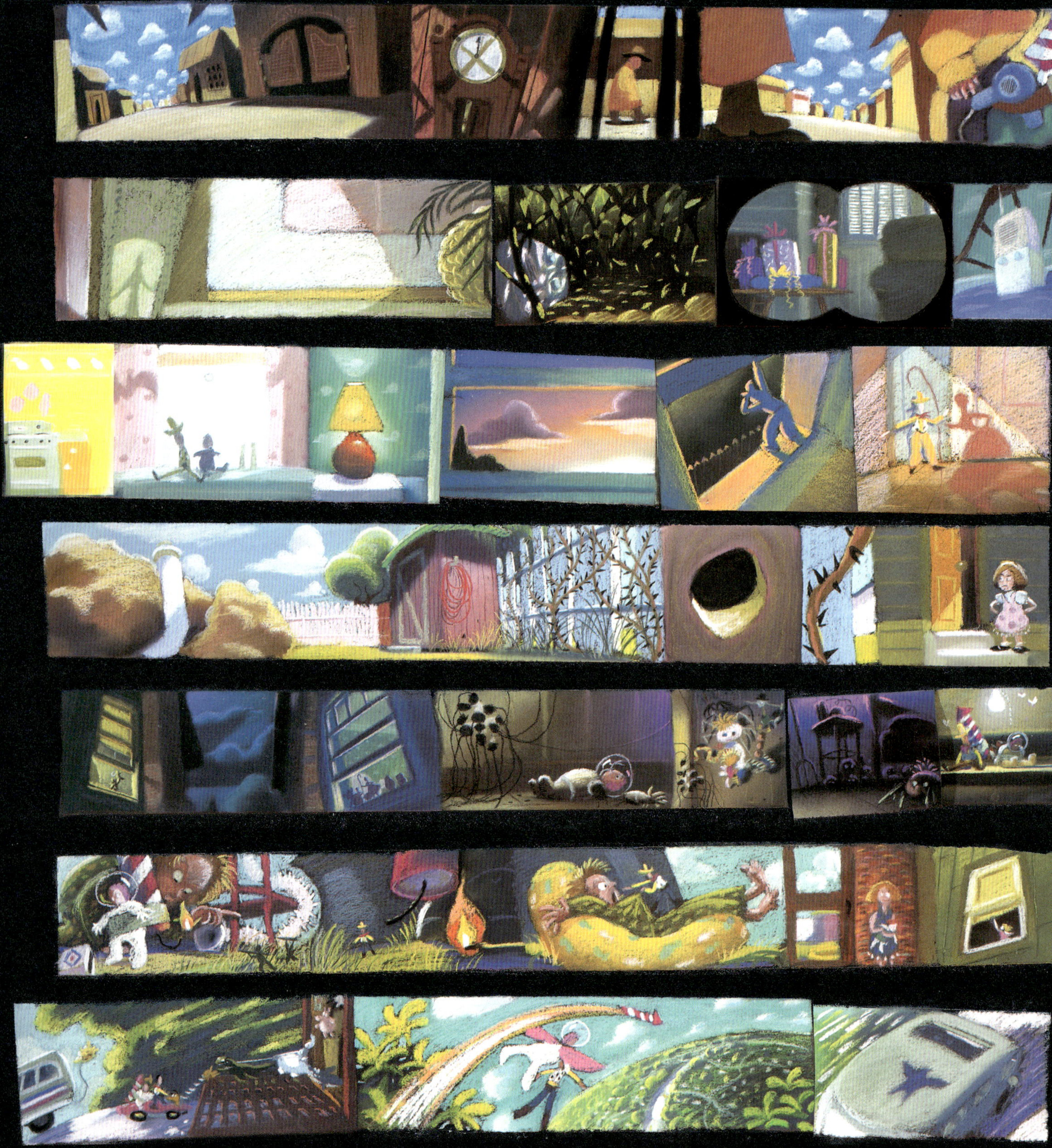

Ralph Eggleston
Colorscript

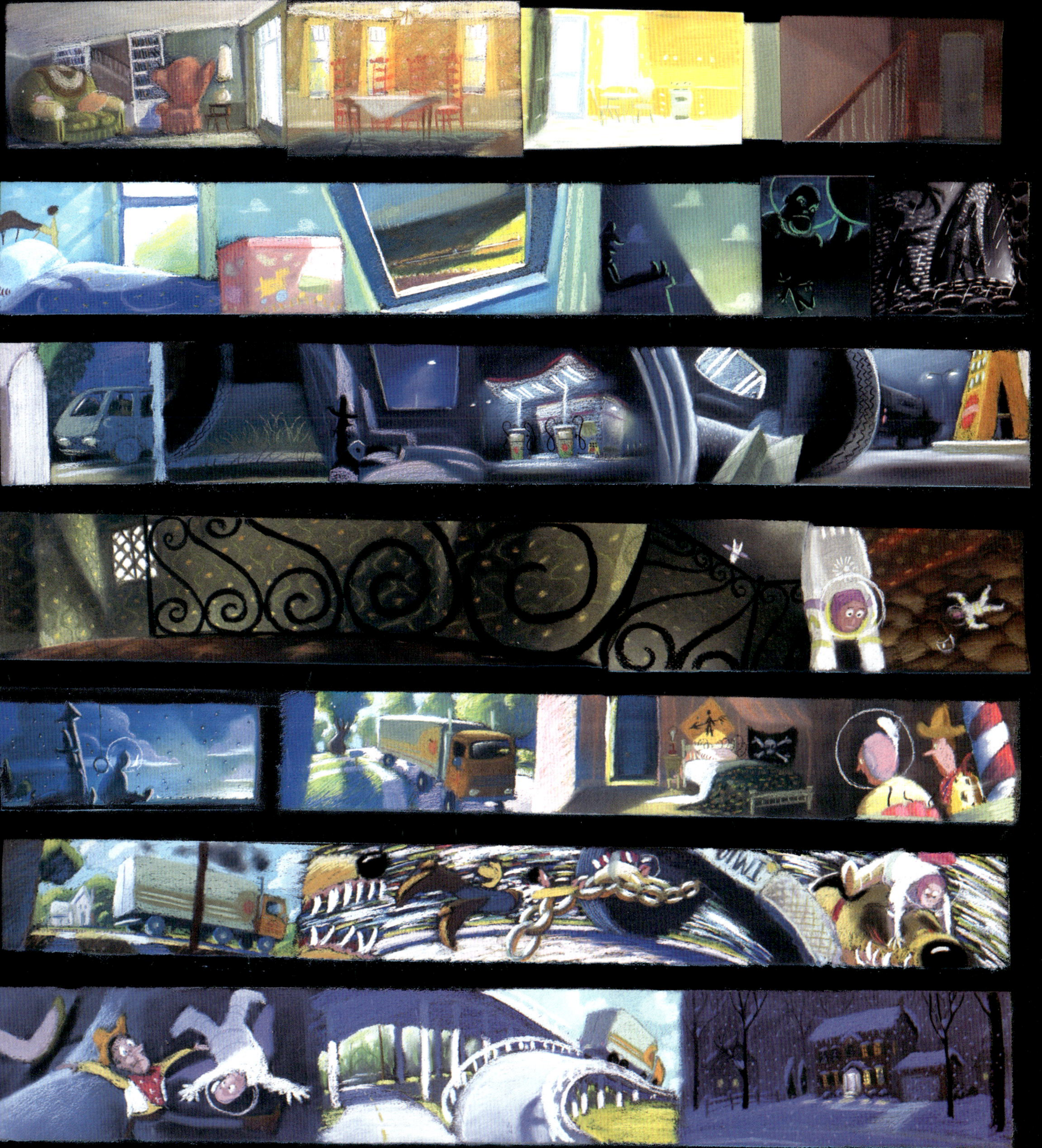

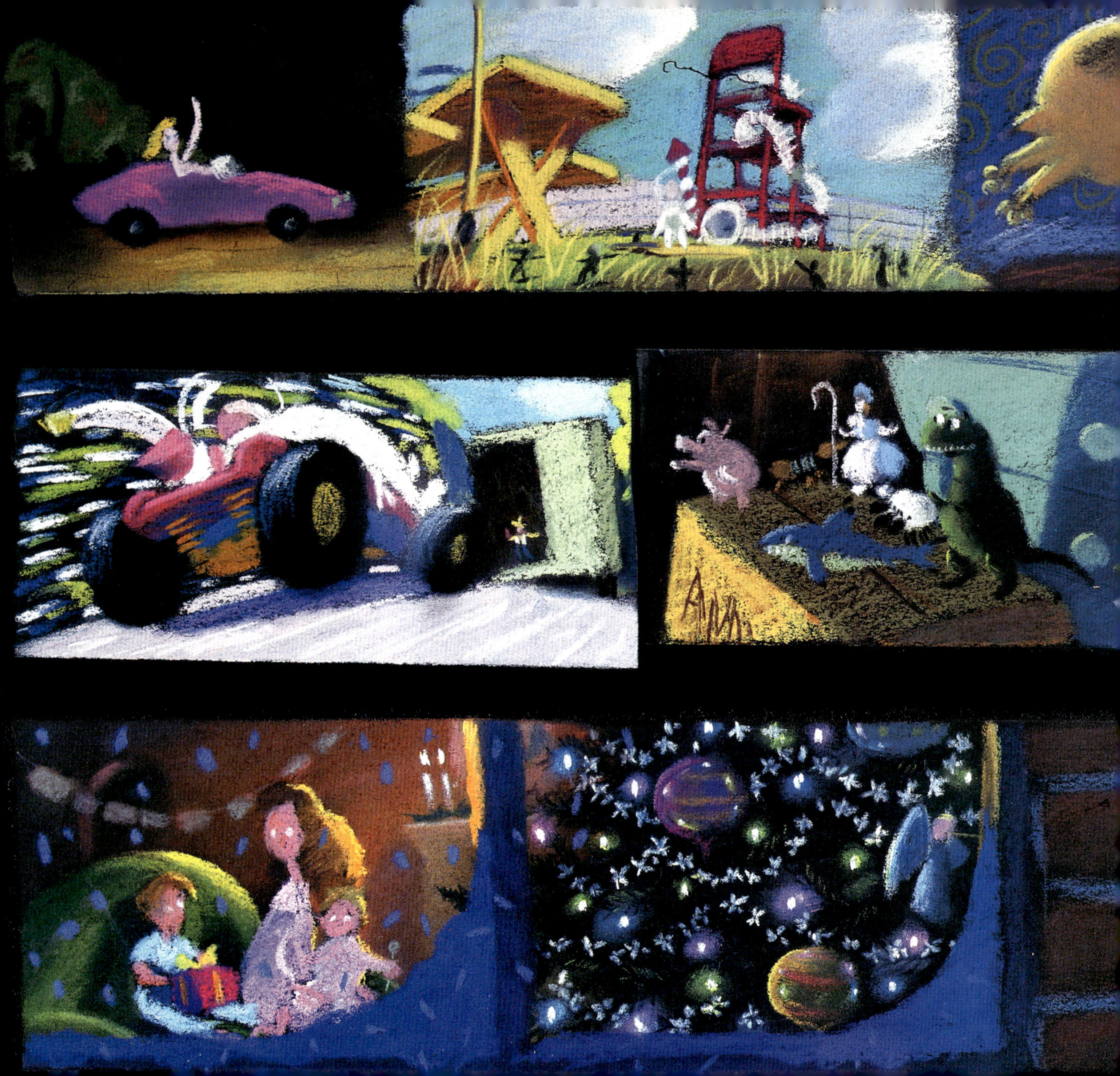

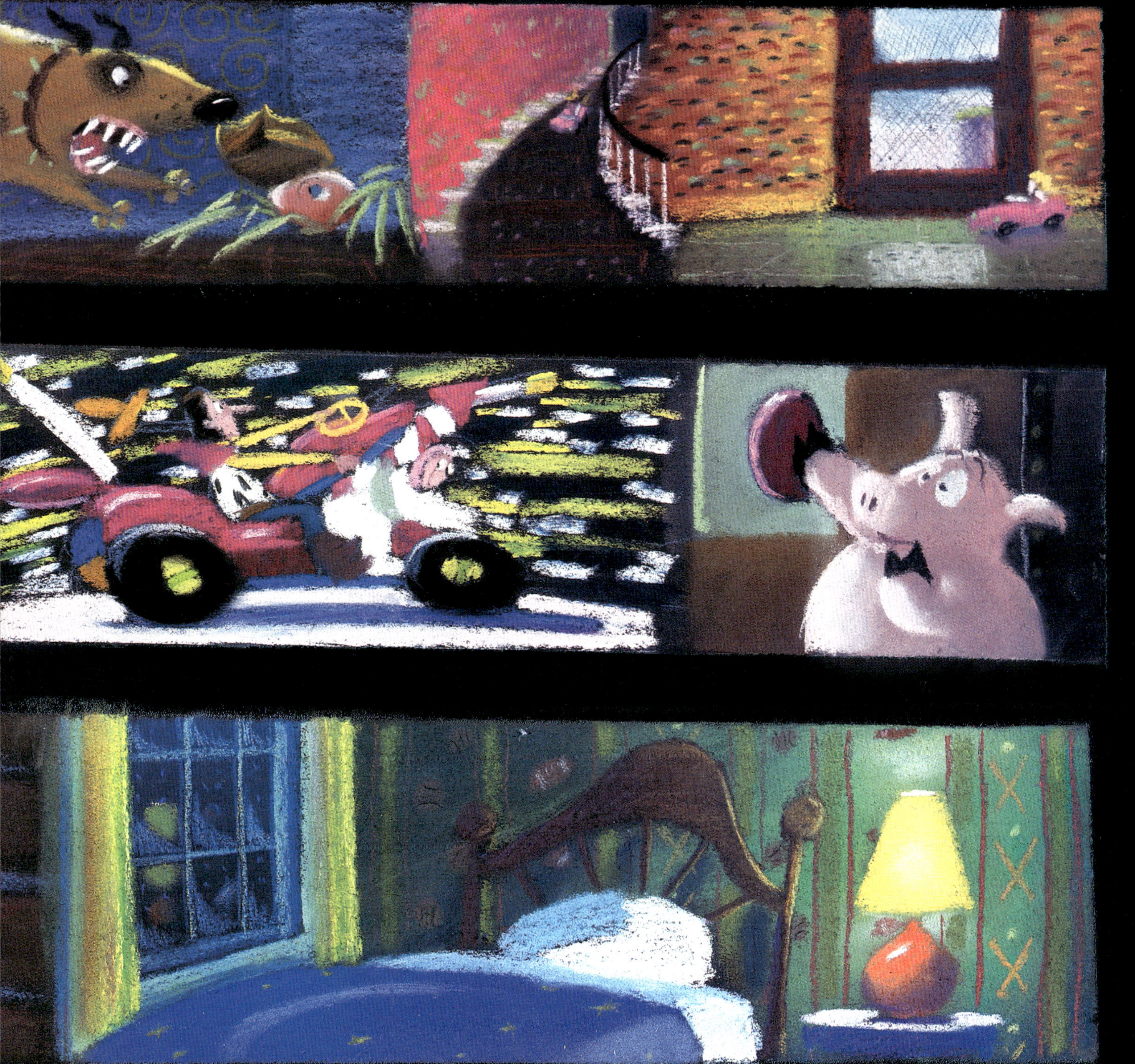

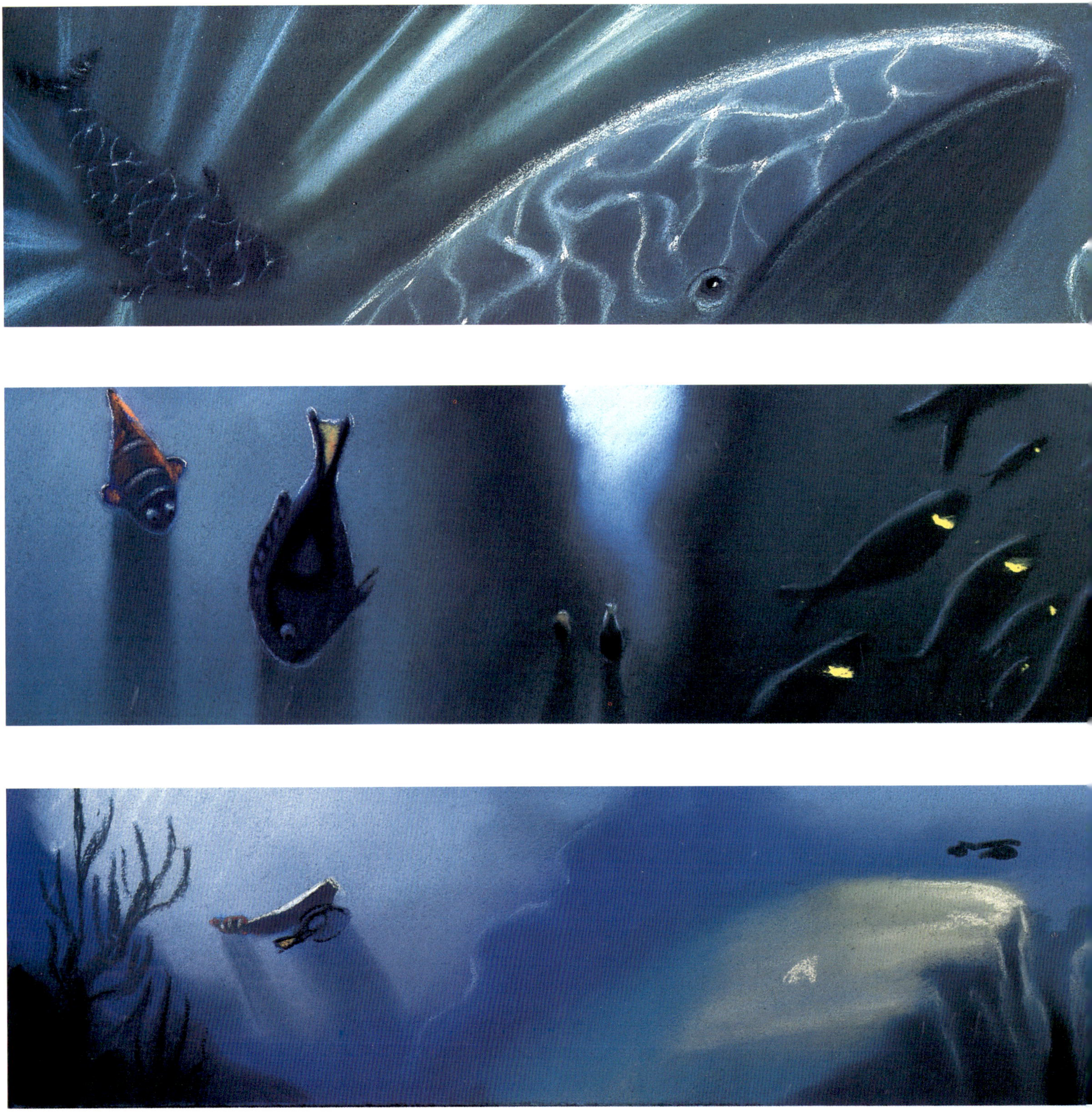

Ralph Eggleston
Early colorscript
FINDING NEMO
Pastel
Dimensions vary

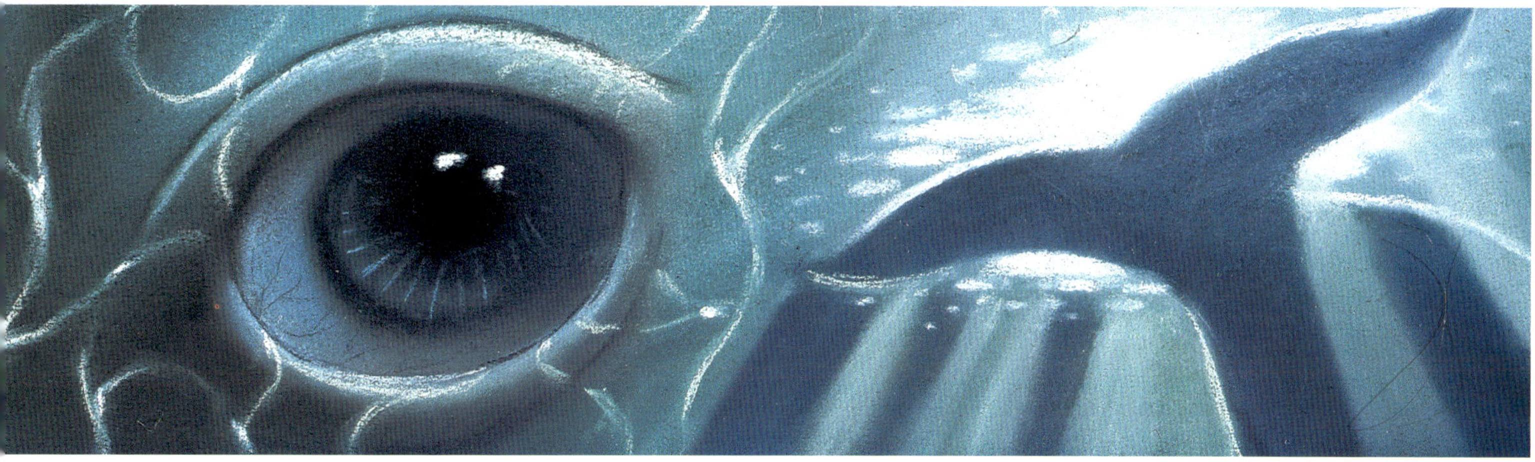

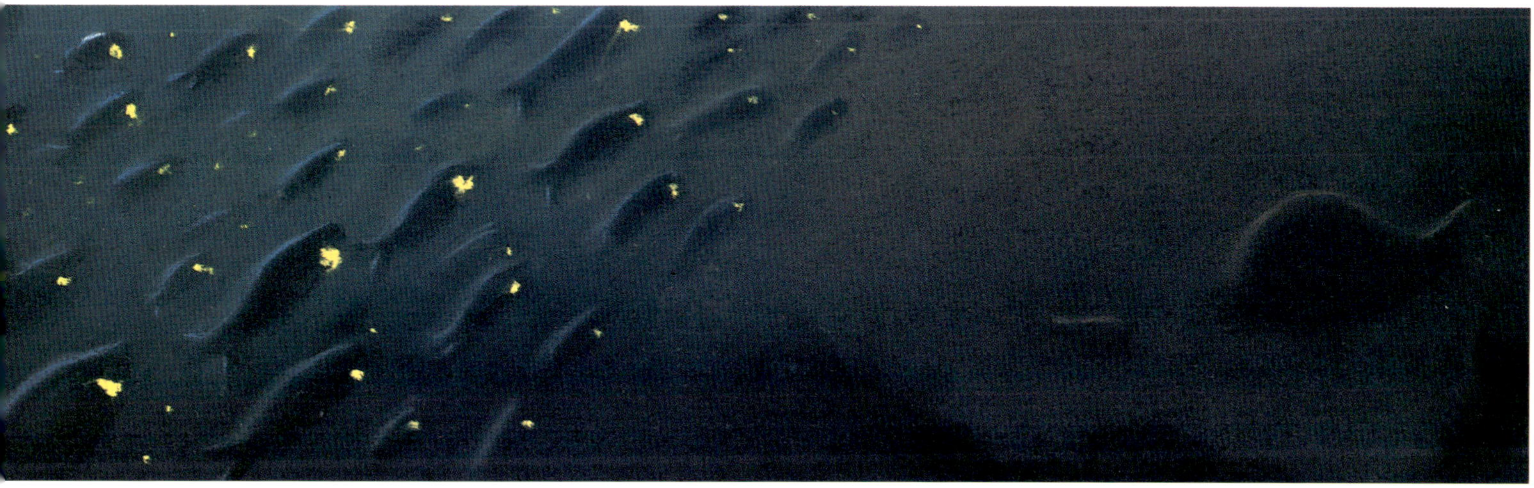

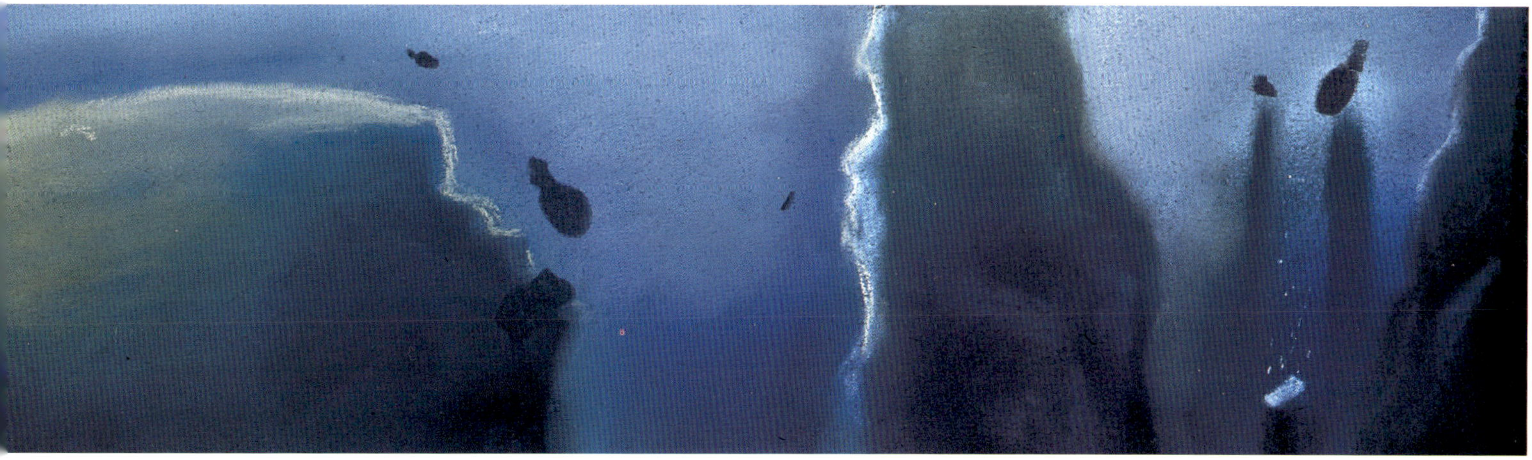

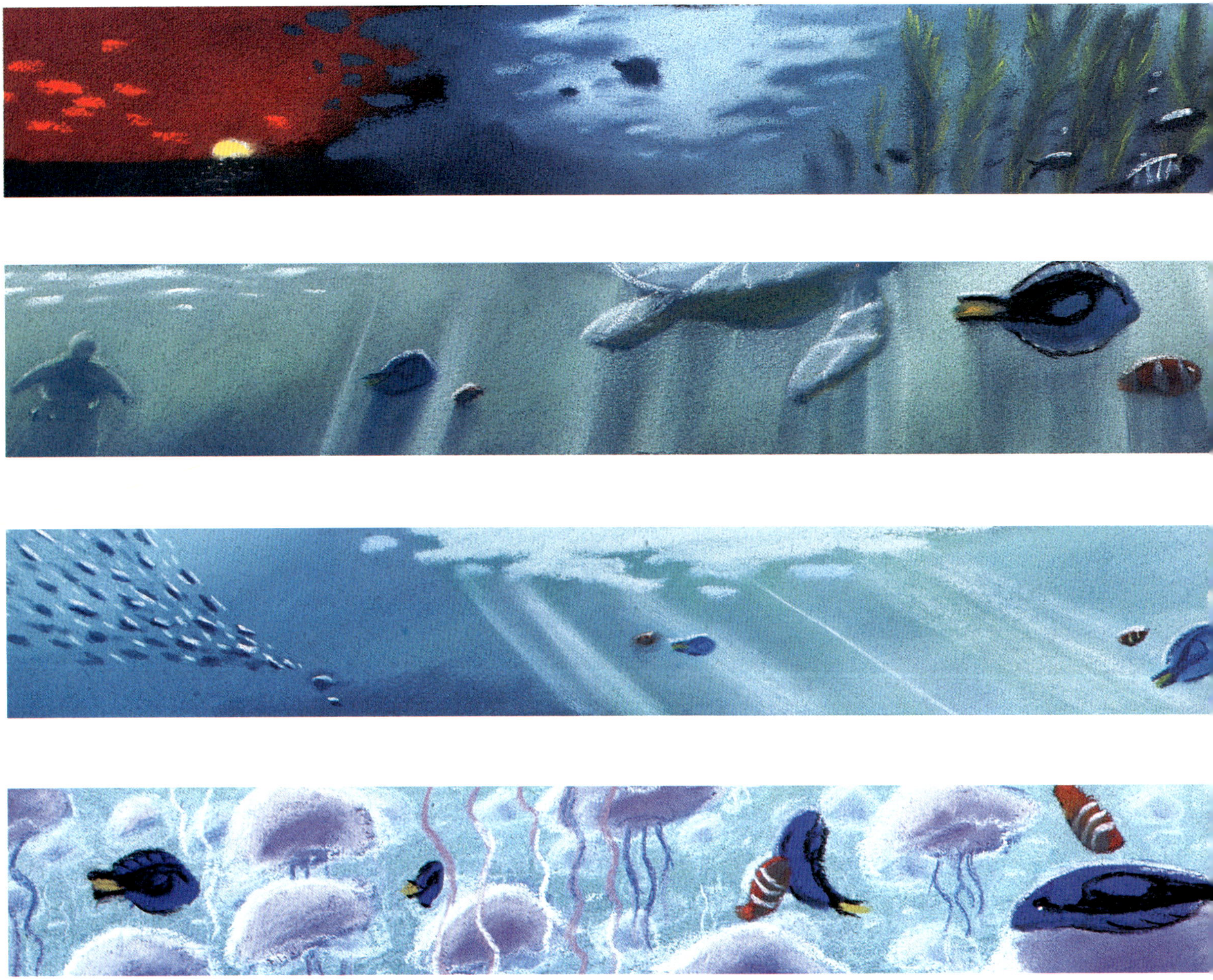

Ralph Eggleston
Early colorscript
FINDING NEMO
Pastel
Dimensions vary

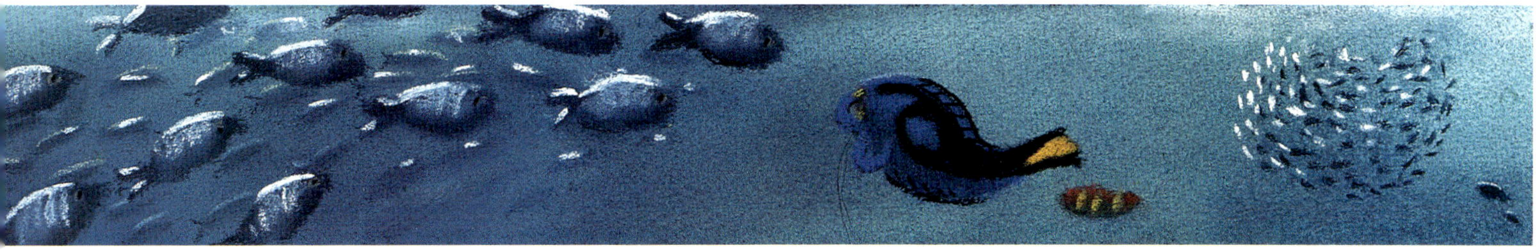

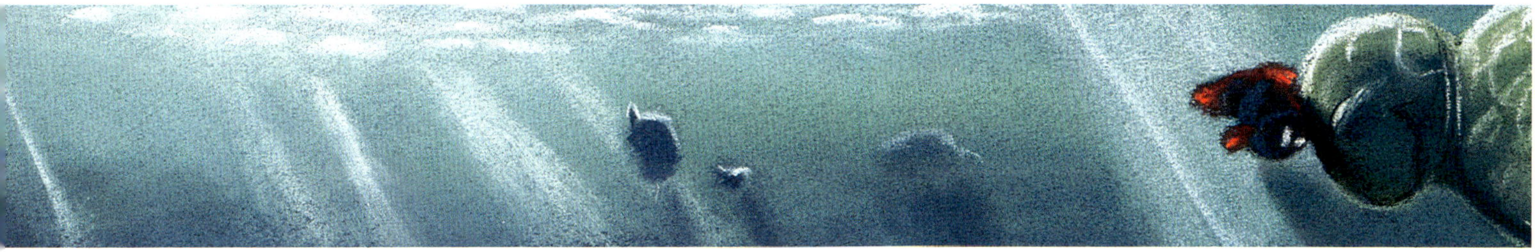

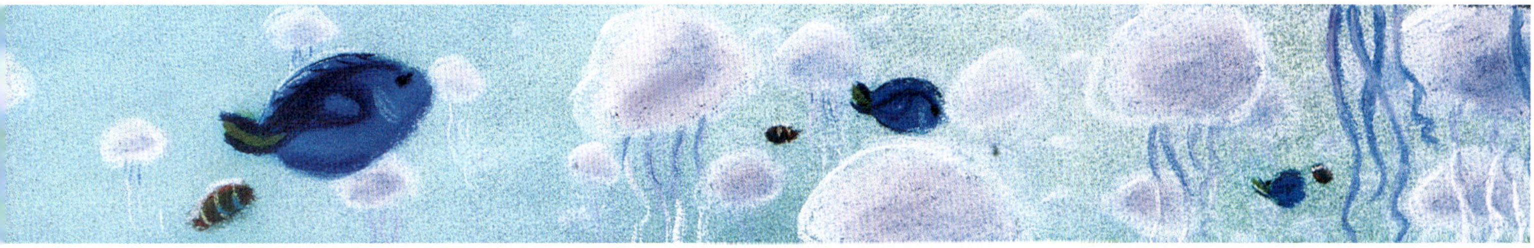

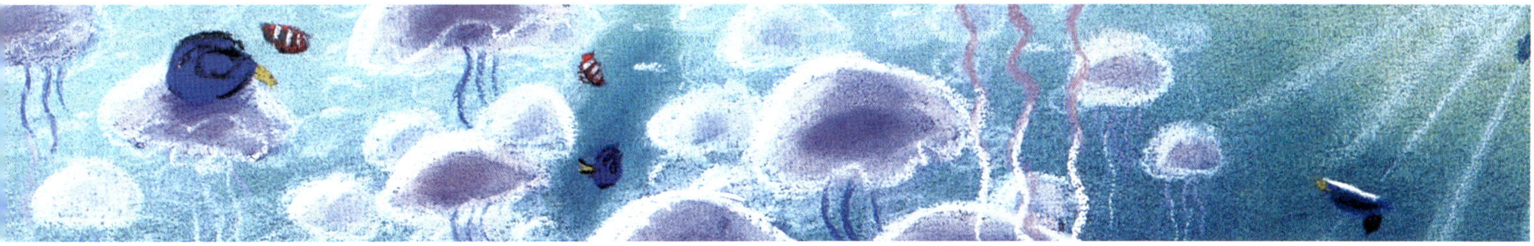

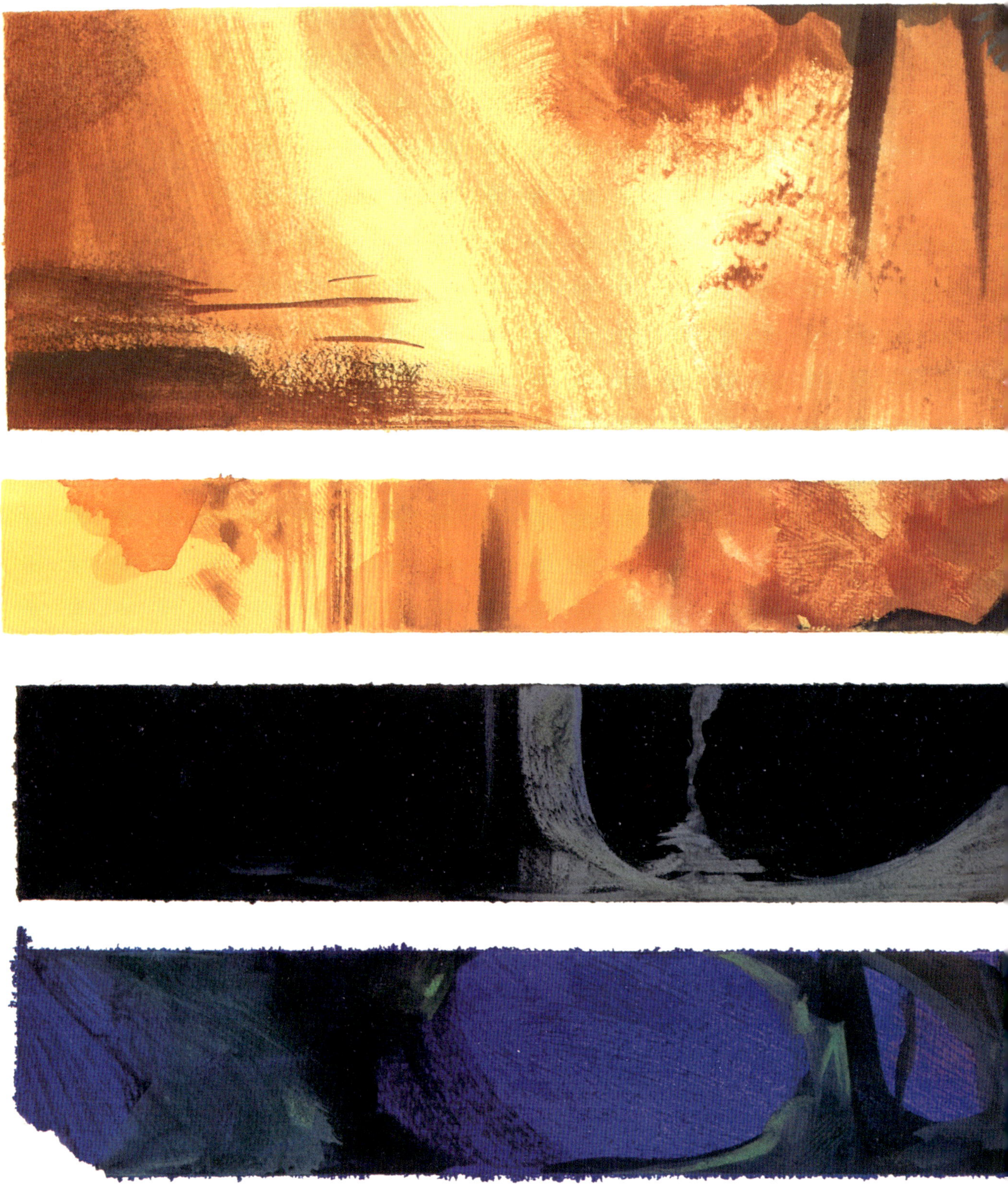

Bill Cone
Study of underground light and forms
A BUG'S LIFE
Acrylic and gouache
8 x 10¾

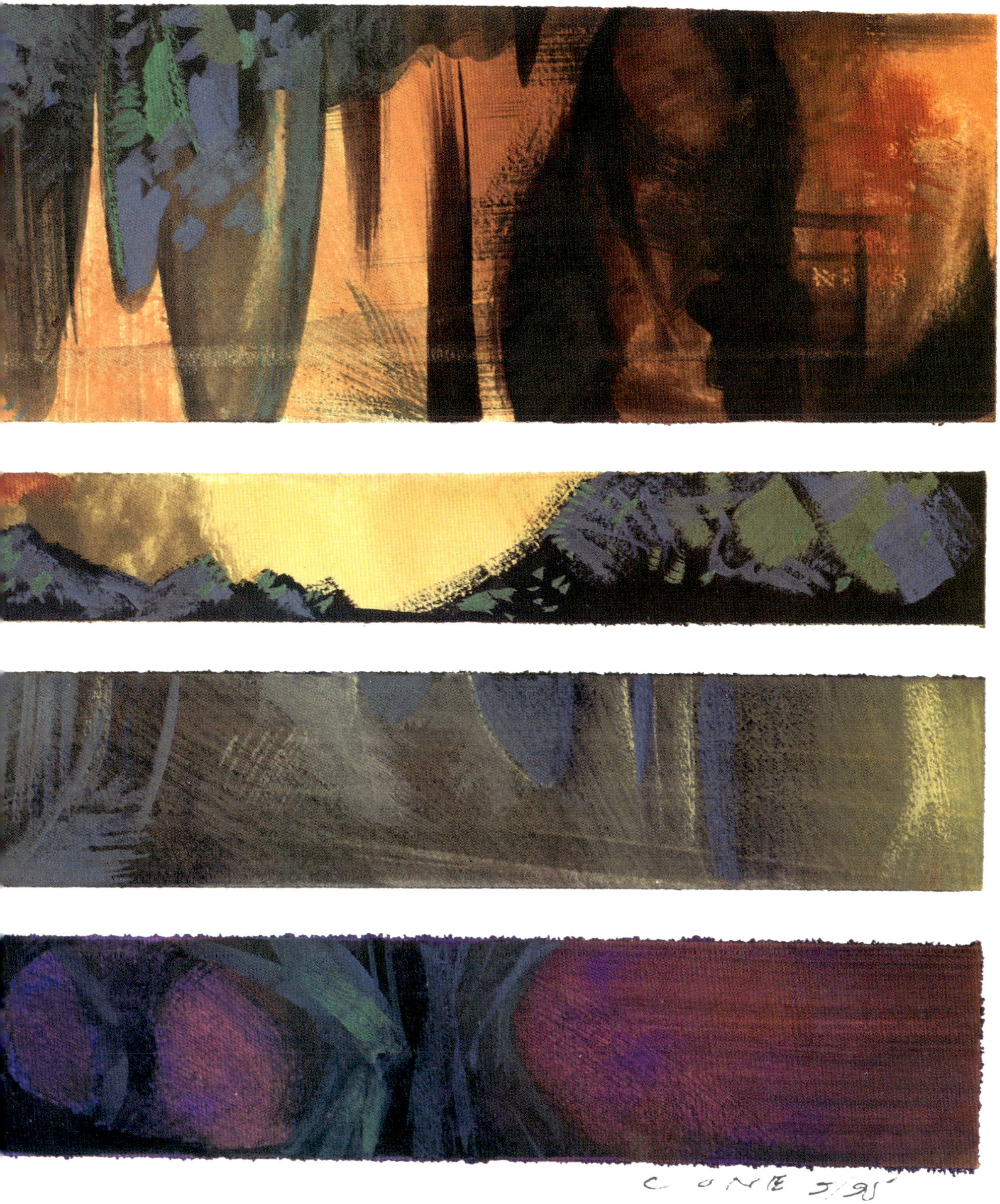
CONE 5/95

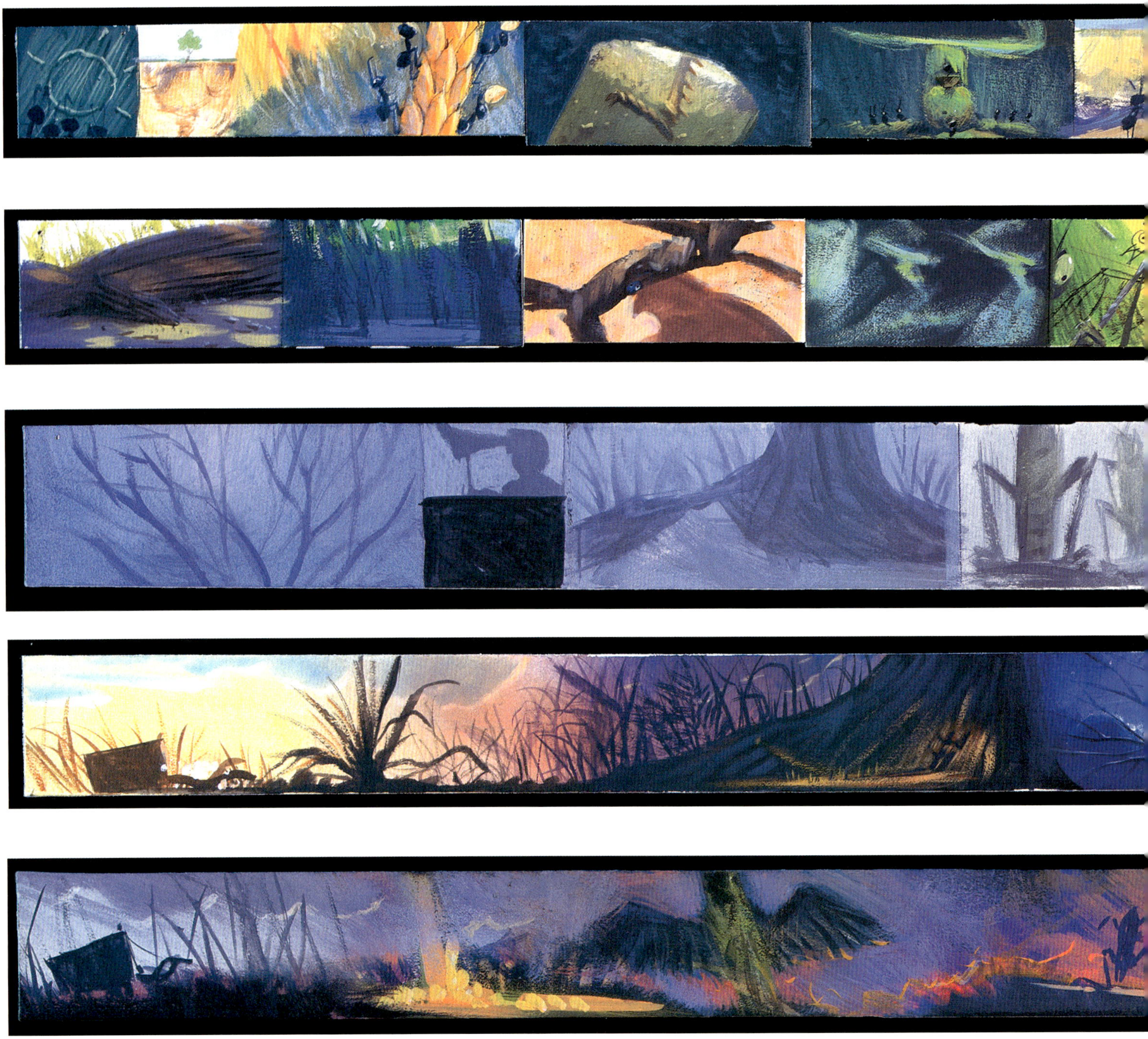

Bill Cone
Early colorscript
A BUG'S LIFE
Acrylic and gouache
Dimensions vary

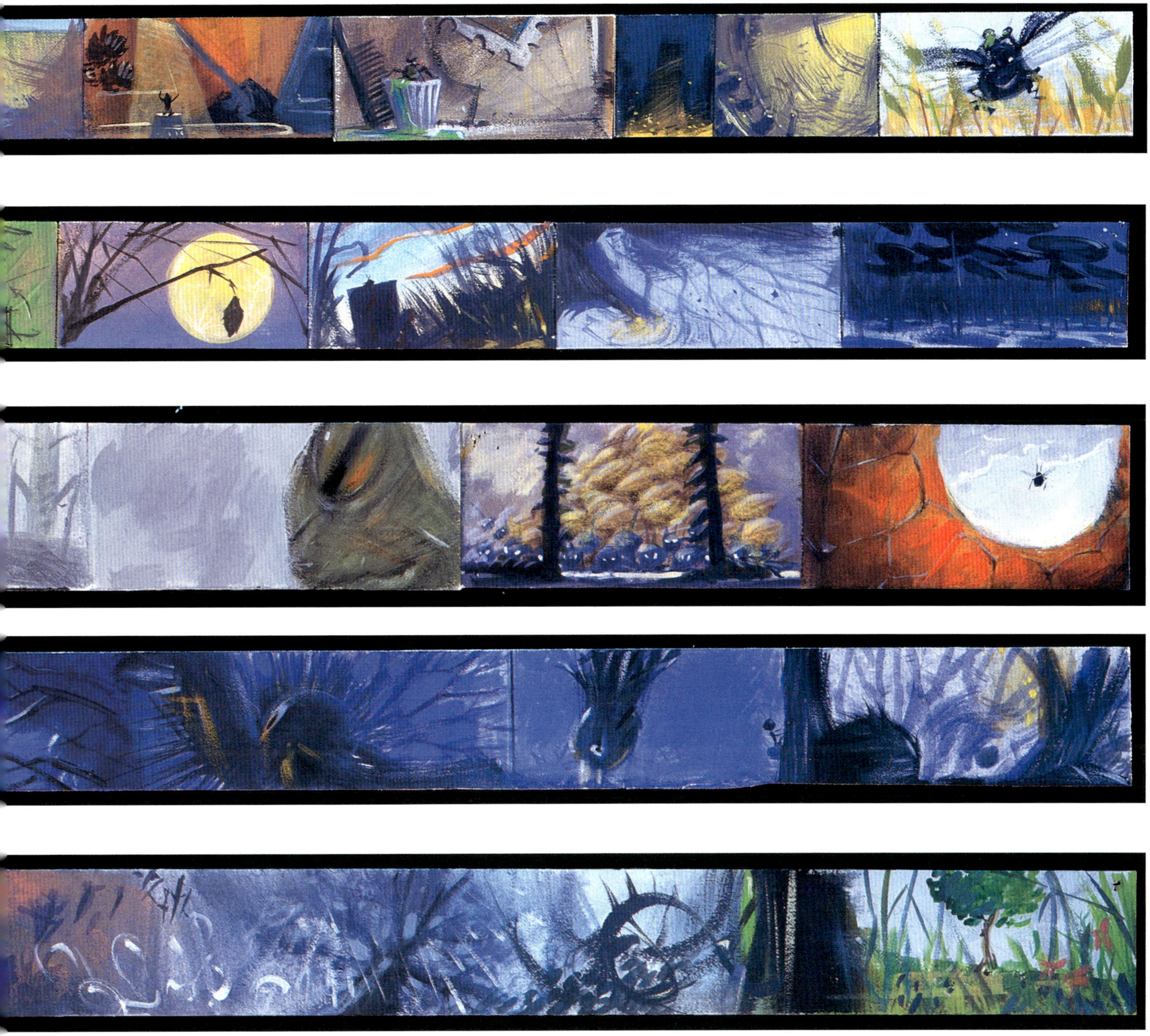

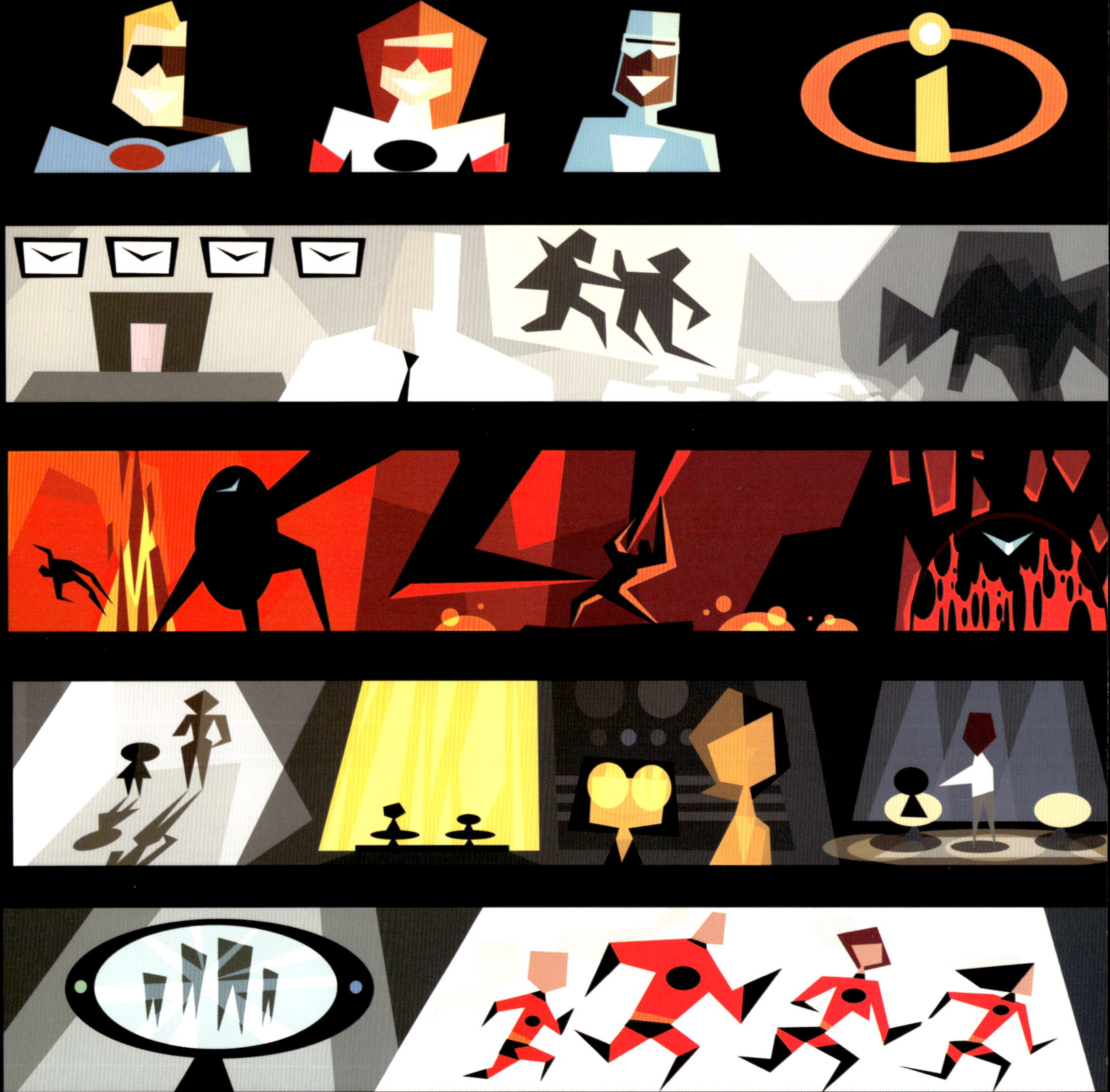

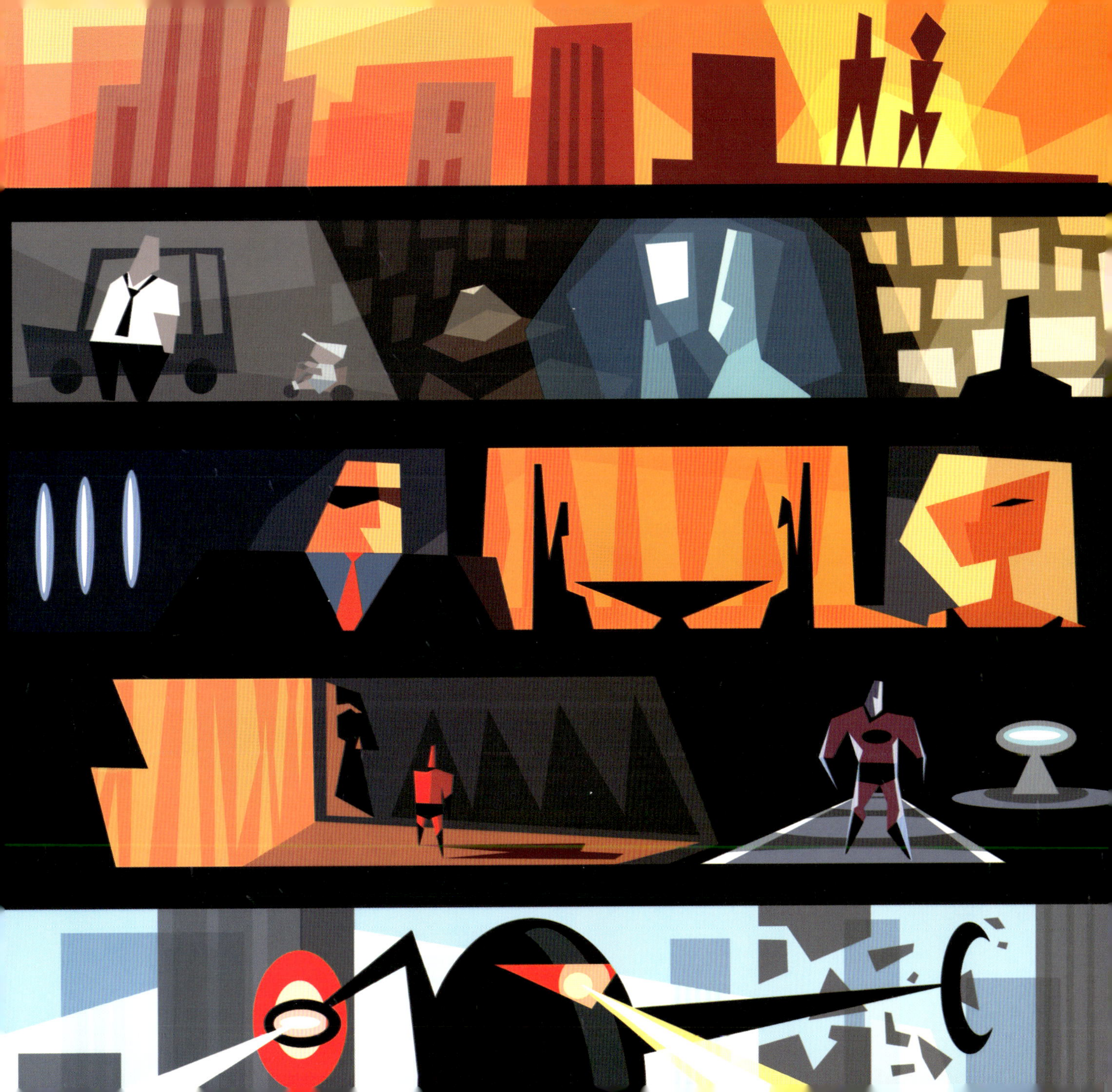

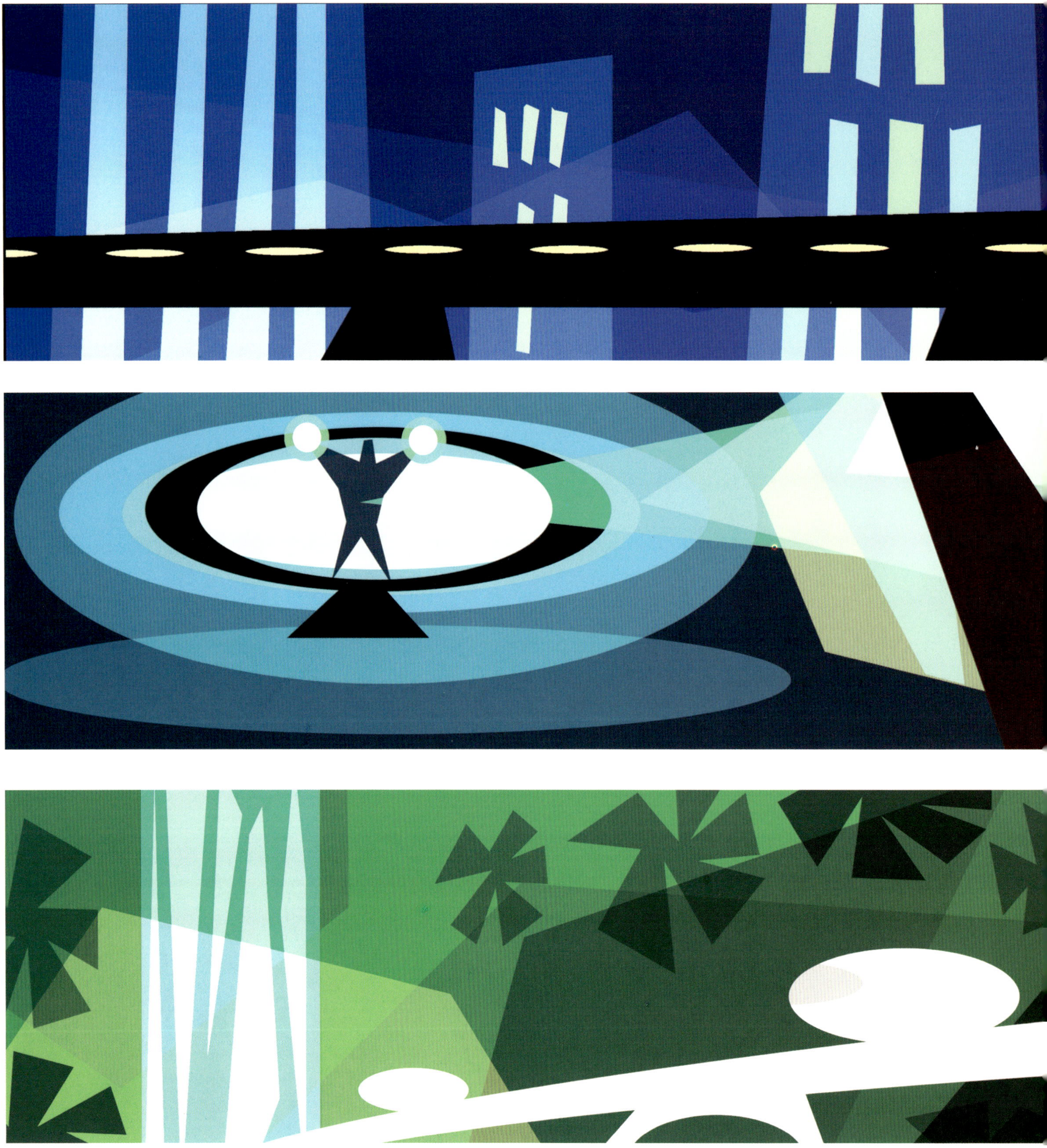

Lou Romano
Colorscript
THE INCREDIBLES
Digital

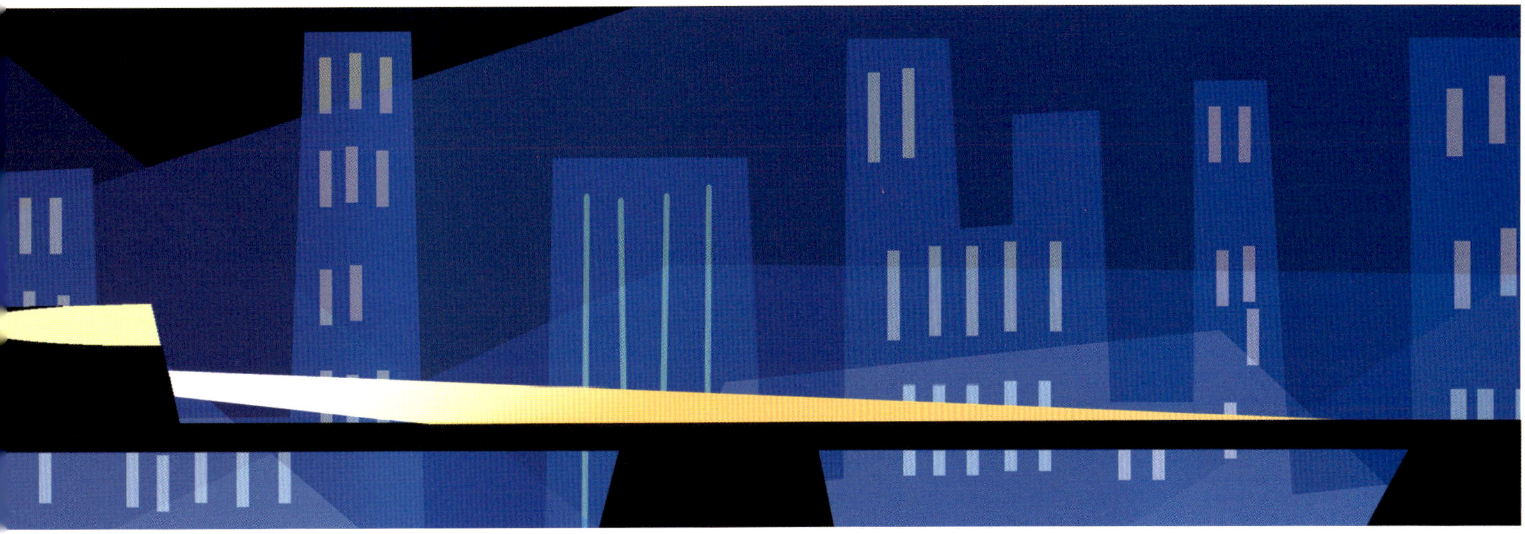

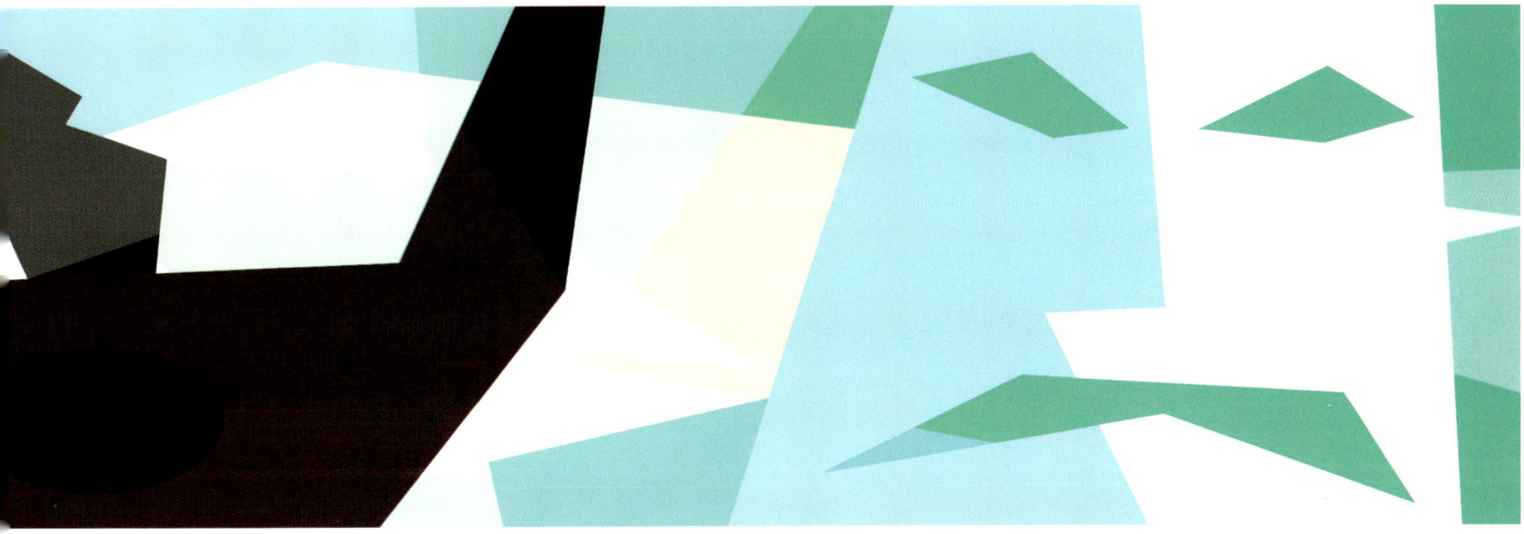

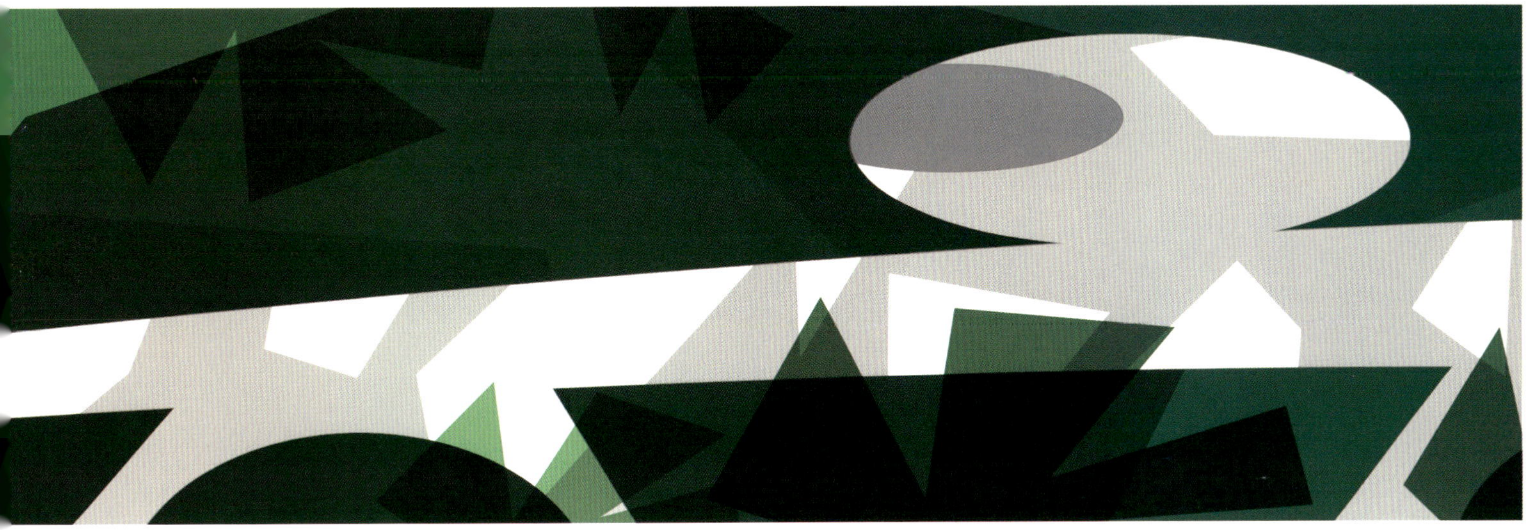

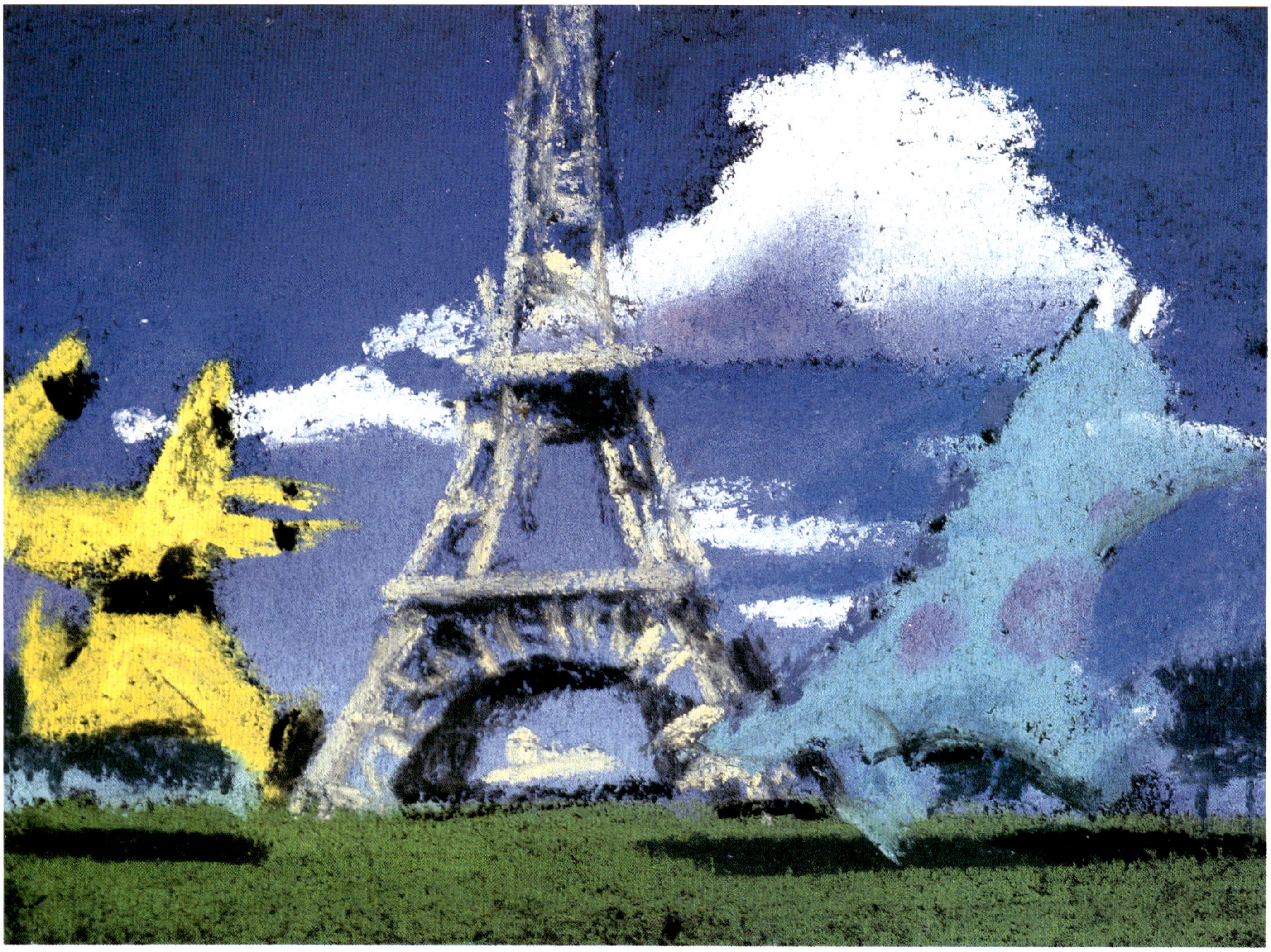

Dominique R. Louis
Colorscript
Layout by Harley Jessup
MONSTERS, INC.
Pastel
3 x 4

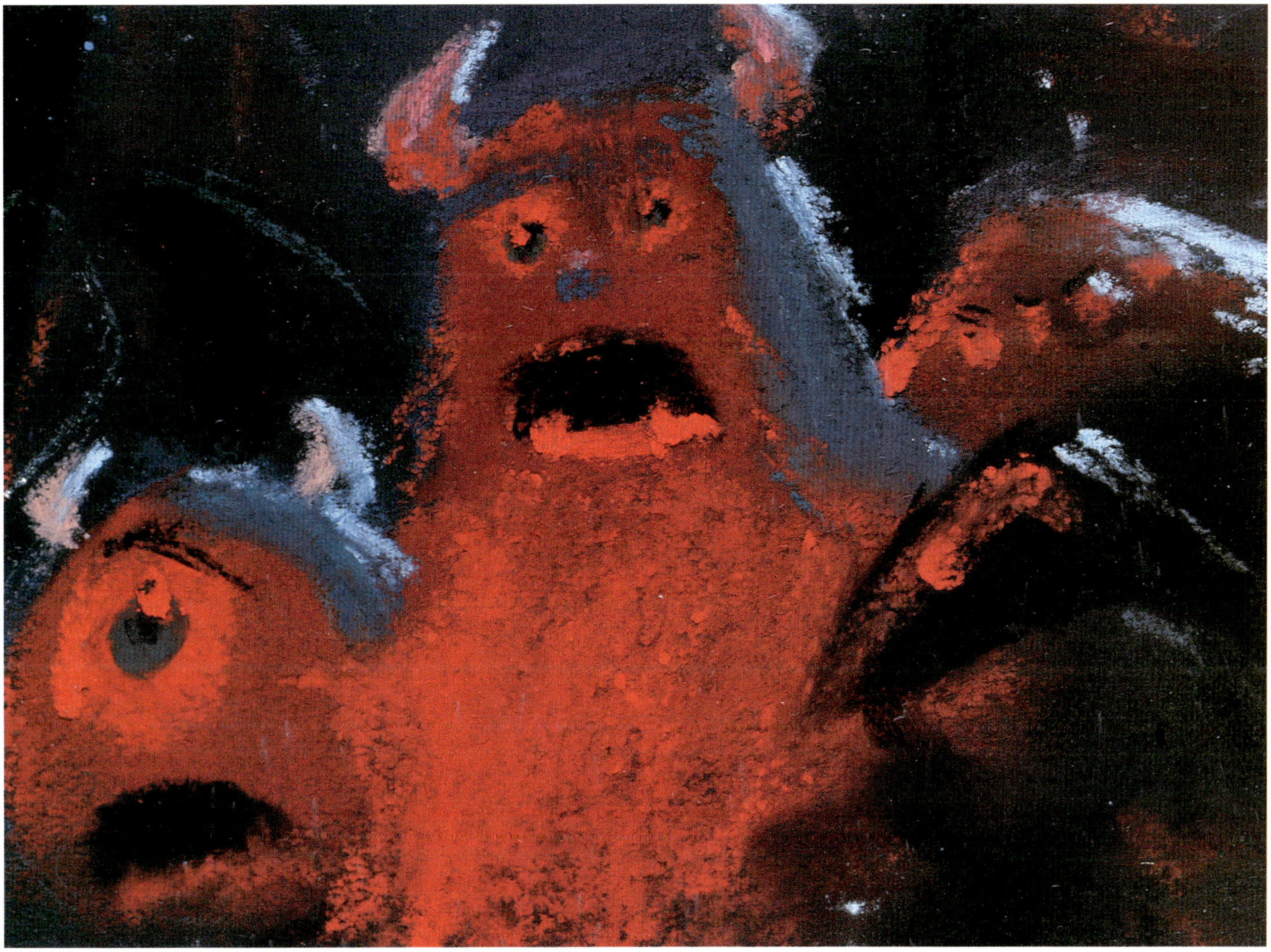

above and overleaf:
Dominique R. Louis
Colorscript
Layout by Harley Jessup
MONSTERS, INC.
Pastel
3 x 4

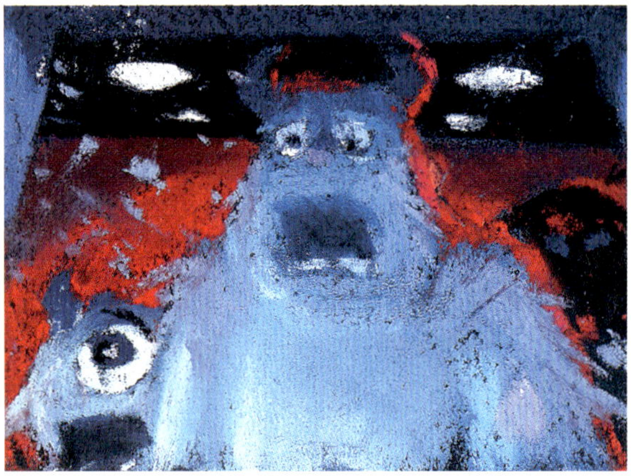
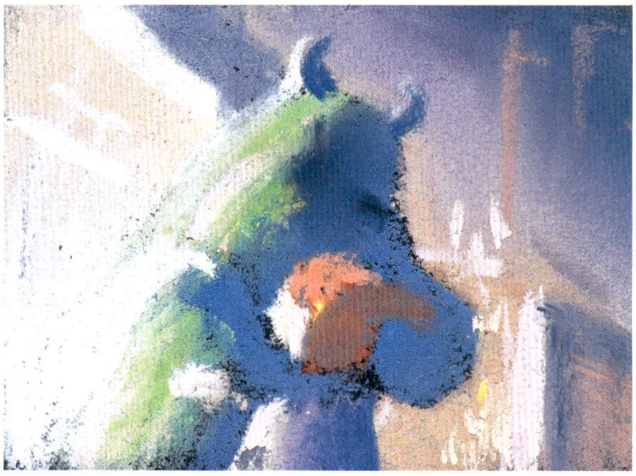
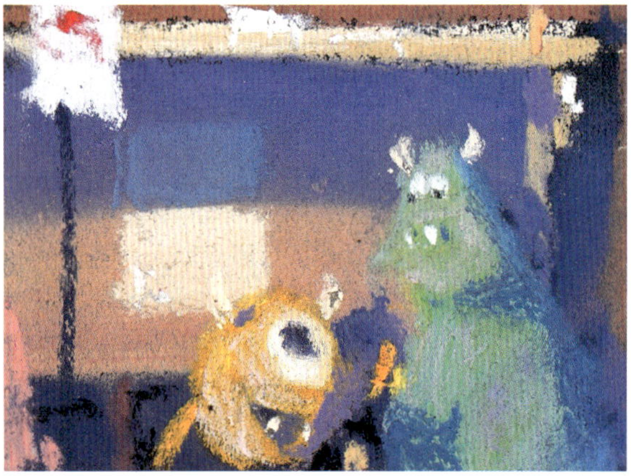
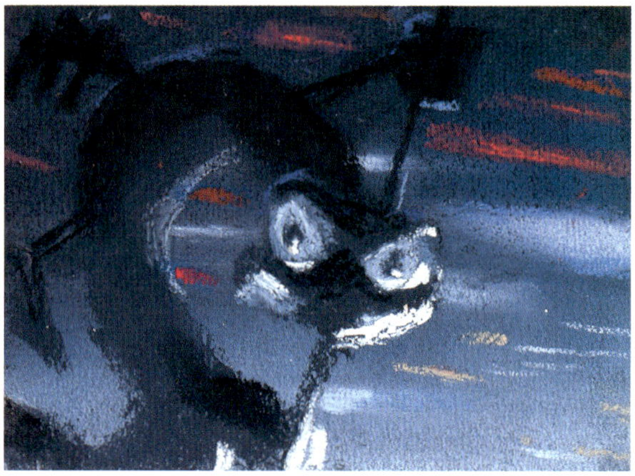
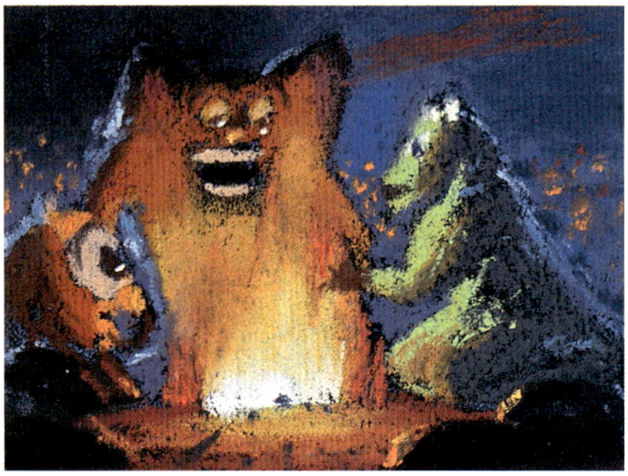
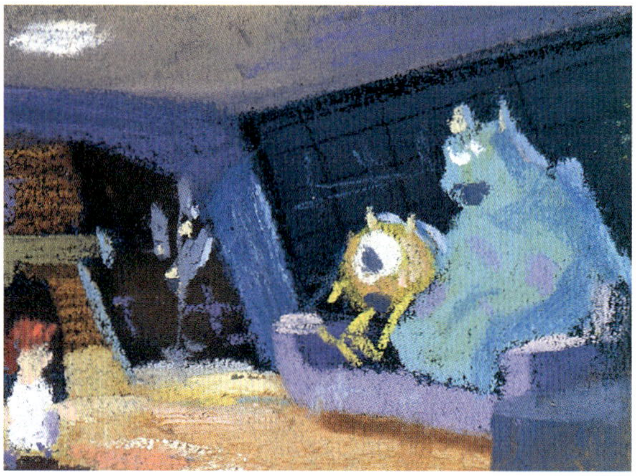
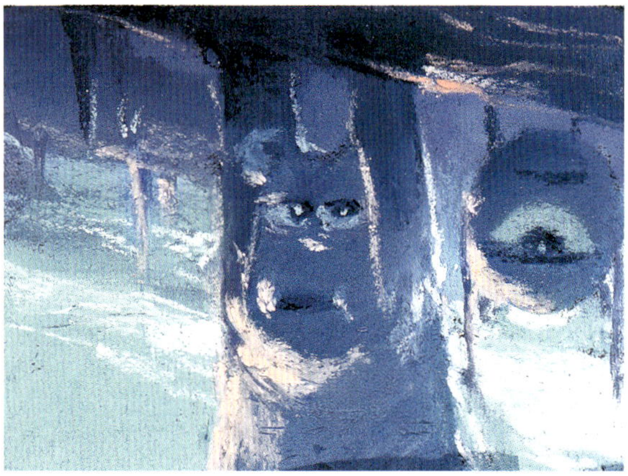
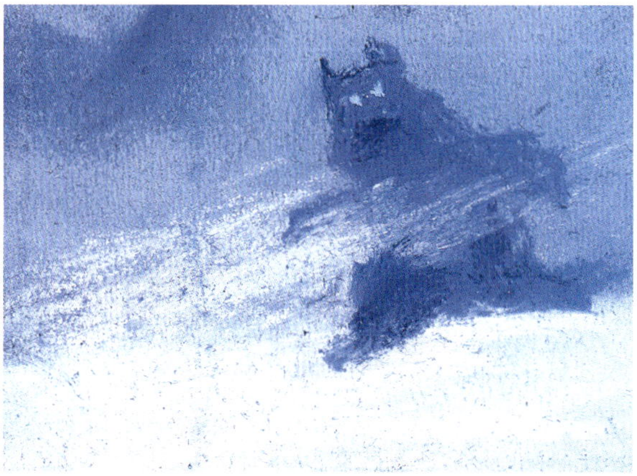

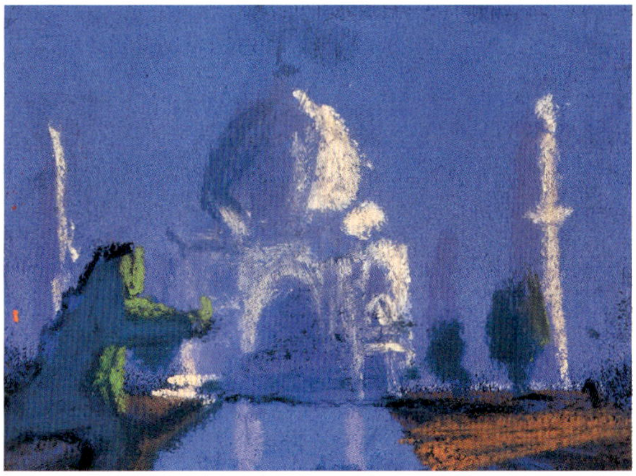
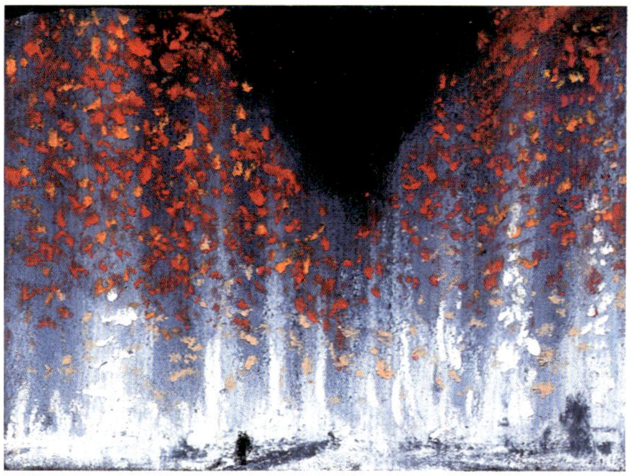
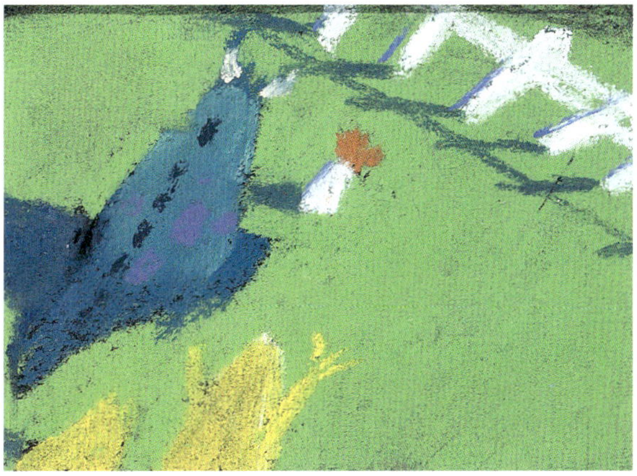
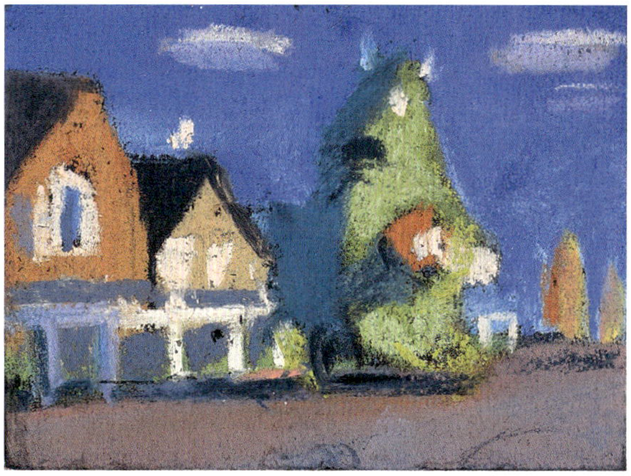
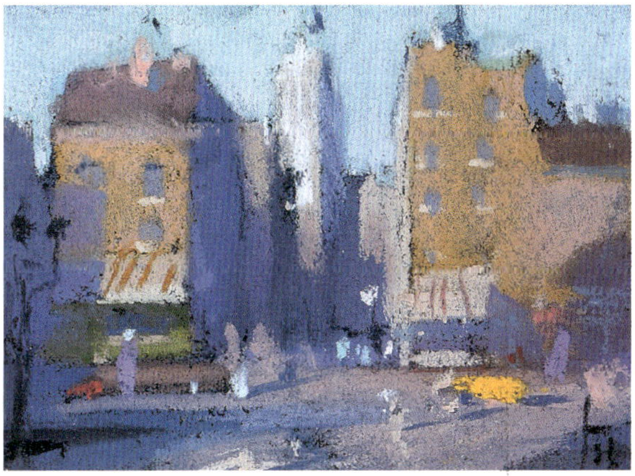
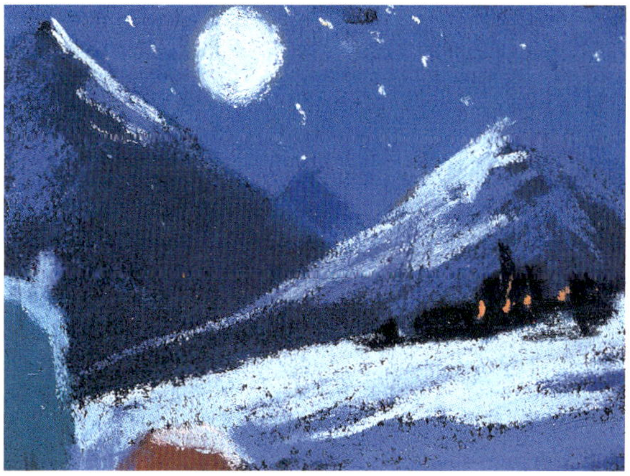
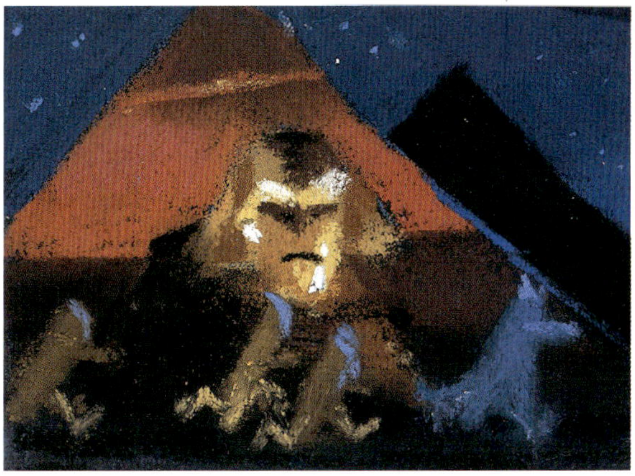
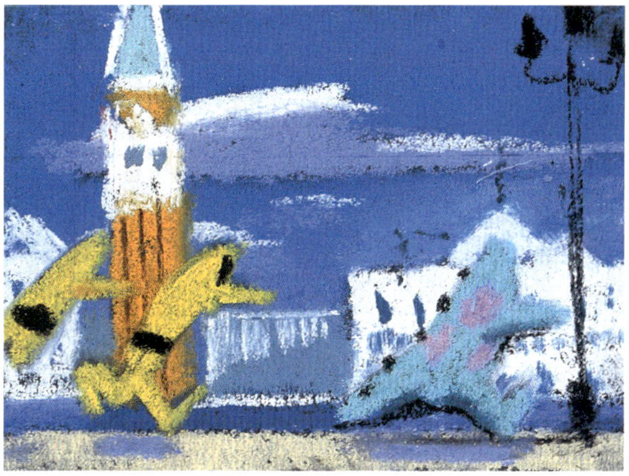

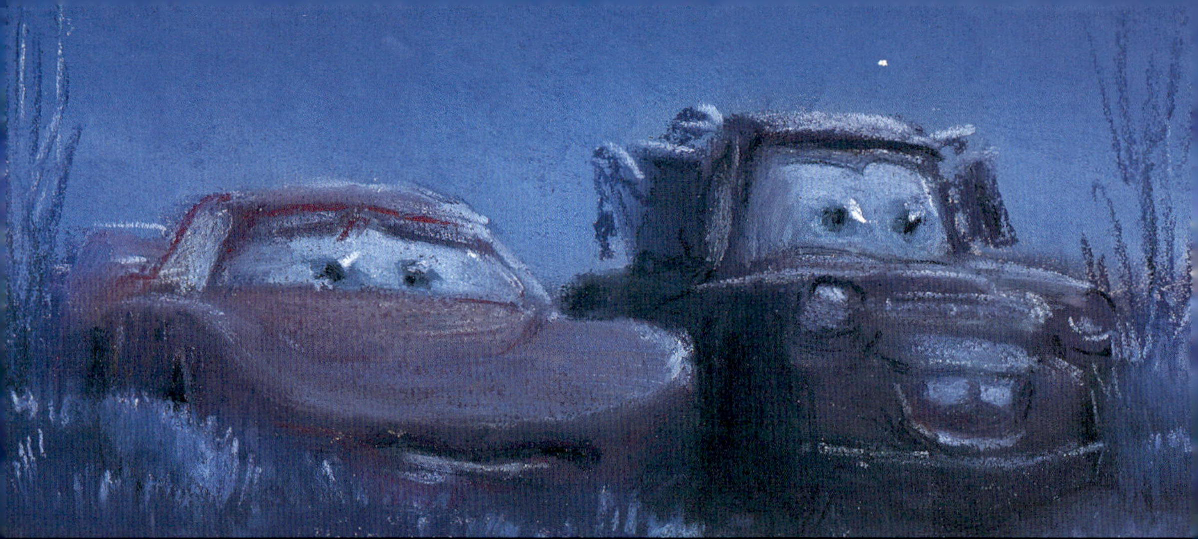

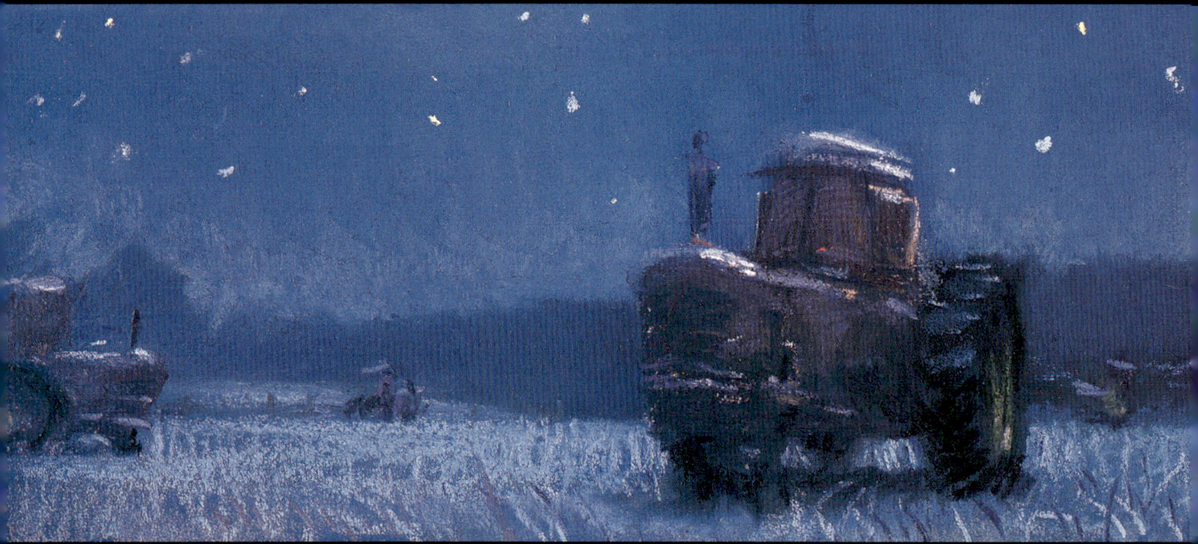

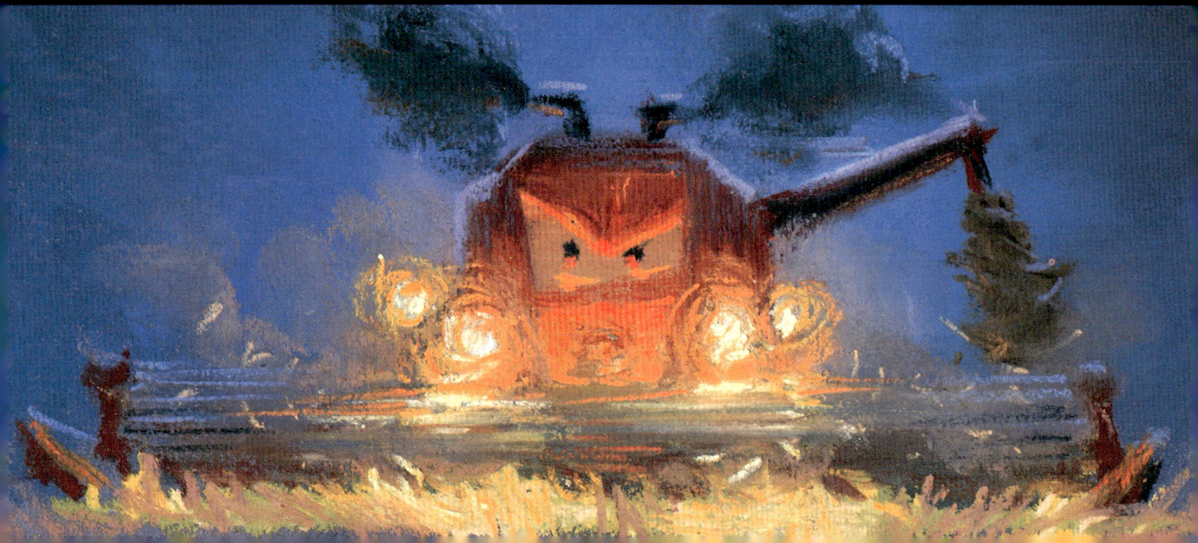

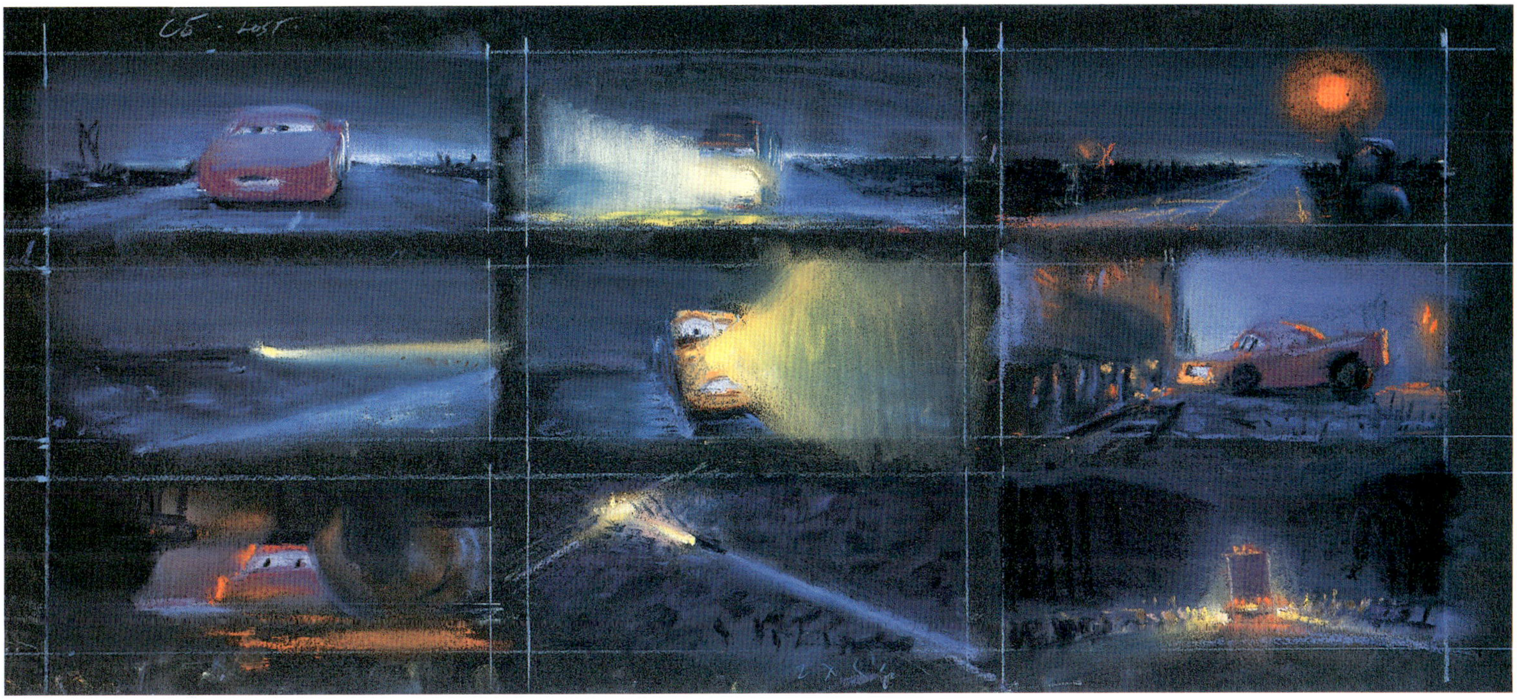

opposite:
Bill Cone
Sequence pastel: Tractor tipping
CARS
Pastel
Dimensions vary

above:
Bill Cone
Sequence pastel: Lost
CARS
Pastel
8 x 18

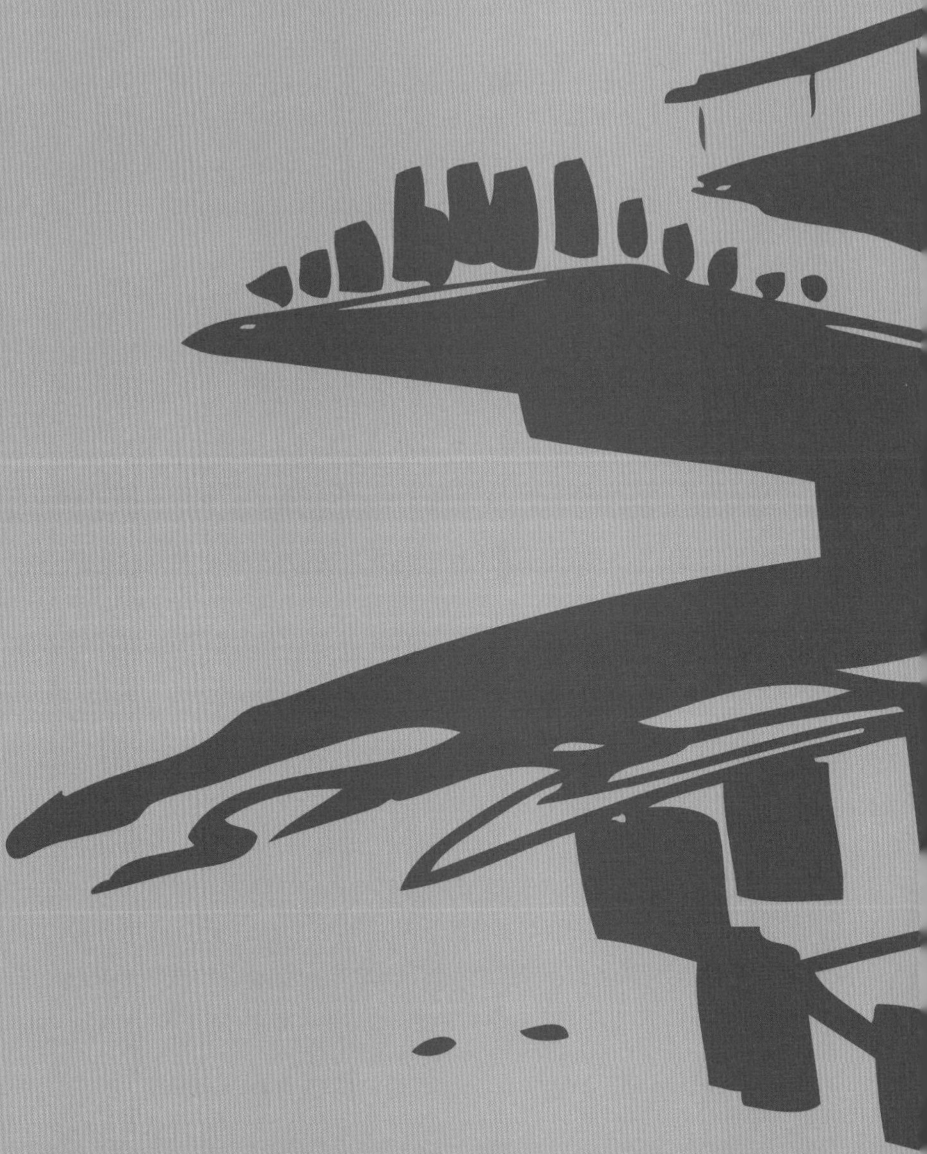

Scott Caple
Edna Mode (aka "E") house
THE INCREDIBLES
Digital. Original, marker

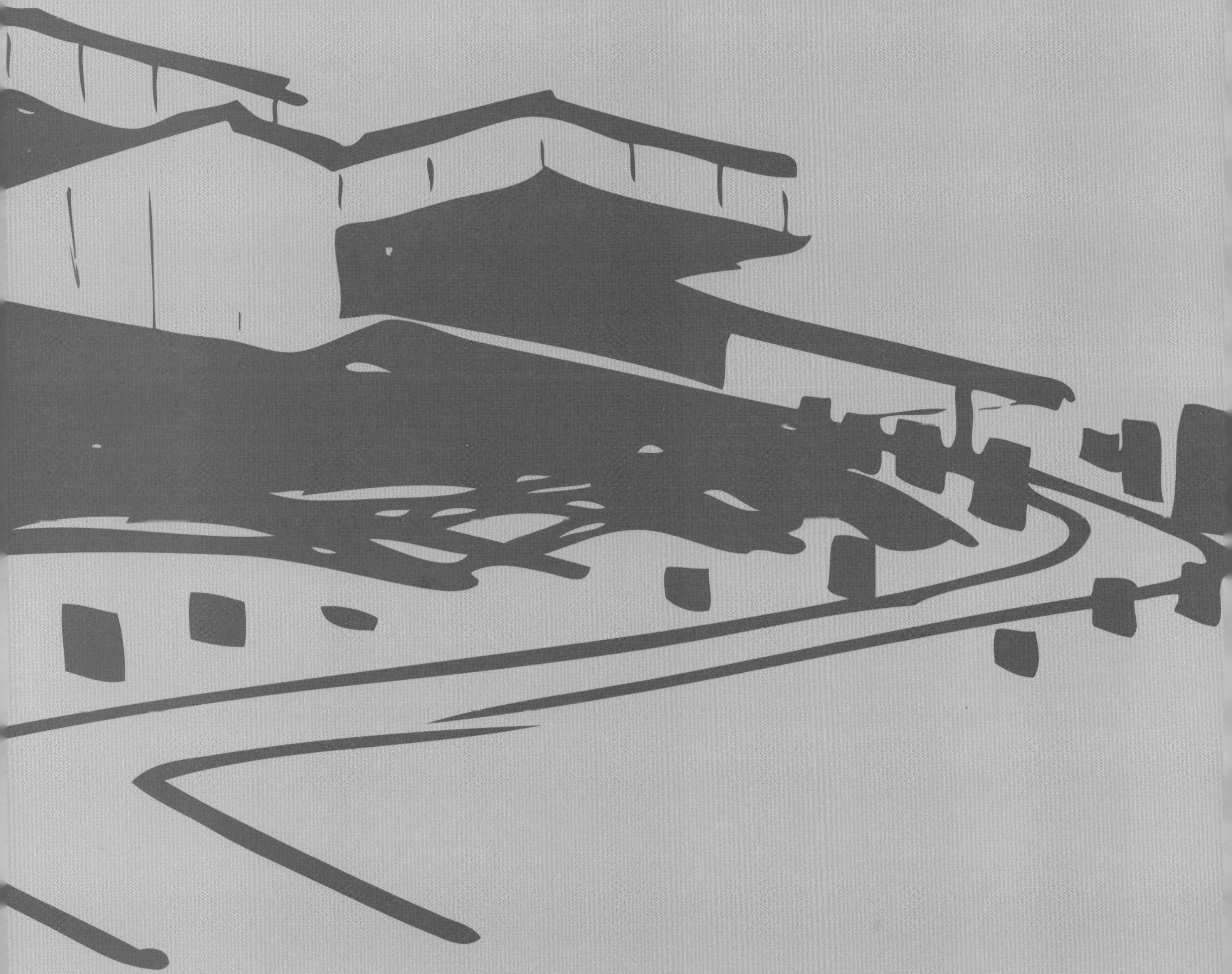

WORLDS

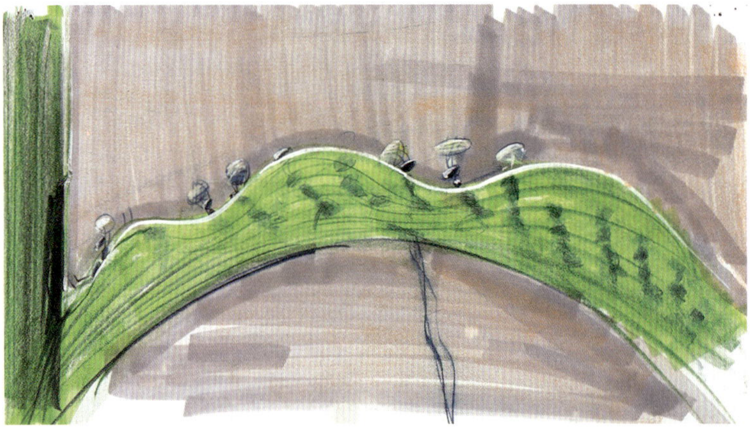

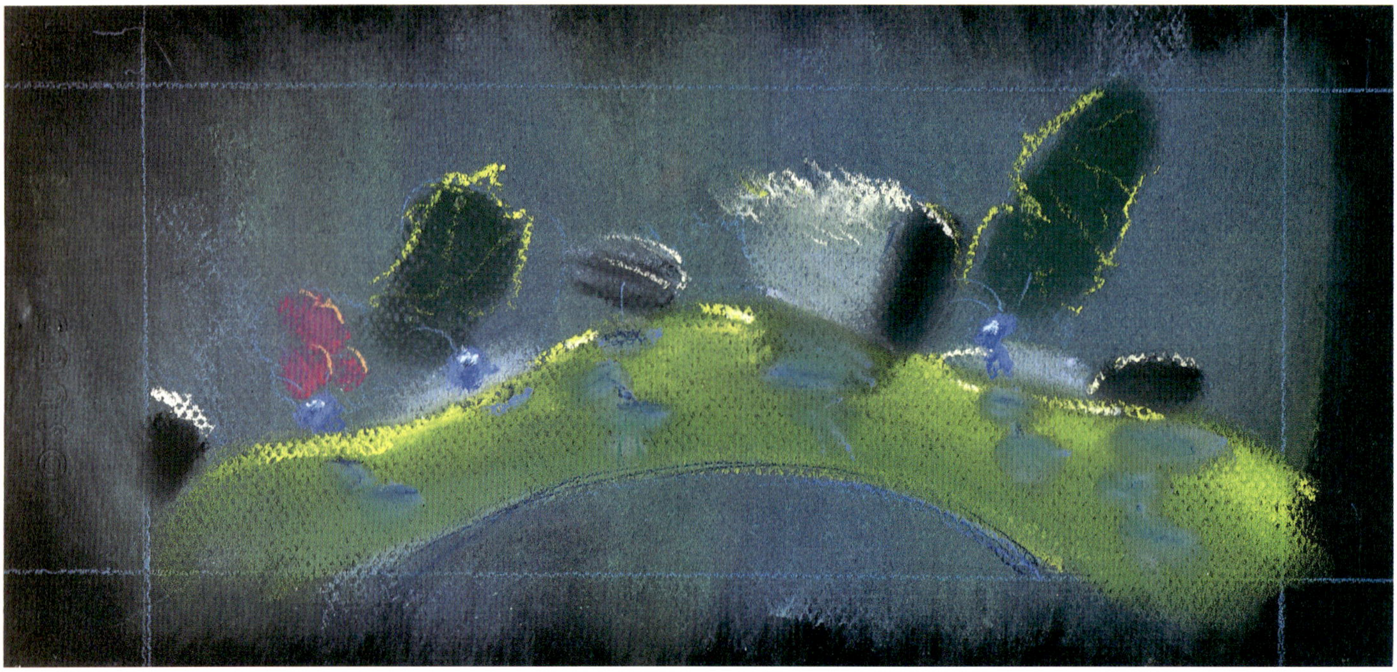

top:
Bill Cone
Leaf Bridge concept art
A BUG'S LIFE
Marker and pencil
5½ x 10

above:
Bill Cone
Leaf Bridge pastel
A BUG'S LIFE
Pastel
5½ x 12

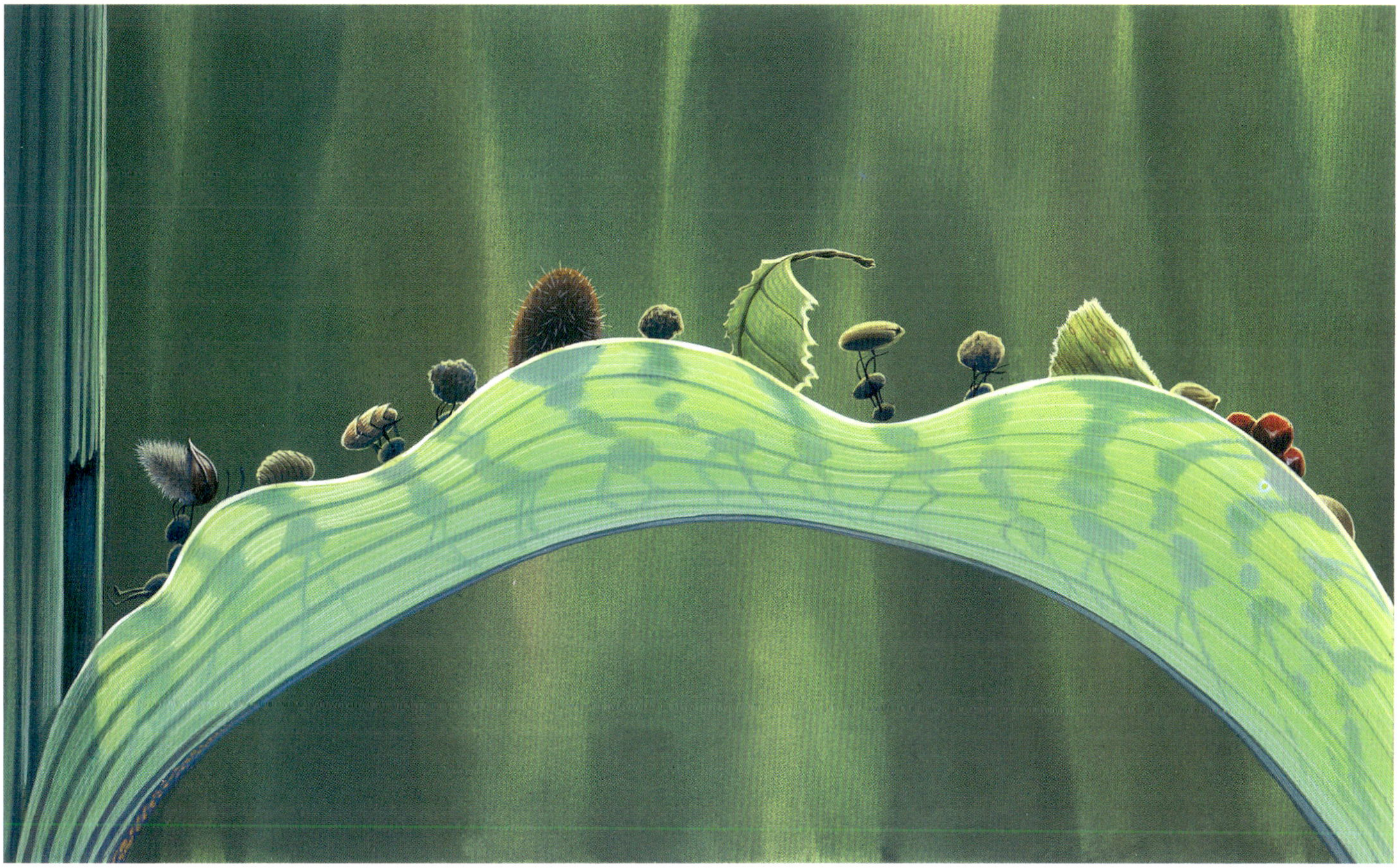

Tia Kratter
The Leaf Bridge
Layout by Bill Cone
A BUG'S LIFE
Acrylic
8 x 12

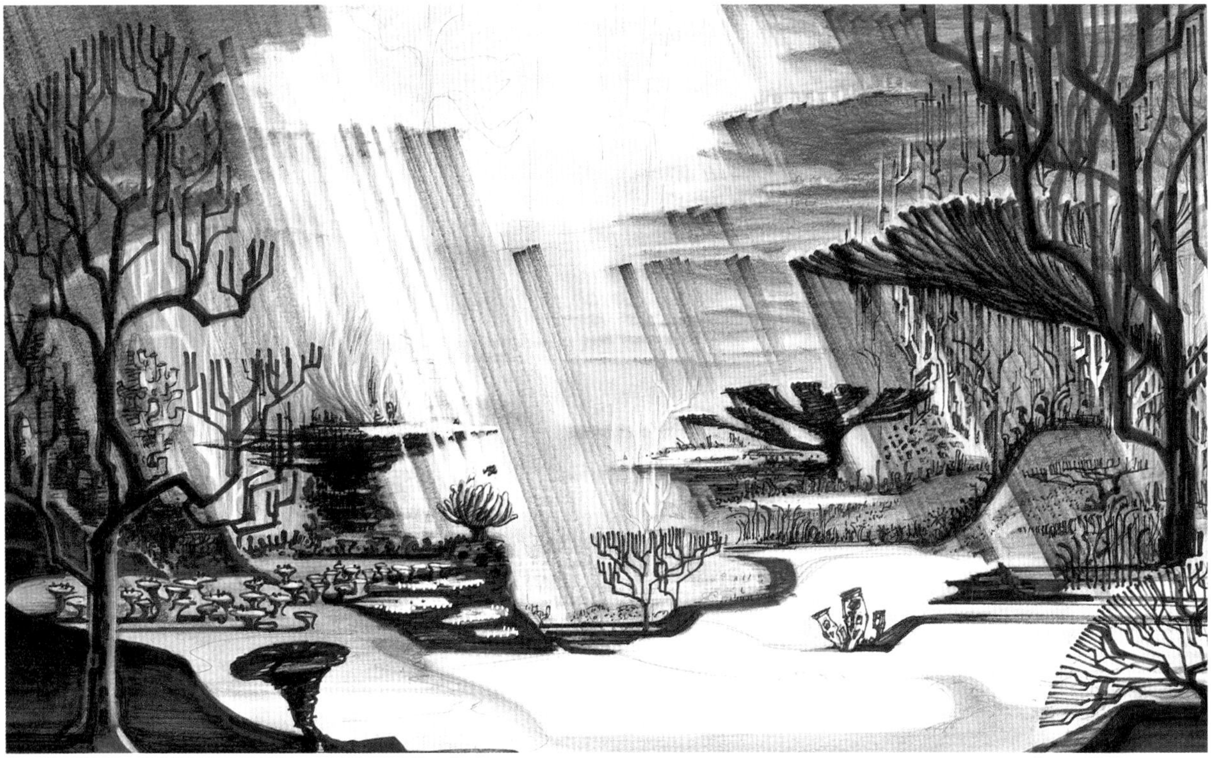

above:
Nelson "Rey" Bohol
Home reef
FINDING NEMO
Marker and pencil
11 x 17

opposite:
Glenn Kim
The door vault
MONSTERS, INC.
Marker
11 x 8½

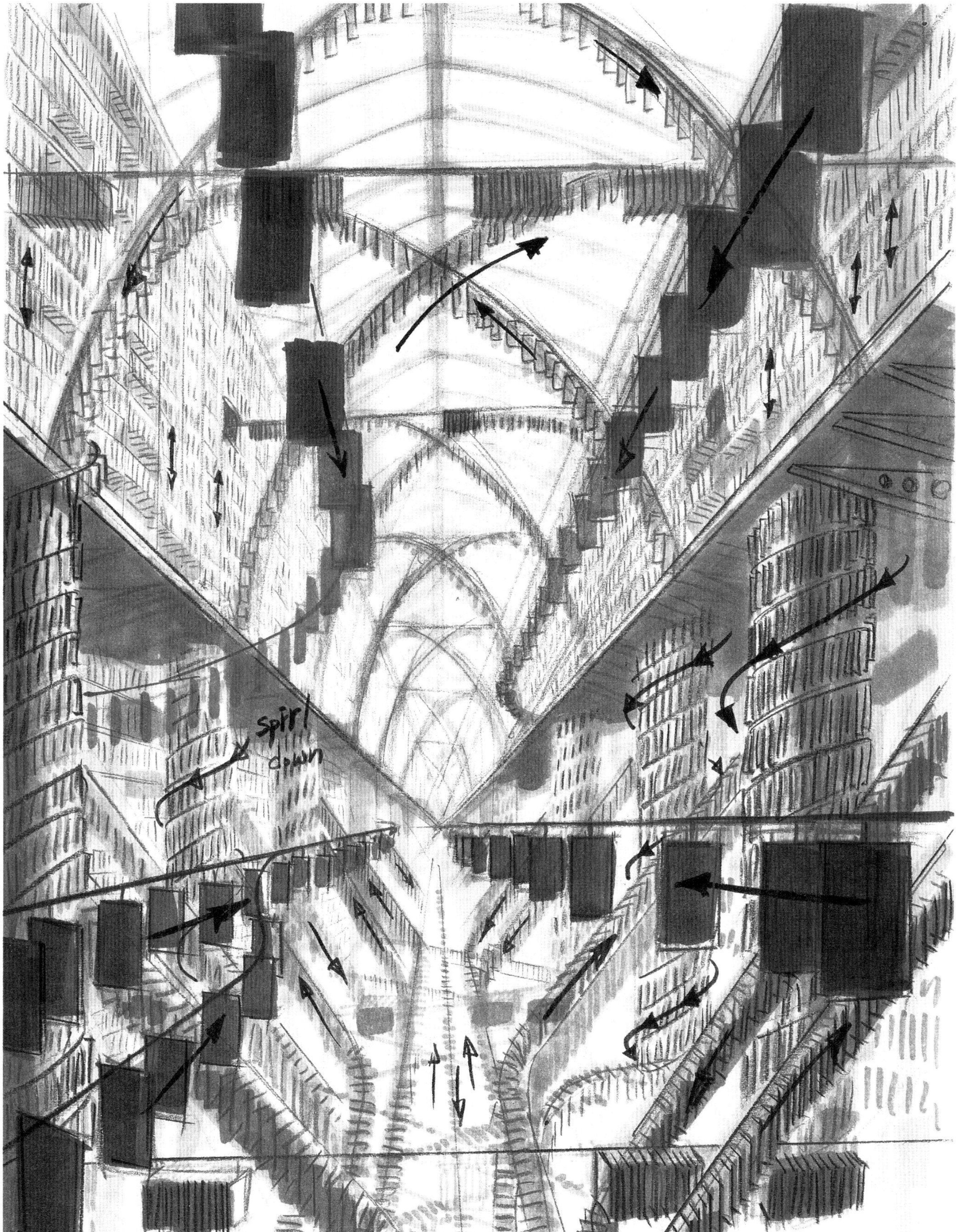
spirl
down

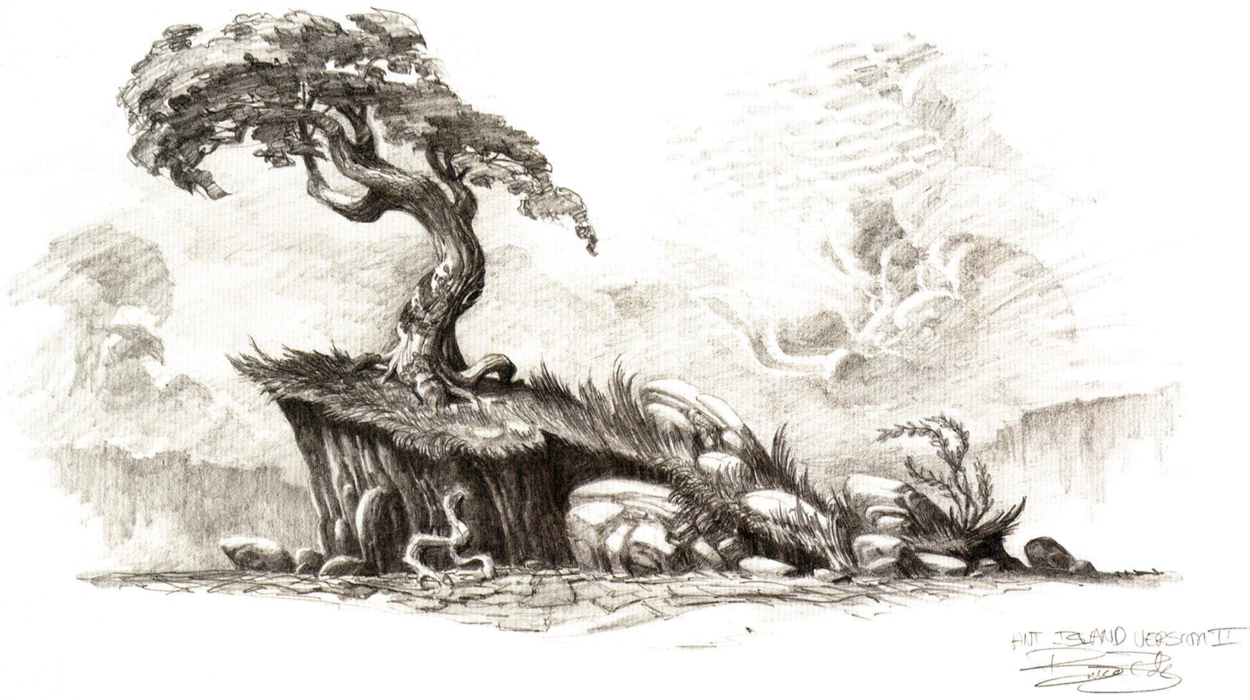

Bruce Zick
Ant Island
A BUG'S LIFE
Pencil
13¼ x 20⅝

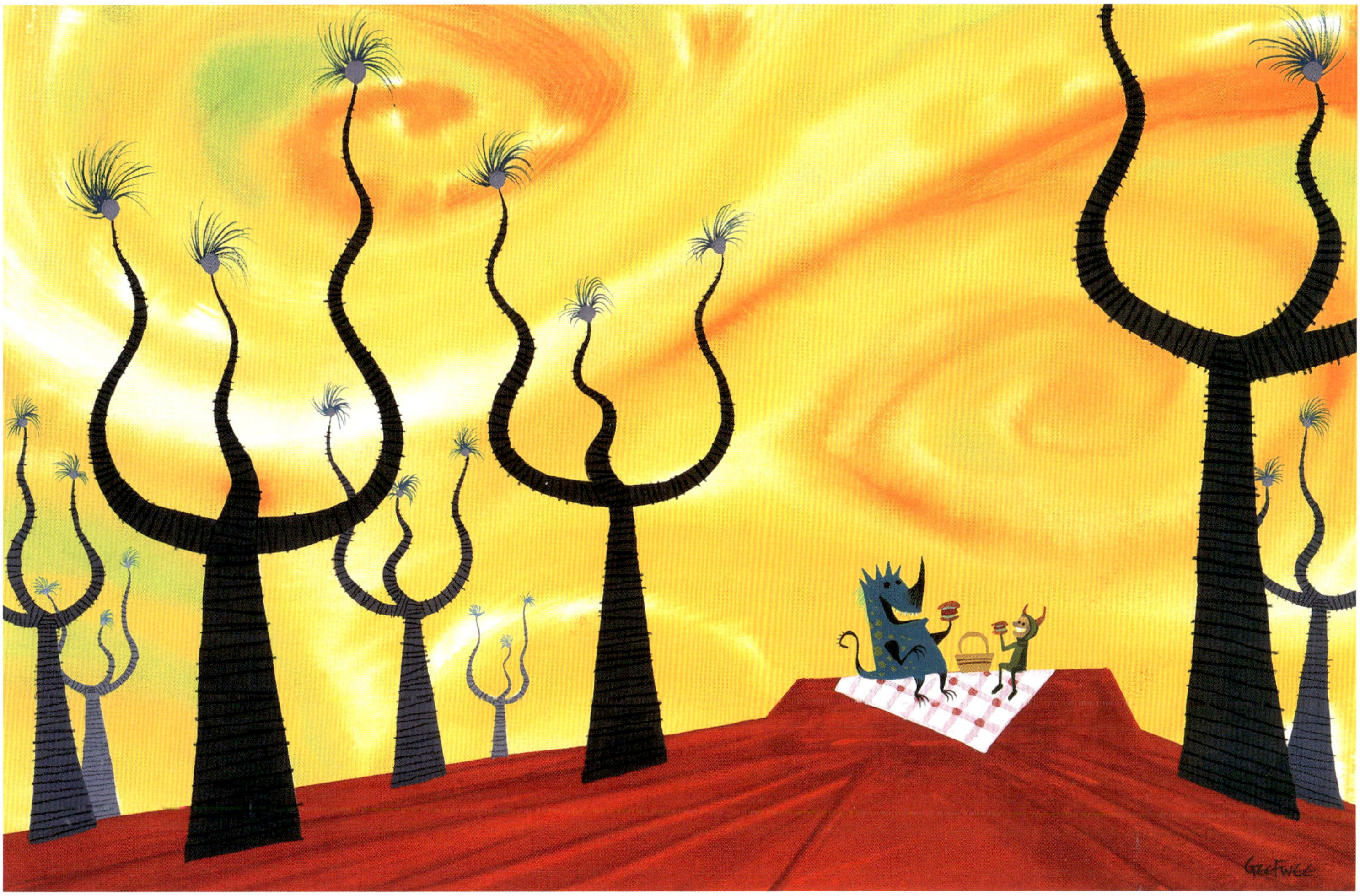

Geefwee Boedoe
Sullivan and Boo
MONSTERS, INC.
Mixed media
8¼ x 12½

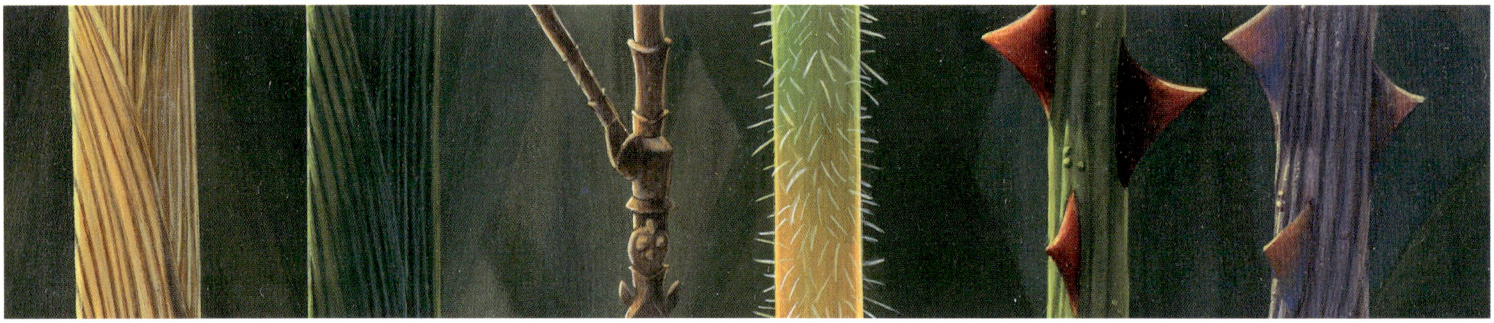

Robin Cooper
Stem study
Layout by Bill Cone
A BUG'S LIFE
Acrylic
5¼ x 17

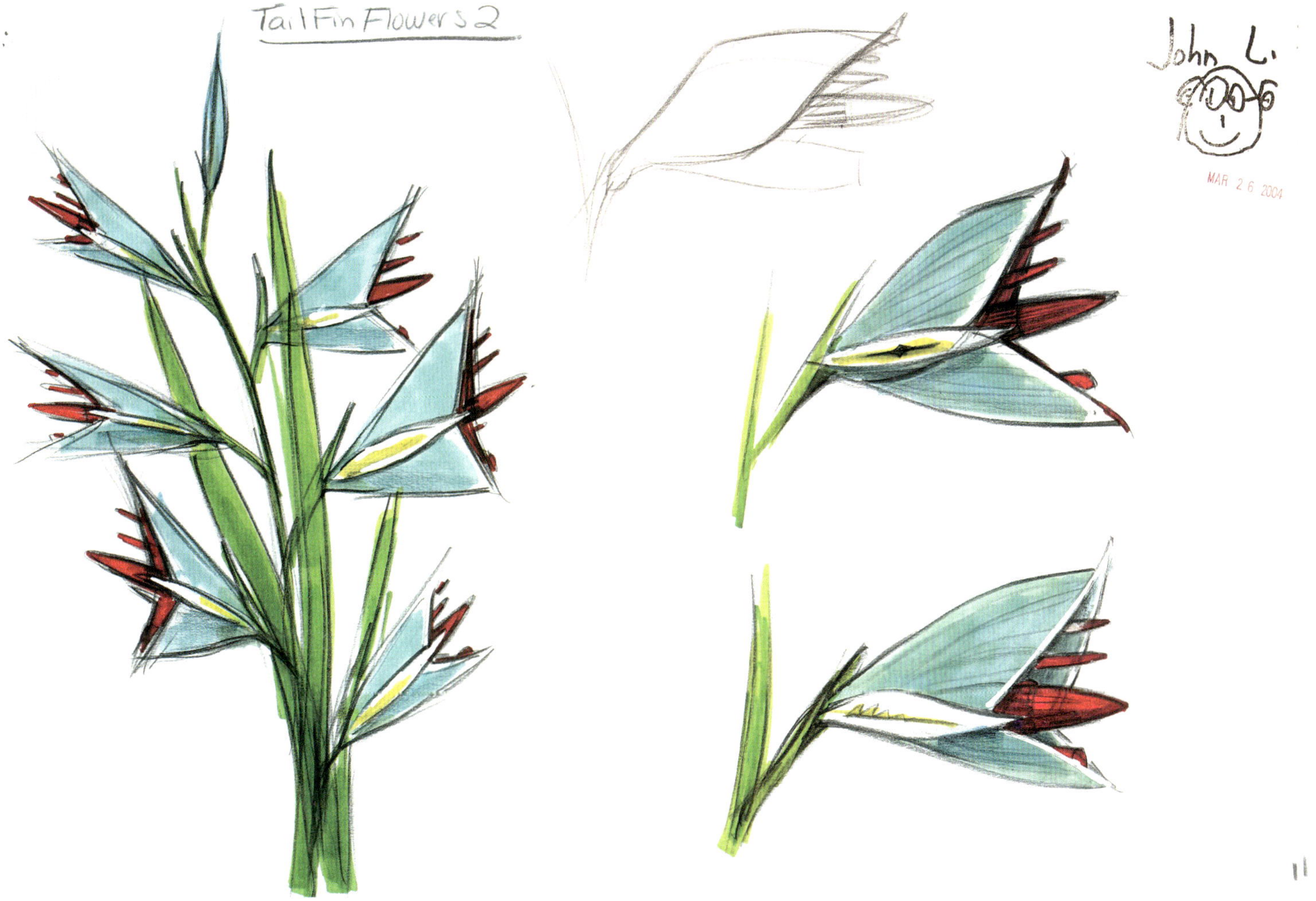

Nat McLaughlin
Tailfin flowers
CARS
Marker and pencil
11 x 17

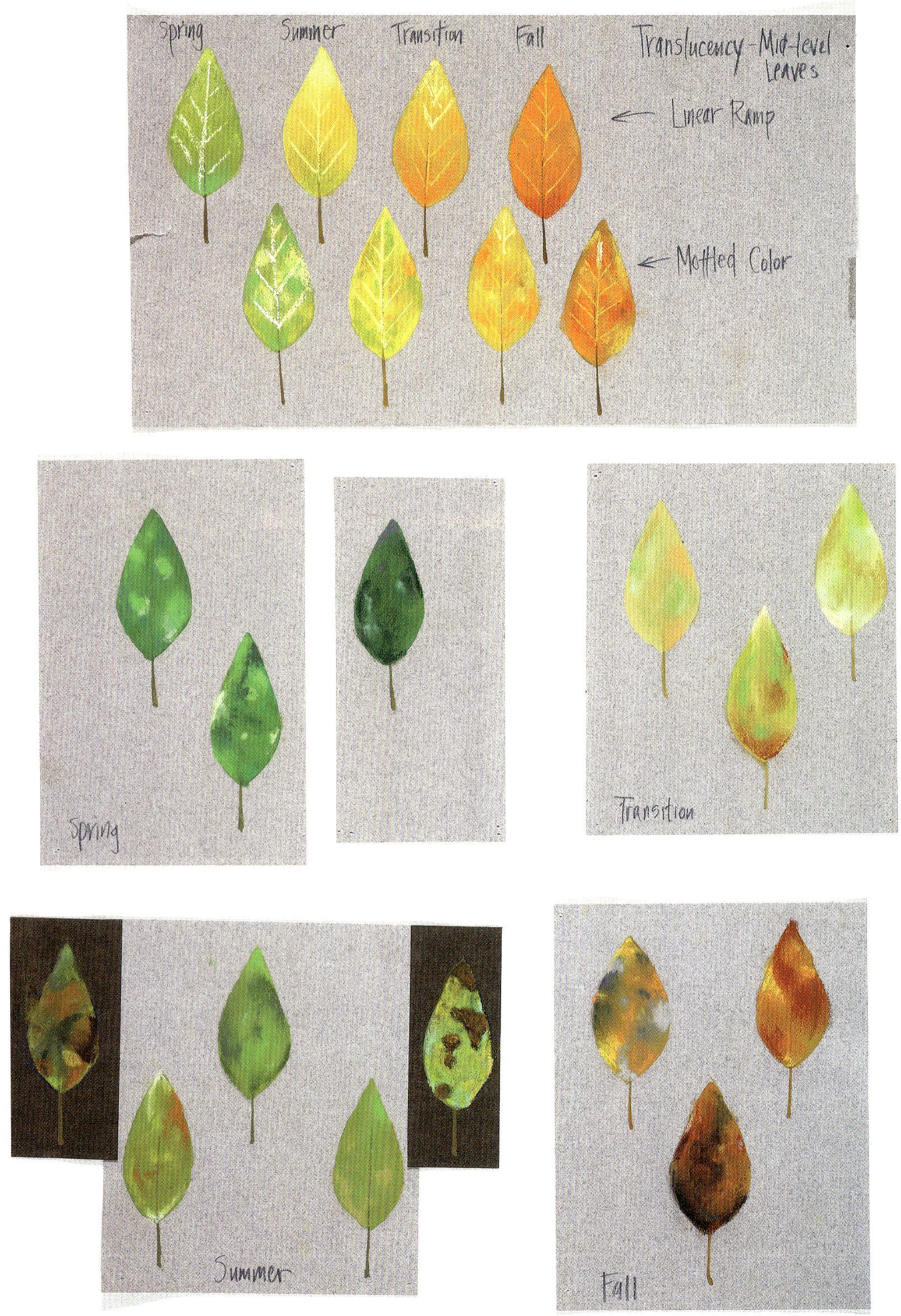

Tia Kratter

Leaf seasonal color palette

A BUG'S LIFE

Acrylic

20 x 15

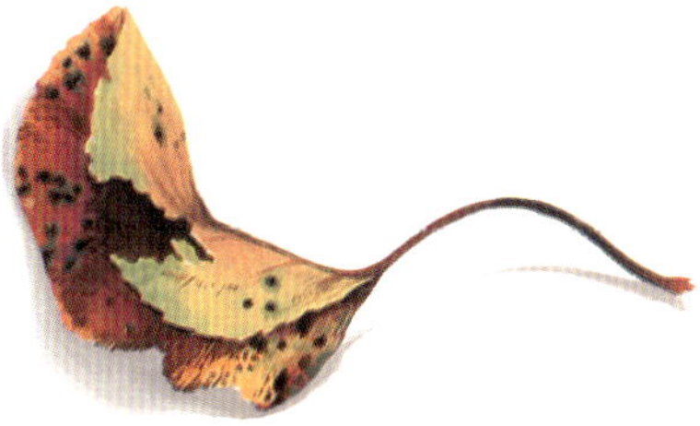

Tia Kratter
Leaf color palette
A BUG'S LIFE
Acrylic
8½ x 11

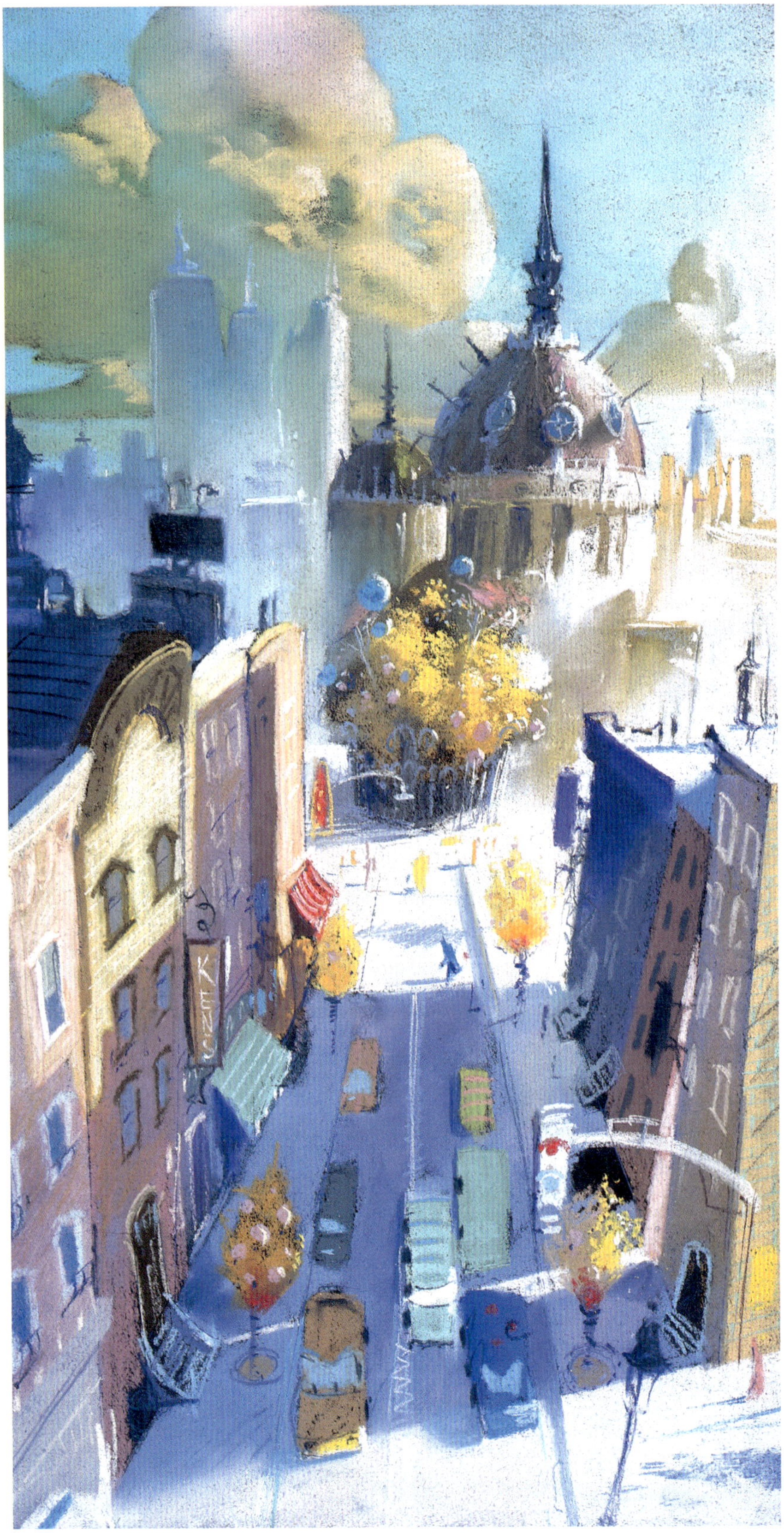

Dominique R. Louis
Downtown Monstropolis
Layout by Harley Jessup
MONSTERS, INC.
Pastel
25½ x 19½

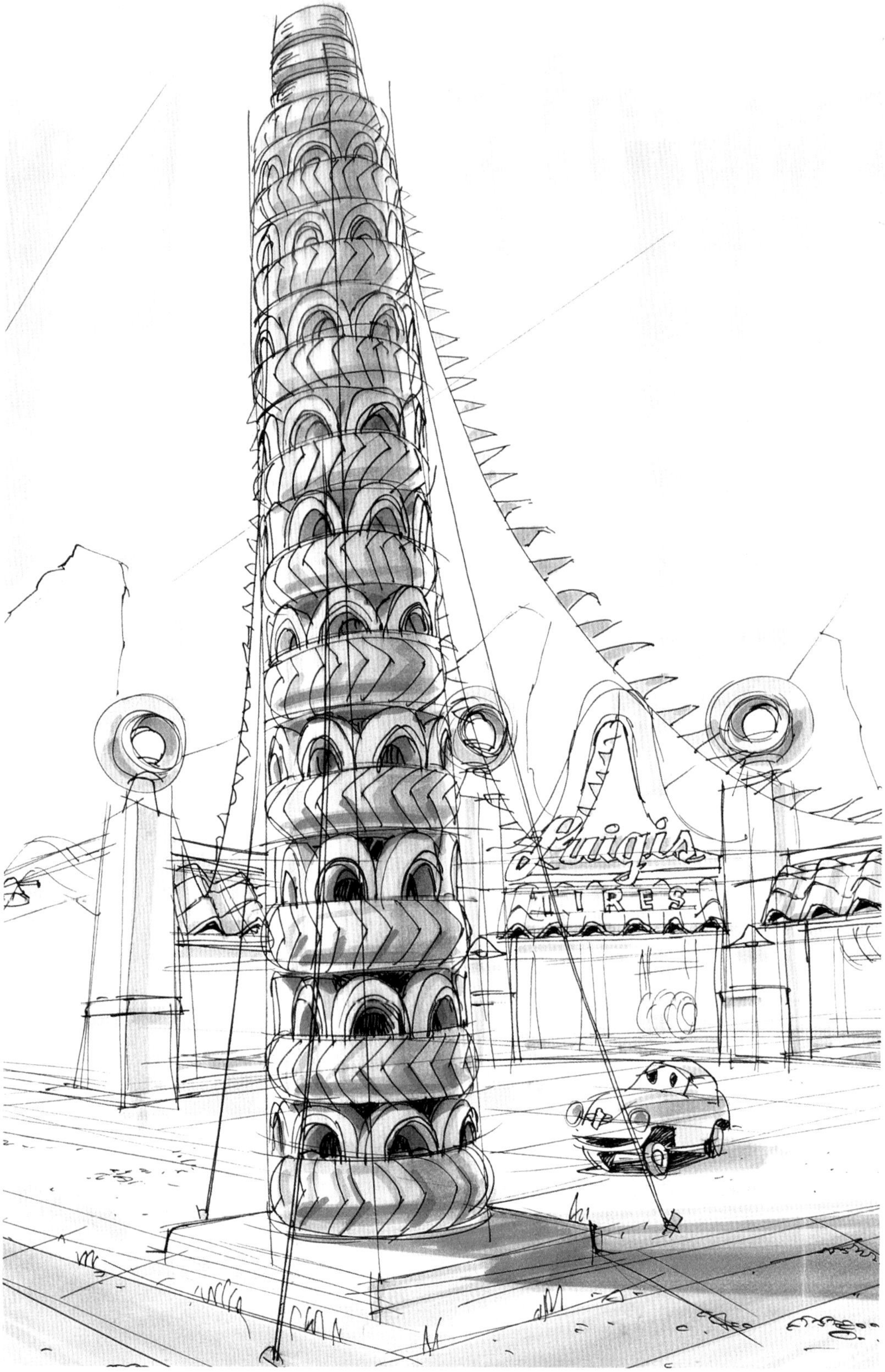

Jay Shuster
Luigi's Tire Shop (detail)
CARS
Marker and pen
11 x 17

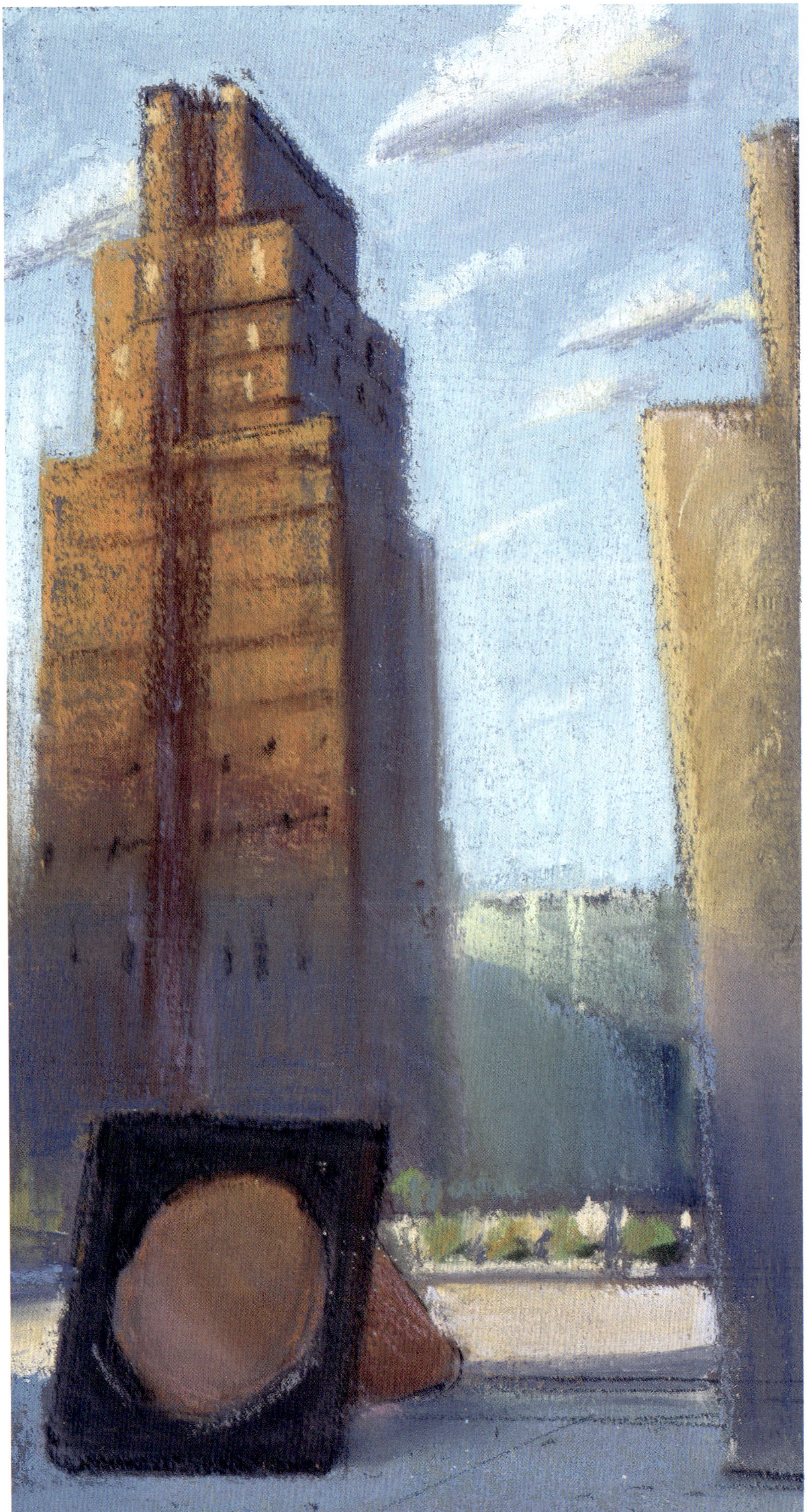

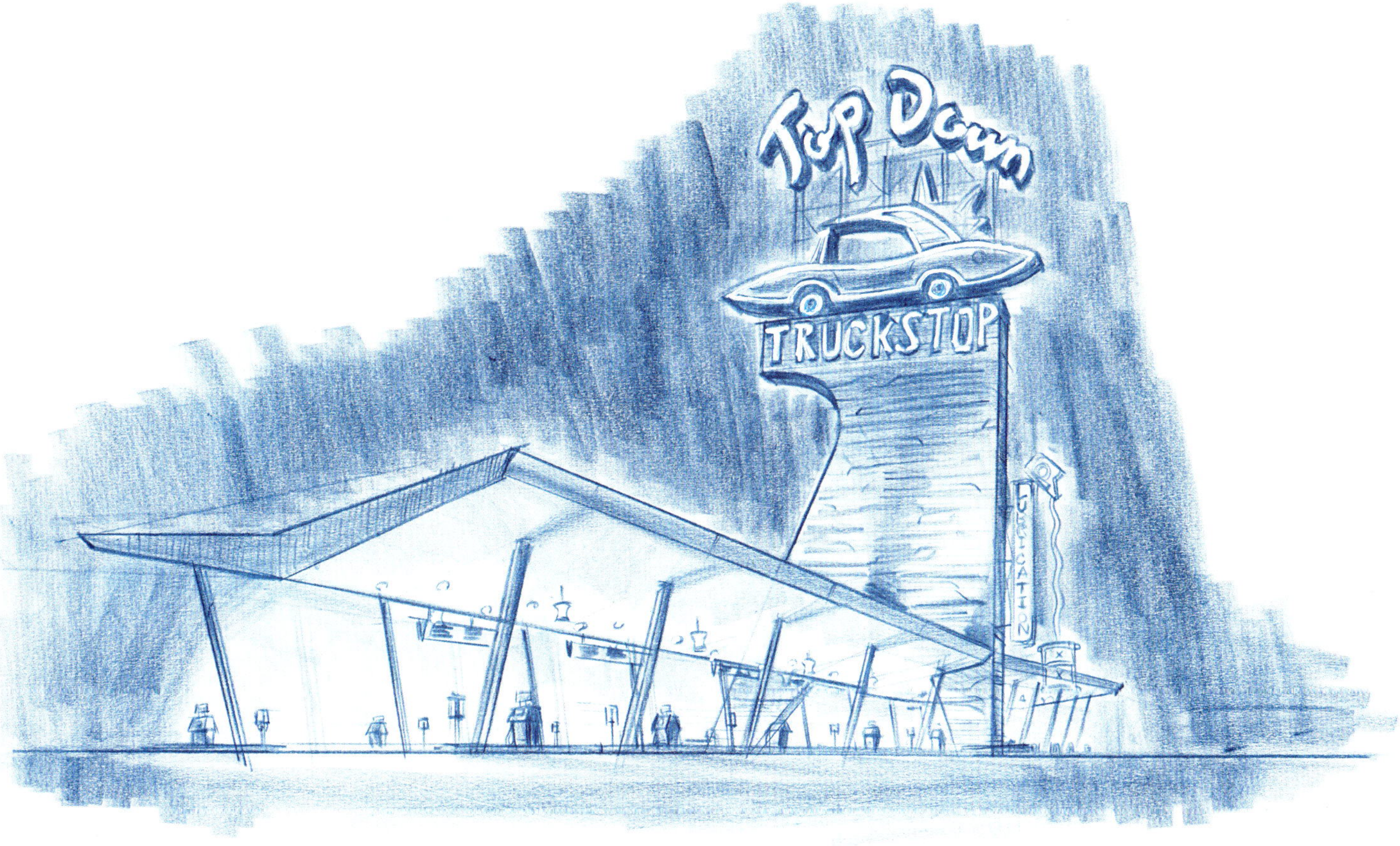

opposite:
Bill Cone
Crossing the road
TOY STORY 2
Pastel
11½ x 8⅜

above:
Nat McLaughlin
Top Down Truckstop
CARS
Pencil
11 x 17

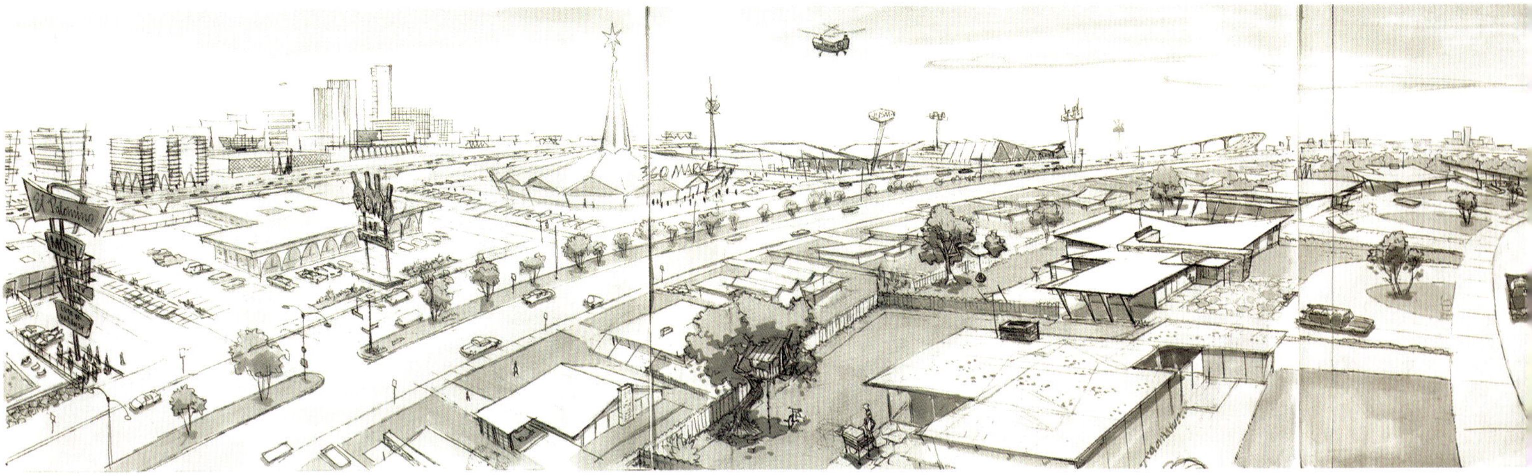

Scott Caple
Suburbia
THE INCREDIBLES
Marker and pencil
9⅛ x 56⅛

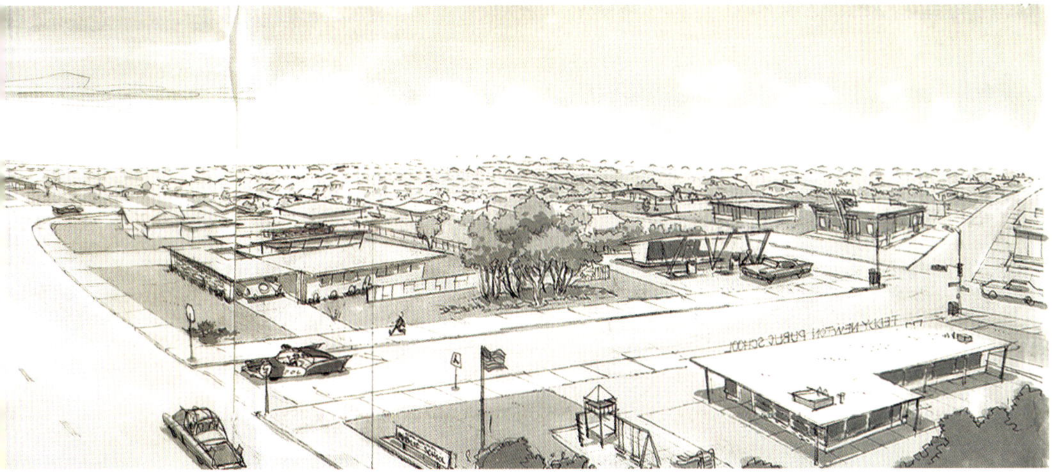

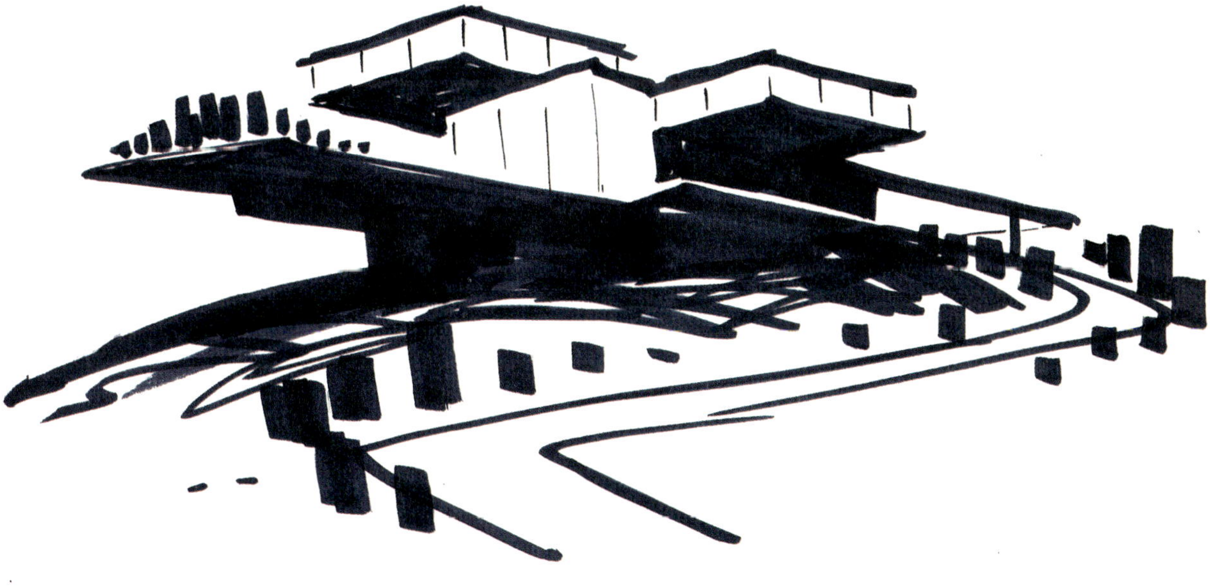

Scott Caple
Edna Mode (aka "E") house
THE INCREDIBLES
Marker
8½ x 11

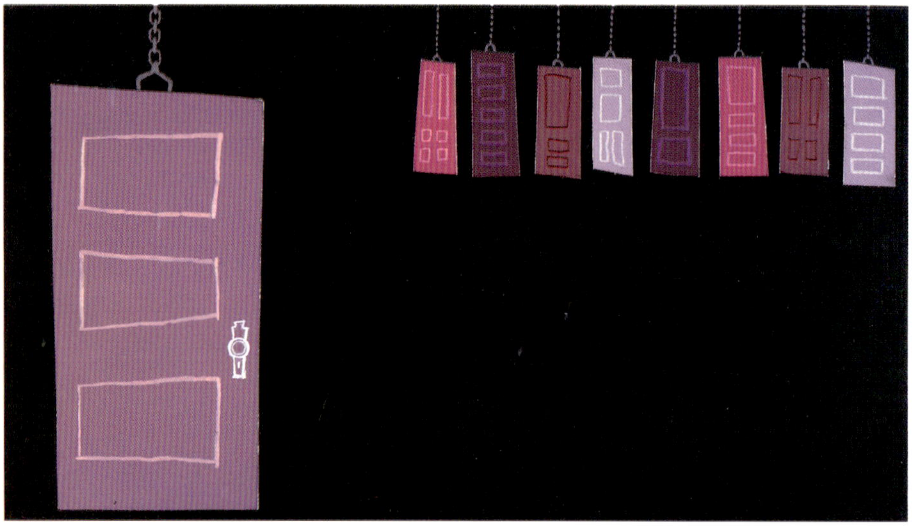

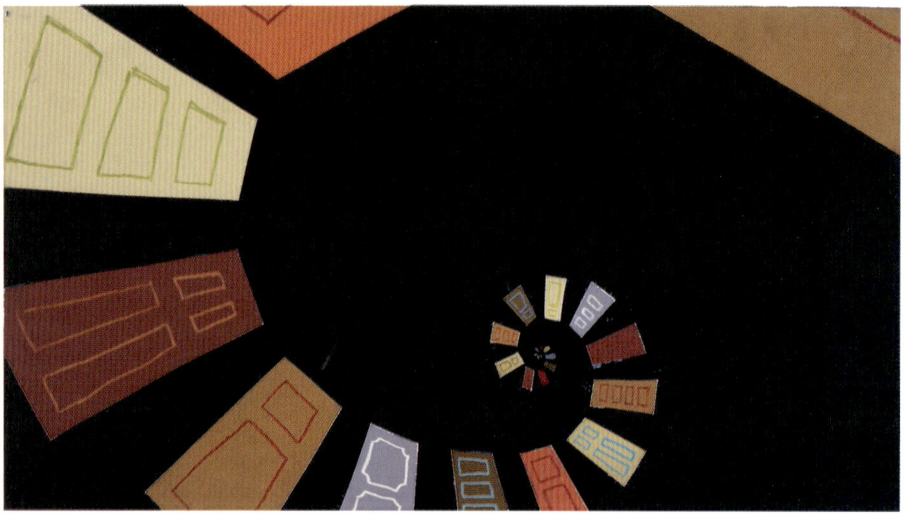

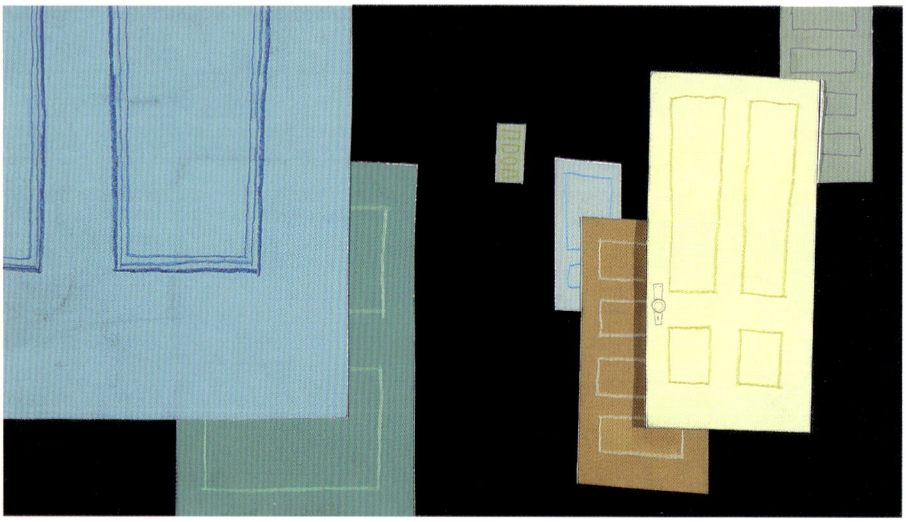

Geefwee Boedoe
Title sequence concept art
MONSTERS, INC.
Collage
5½ x 10 (each)

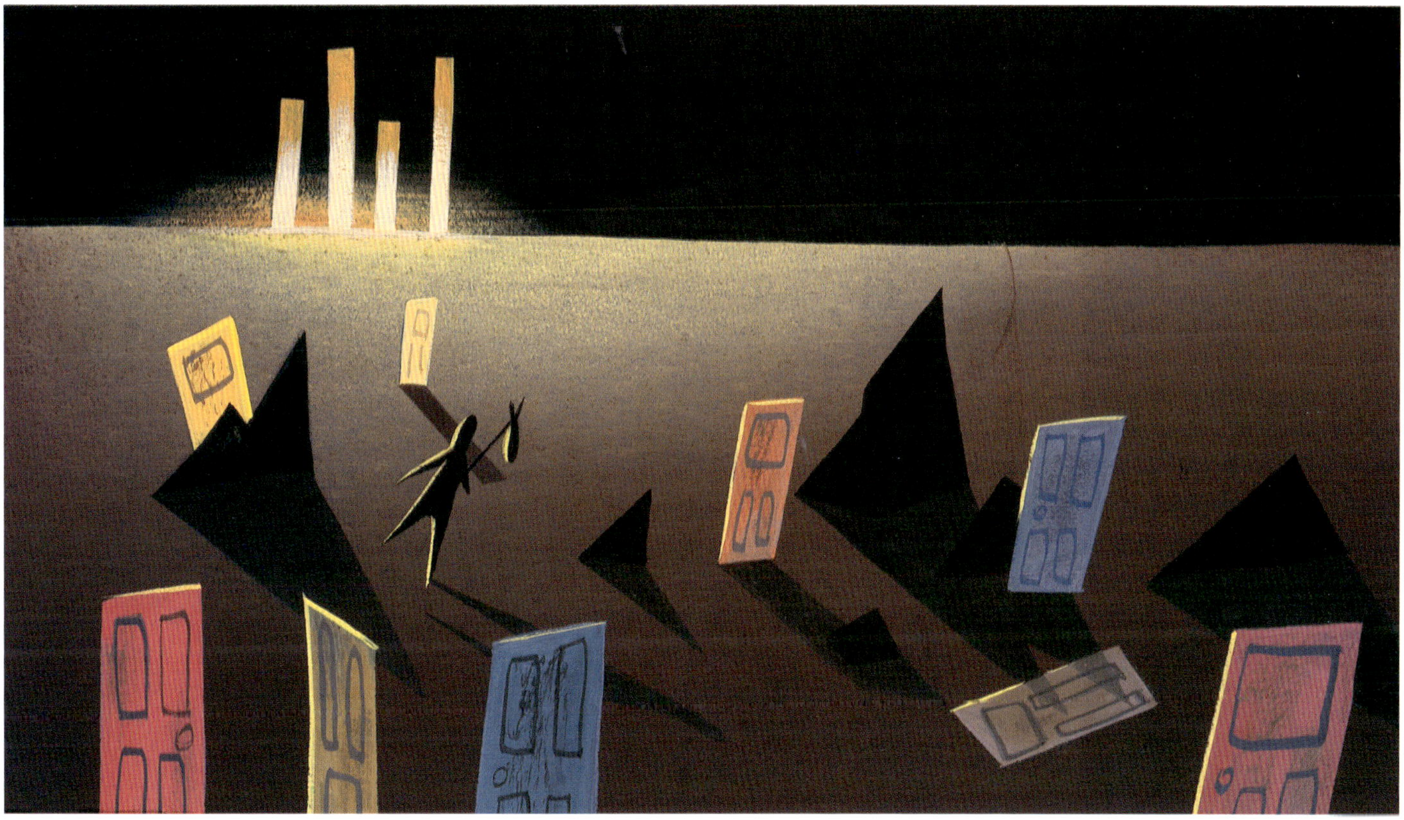

Lou Romano
The outskirts of Monstropolis
MONSTERS, INC.
Gouache and pastel
4½ x 7¼

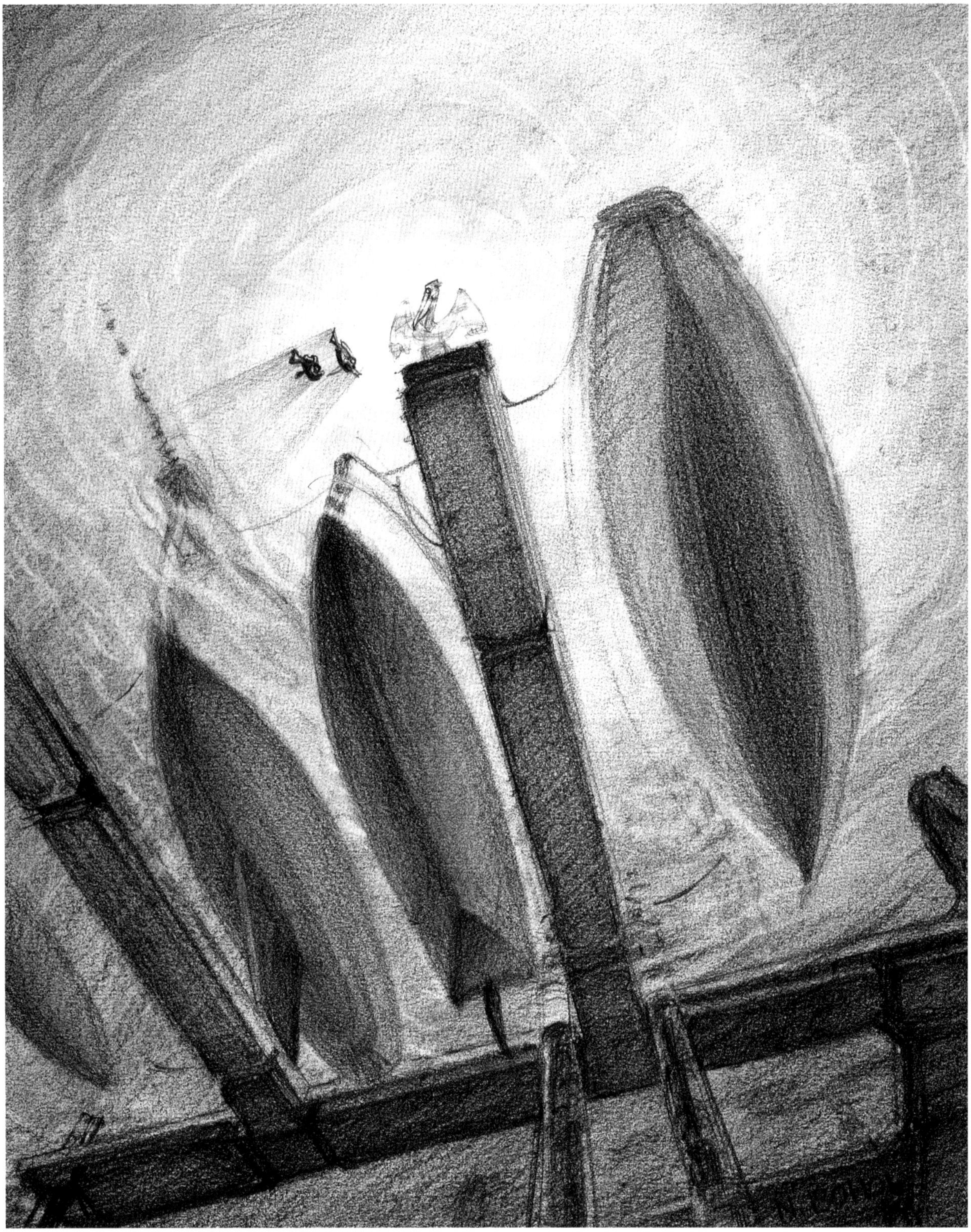

Nelson "Rey" Bohol
Under the docks
FINDING NEMO
Pencil
14 x 11

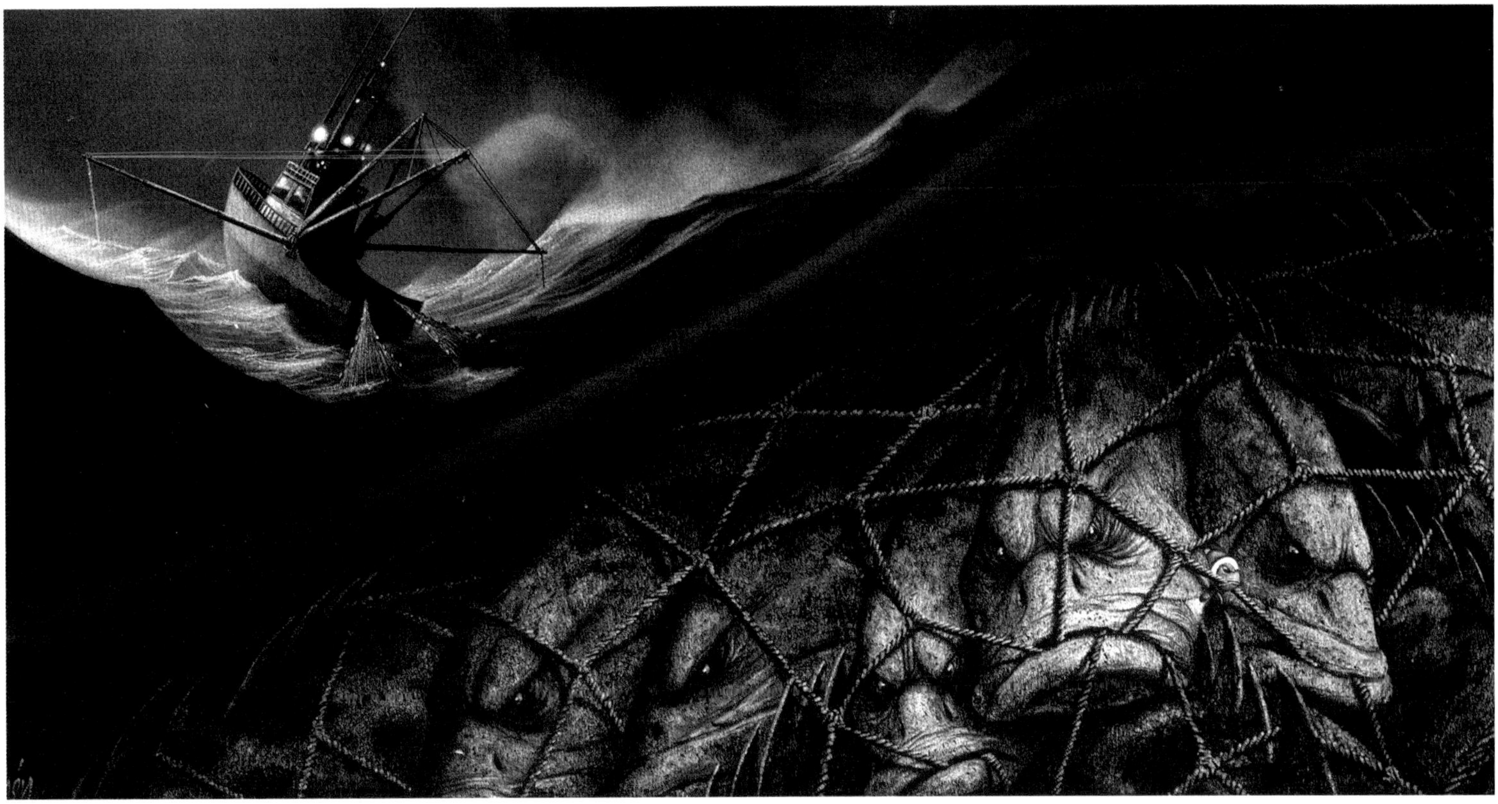

Simón Varela
Fishing net
FINDING NEMO
Charcoal
17 x 29

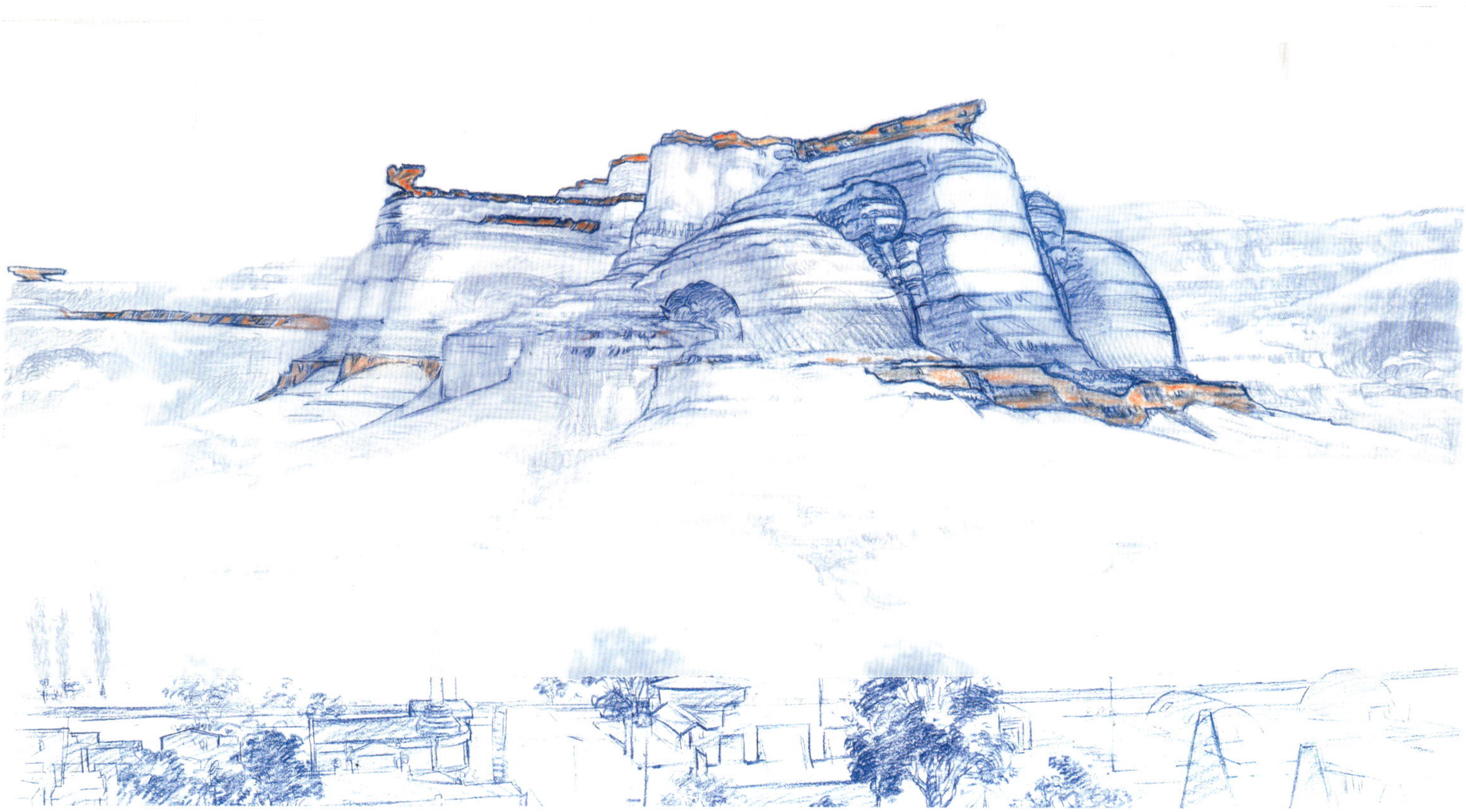

Anthony Christov
Ornament Valley
CARS
Pencil
8 x 15

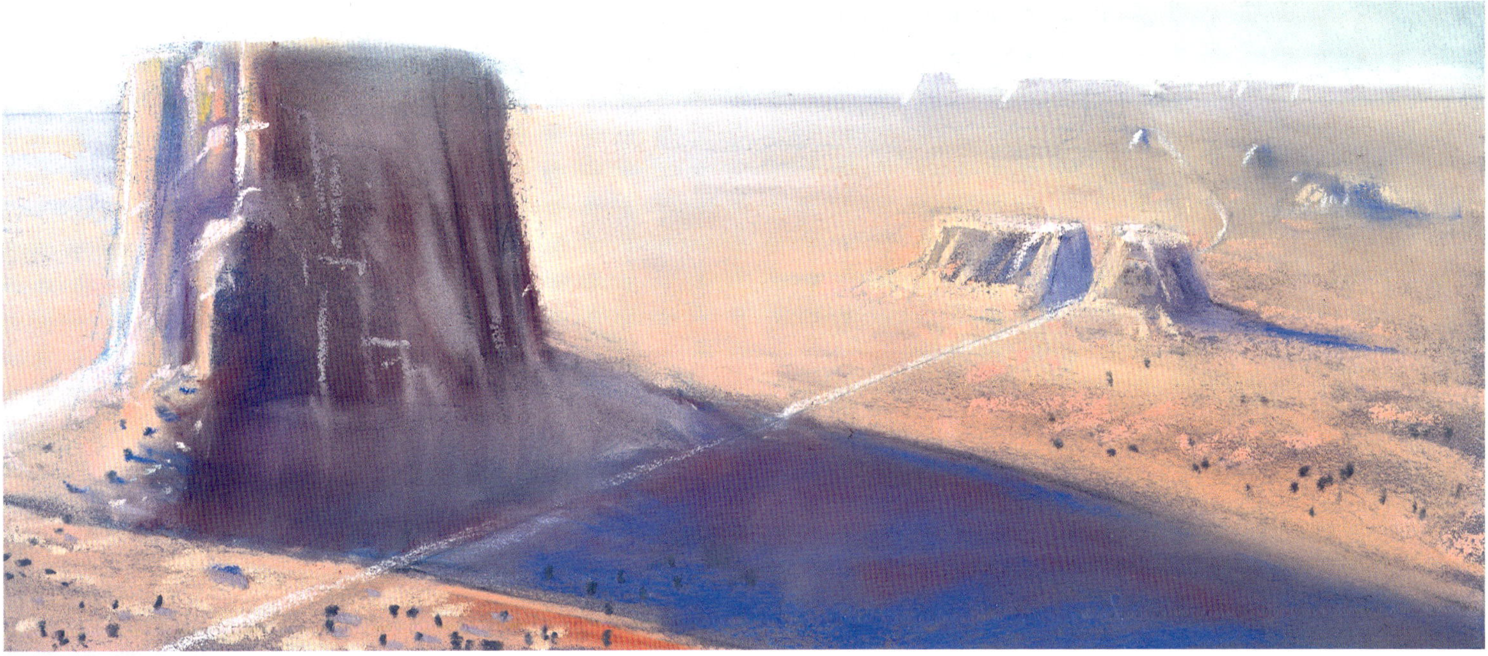

Bill Cone
3D paint projection study
CARS
Pastel
8 x 14⅜

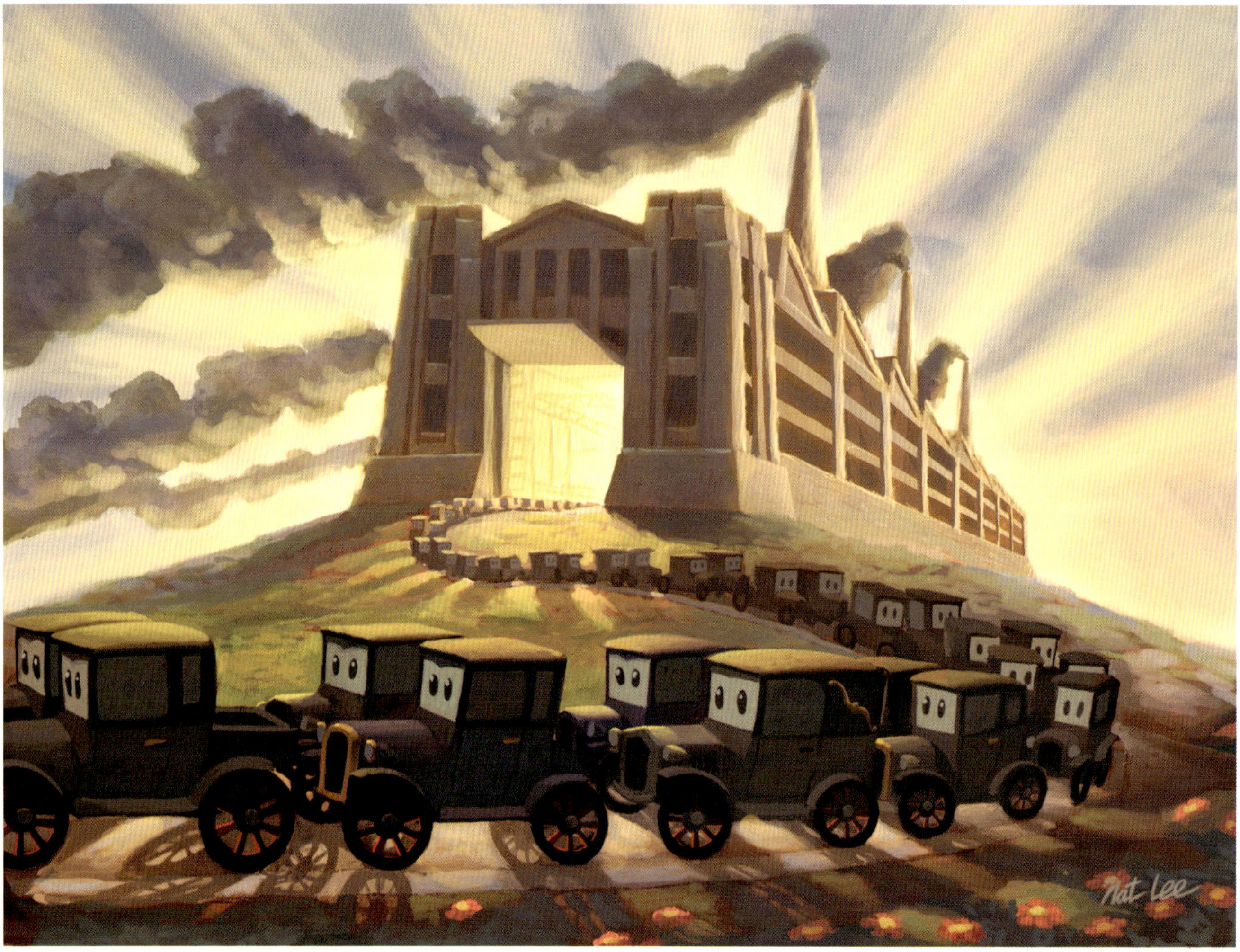

John Lee
Creation
Layout by Nat McLaughlin
CARS
Digital

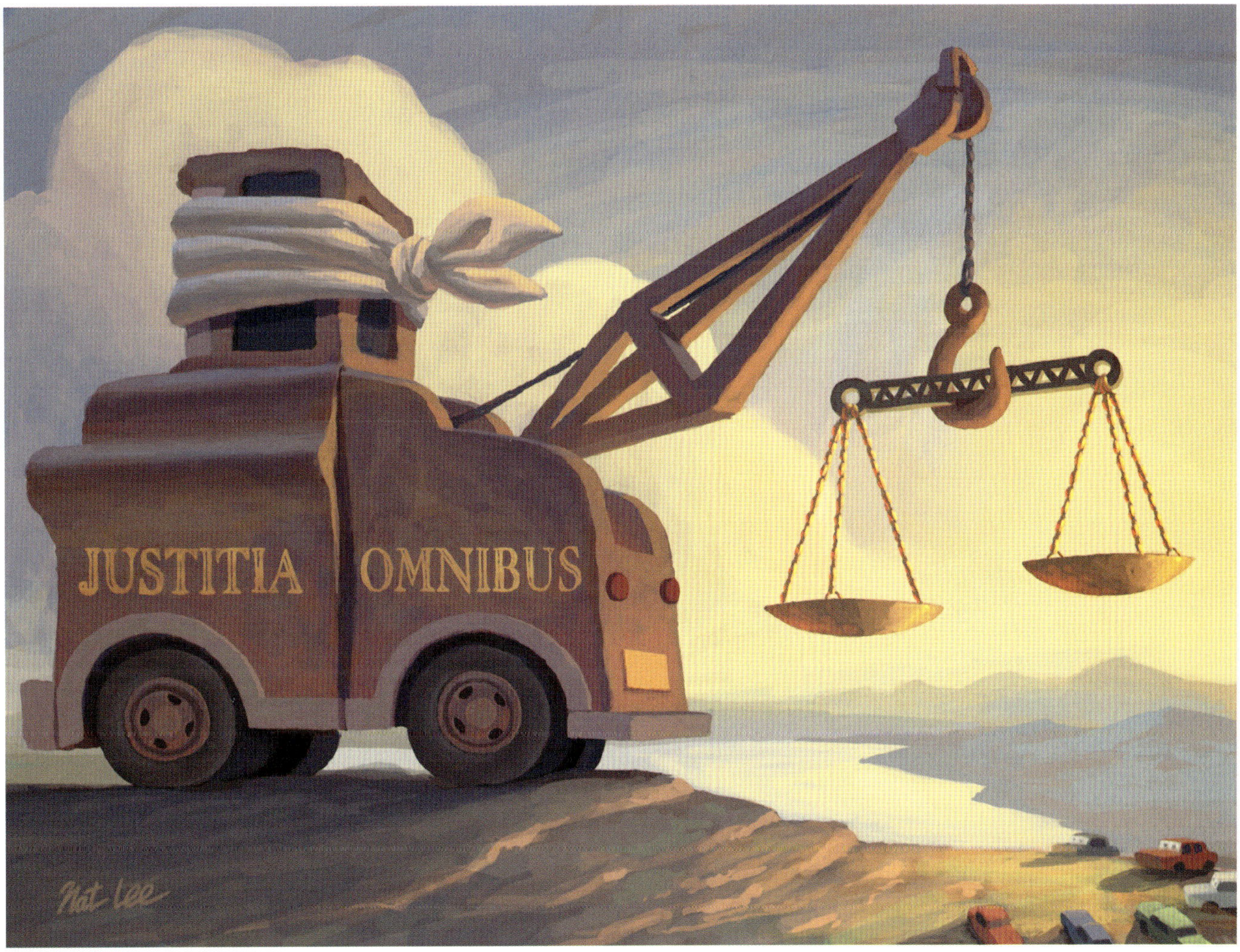

John Lee
Blind Justice
Layout by Nat McLaughlin
CARS
Digital

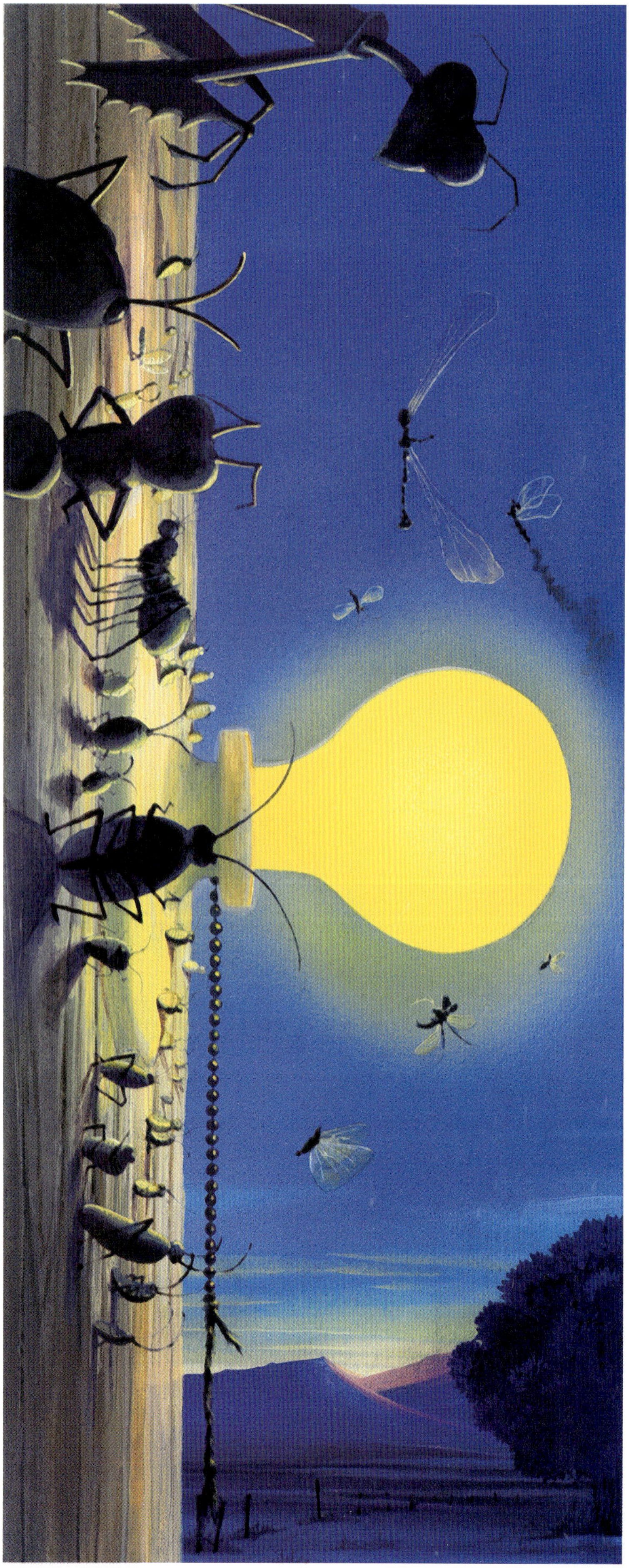

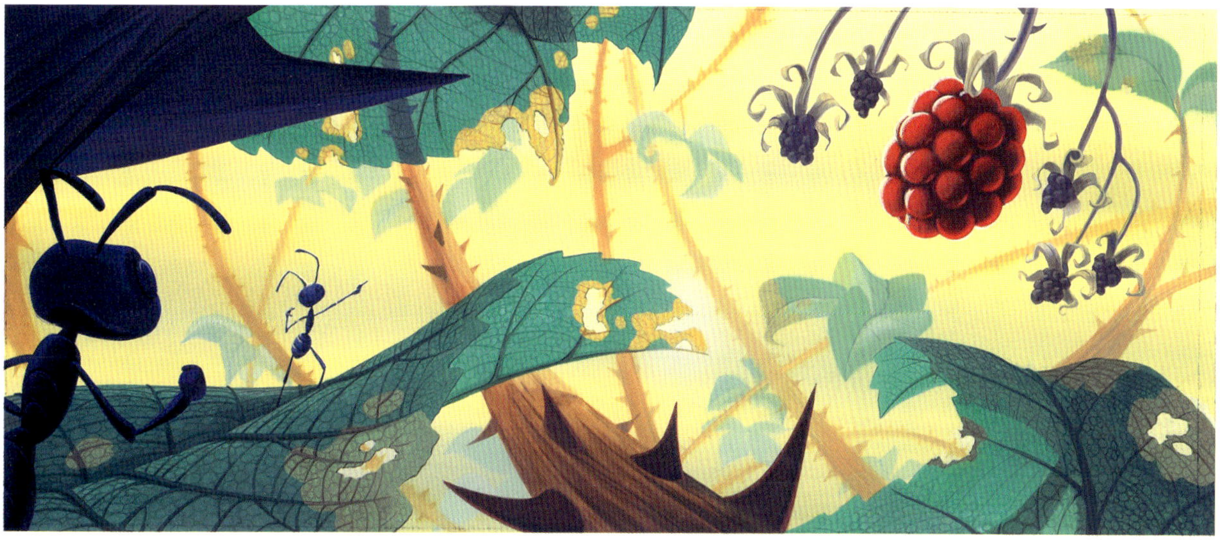

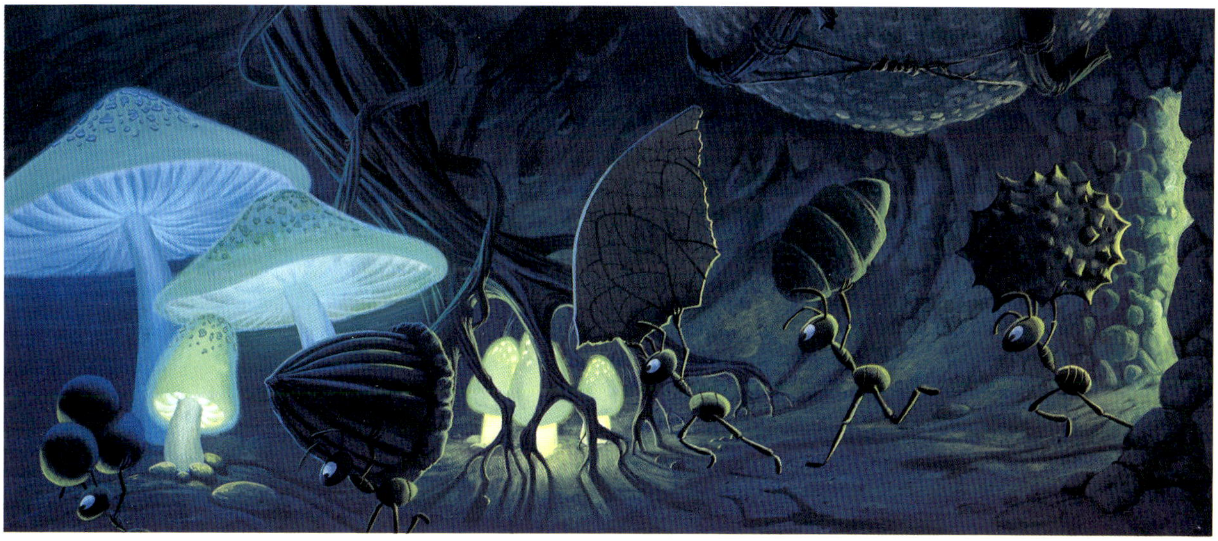

opposite:
Tia Kratter
A human's eye view of the bug world
Layout by Bill Cone
A BUG'S LIFE
Acrylic
13 x 6½

top:
Tia Kratter
Berry vine
Layout by Geefwee Boedoe
A BUG'S LIFE
Acrylic
9 x 18½

above:
Tia Kratter
Bunker
Layout by Bill Cone
A BUG'S LIFE
Acrylic
9 x 18½

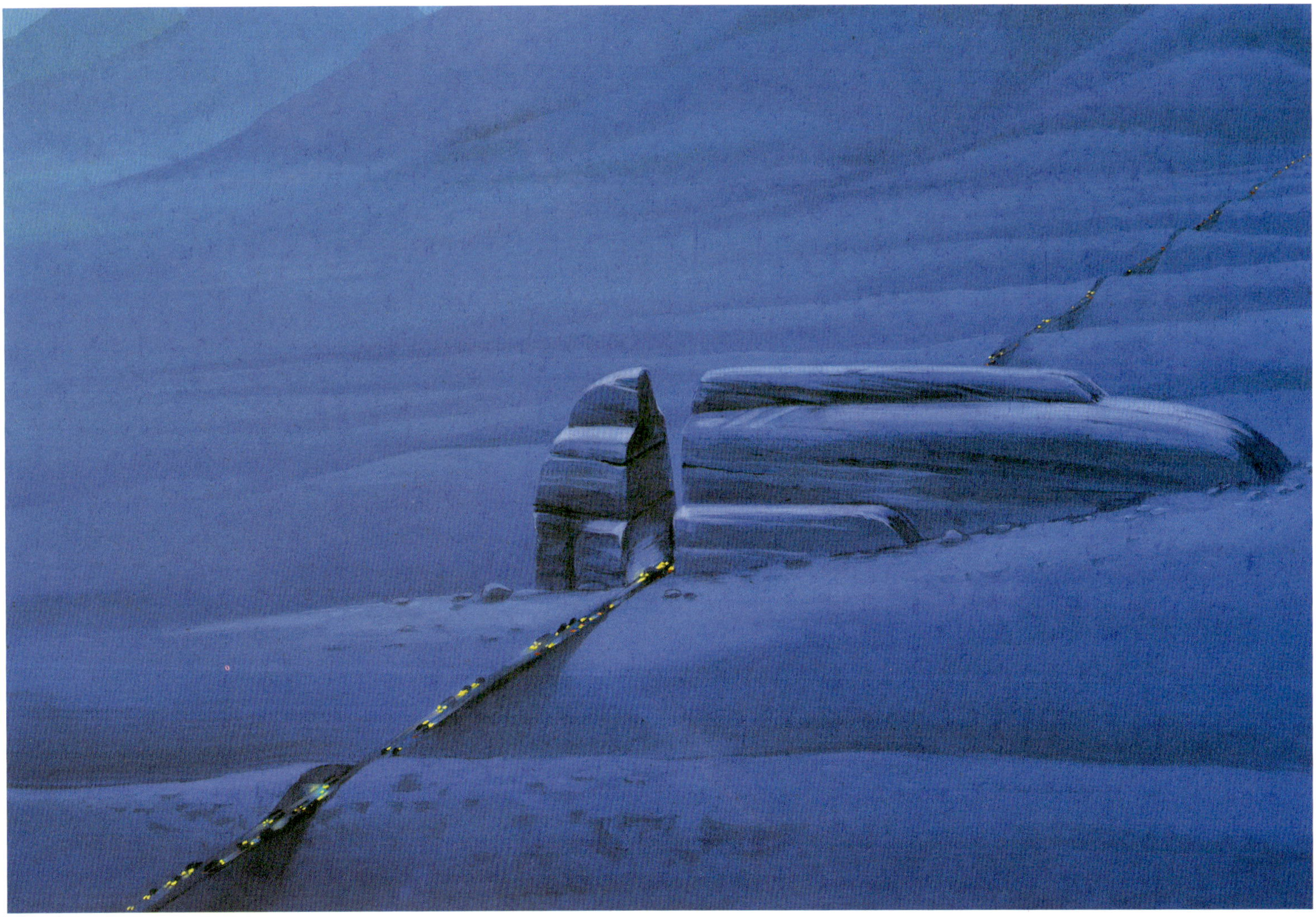

above:
Tia Kratter
Interstate study
CARS
Acrylic
9½ x 13

opposite:
Glenn Kim
Waterfall mechanics
THE INCREDIBLES
Digital

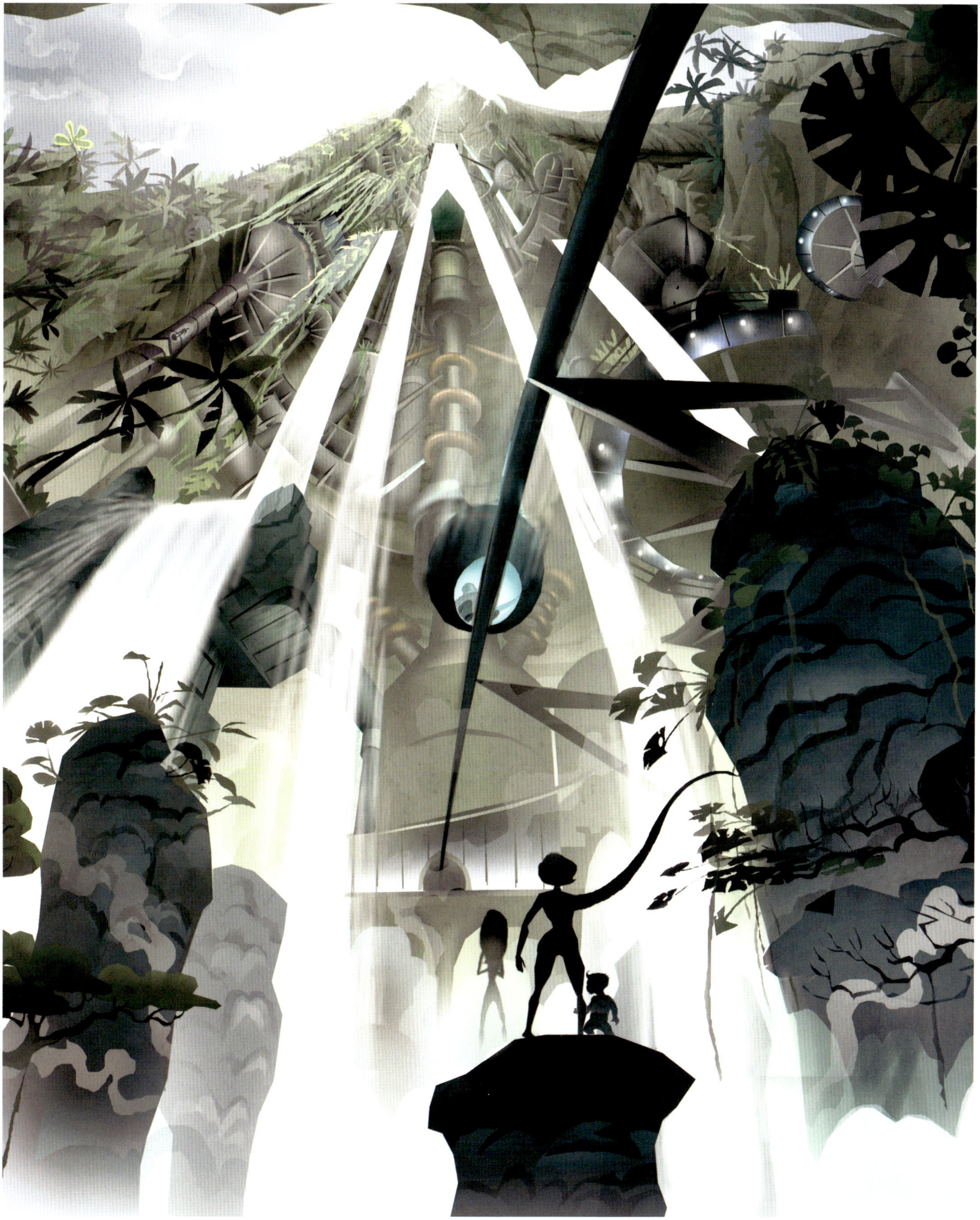

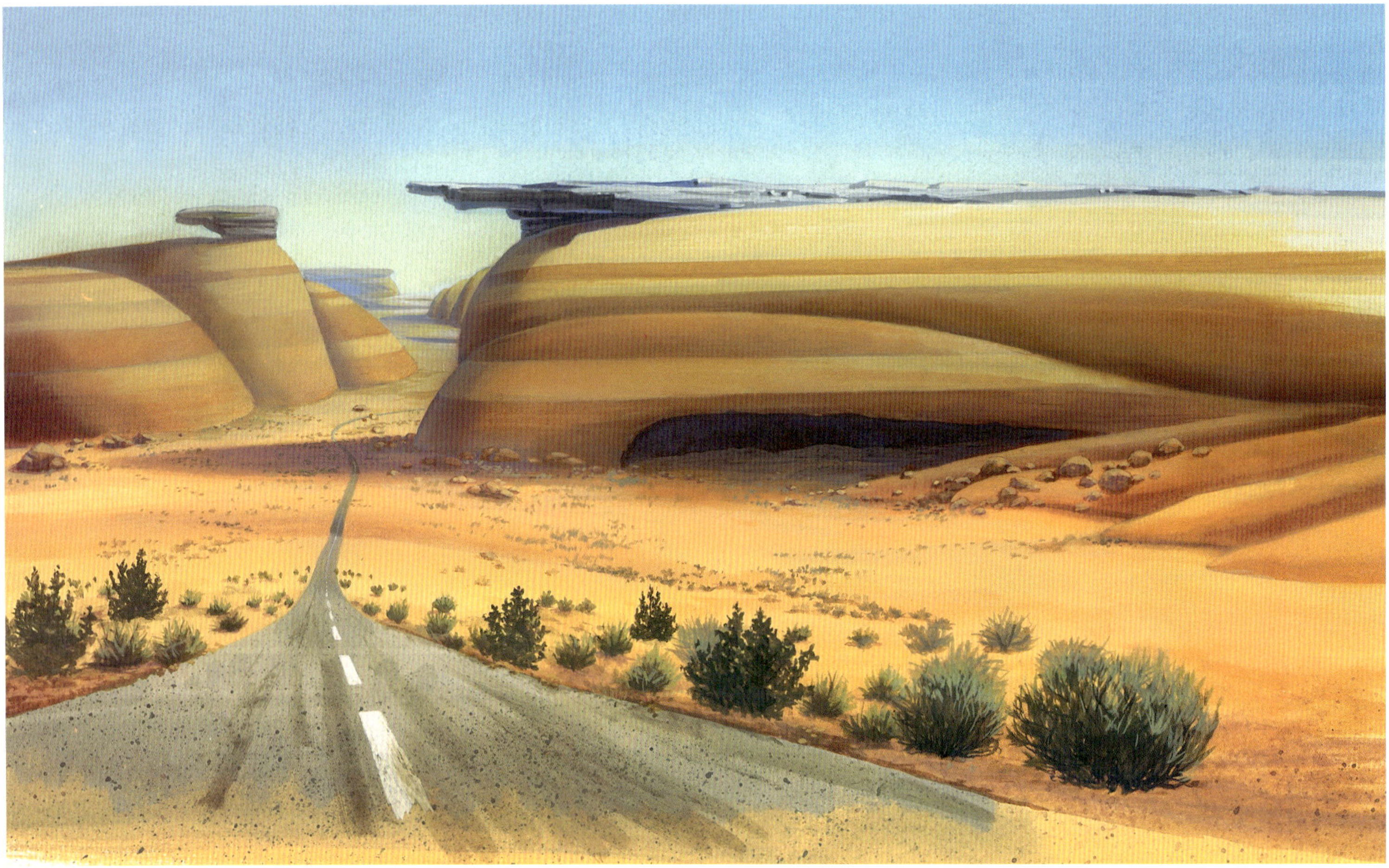

Tia Kratter
Ornament Valley
CARS
Acrylic
$9\frac{5}{8}$ x $13\frac{1}{2}$

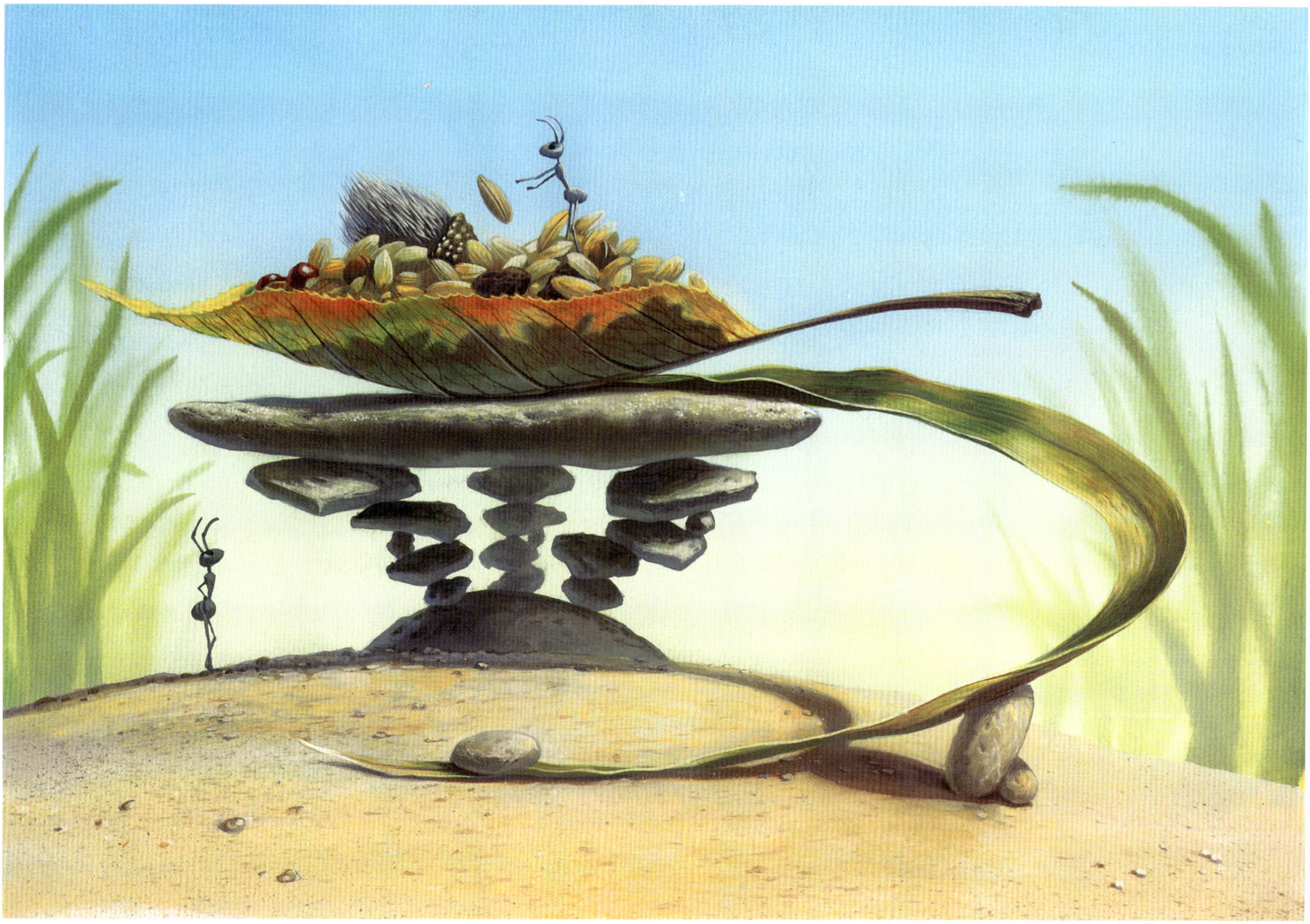

Tia Kratter
The Offering Stone
Layout by Nat McLaughlin
A BUG'S LIFE
Acrylic
8½ x 11

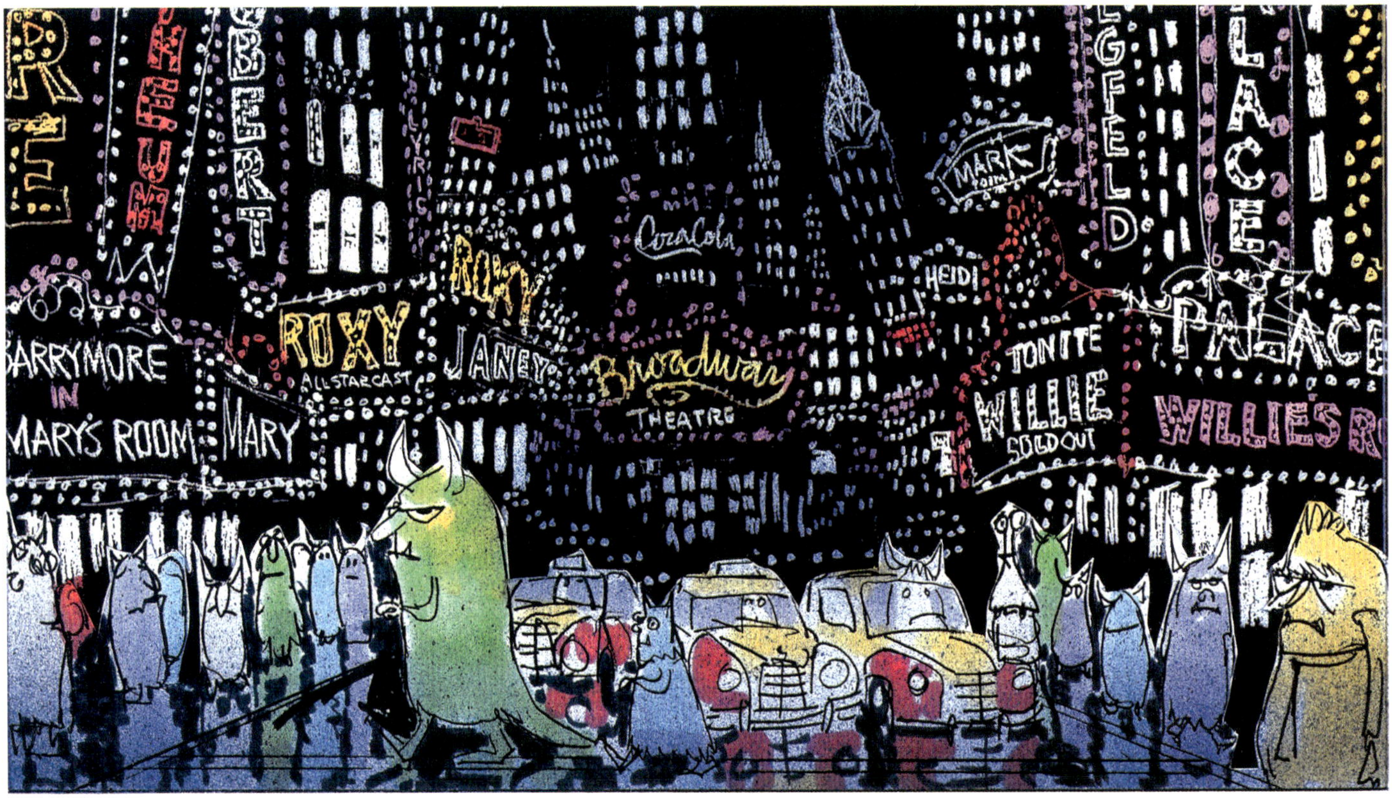

Harley Jessup
Monstropolis
MONSTERS, INC.
Mixed media
11 x 8½

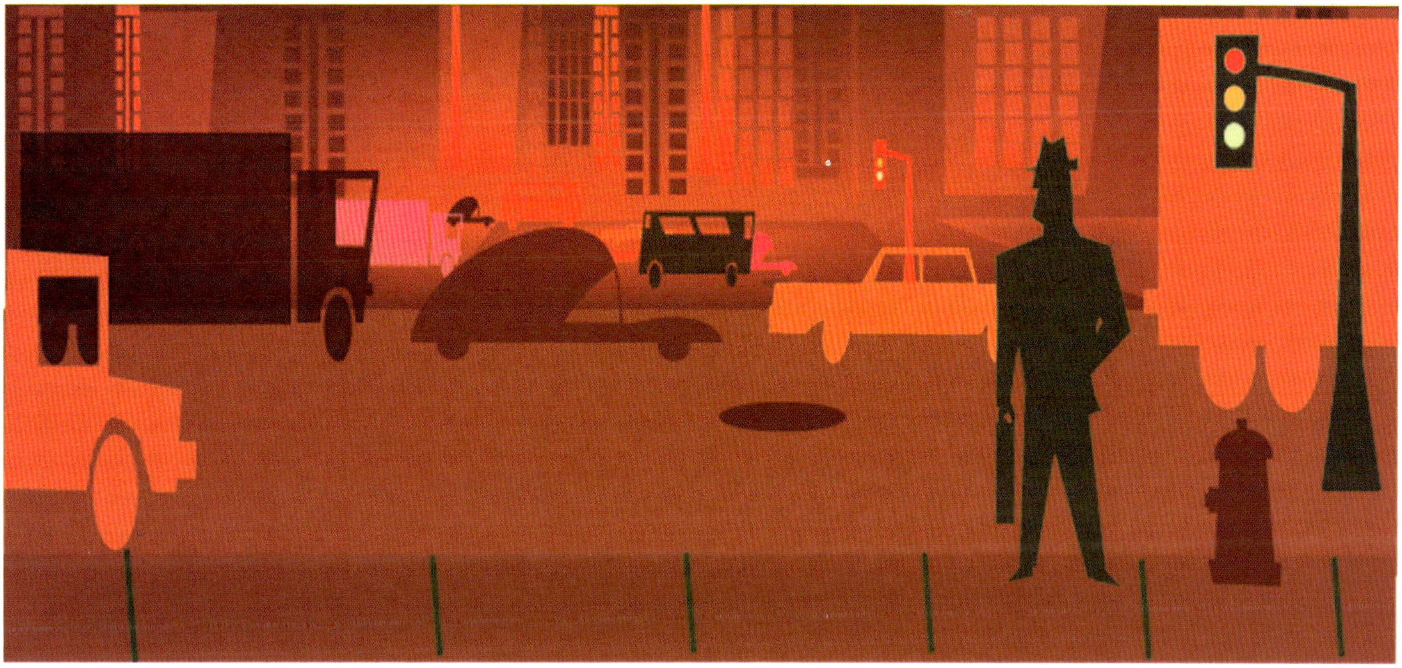

Teddy Newton
Early concept for title sequence
THE INCREDIBLES
Digital

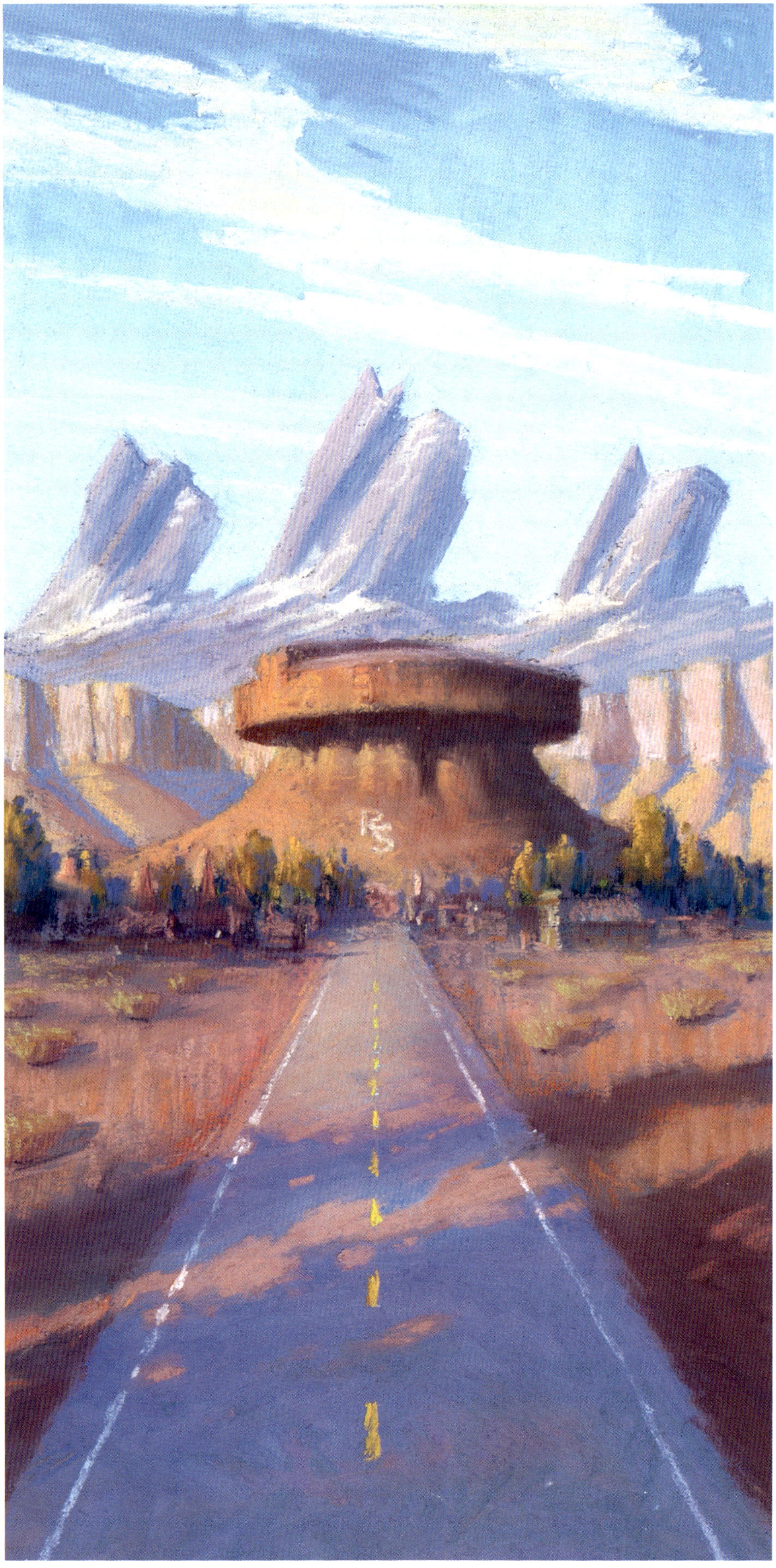

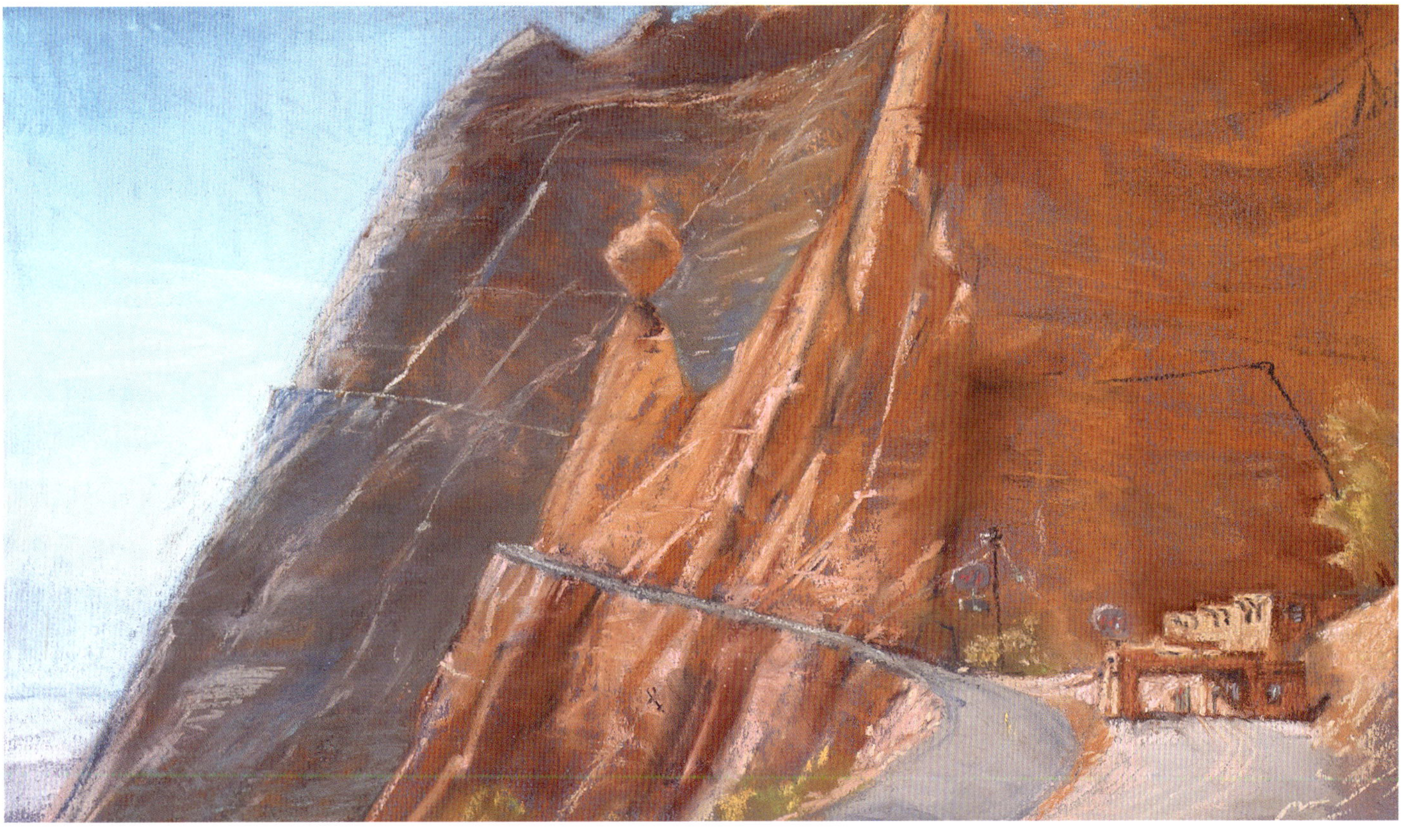

opposite:
Bill Cone
Radiator Cap
CARS
Pastel
17⅜ x 9⅞

above:
Bill Cone
Wheel Well Motel
CARS
Pastel
11 x 17⅞

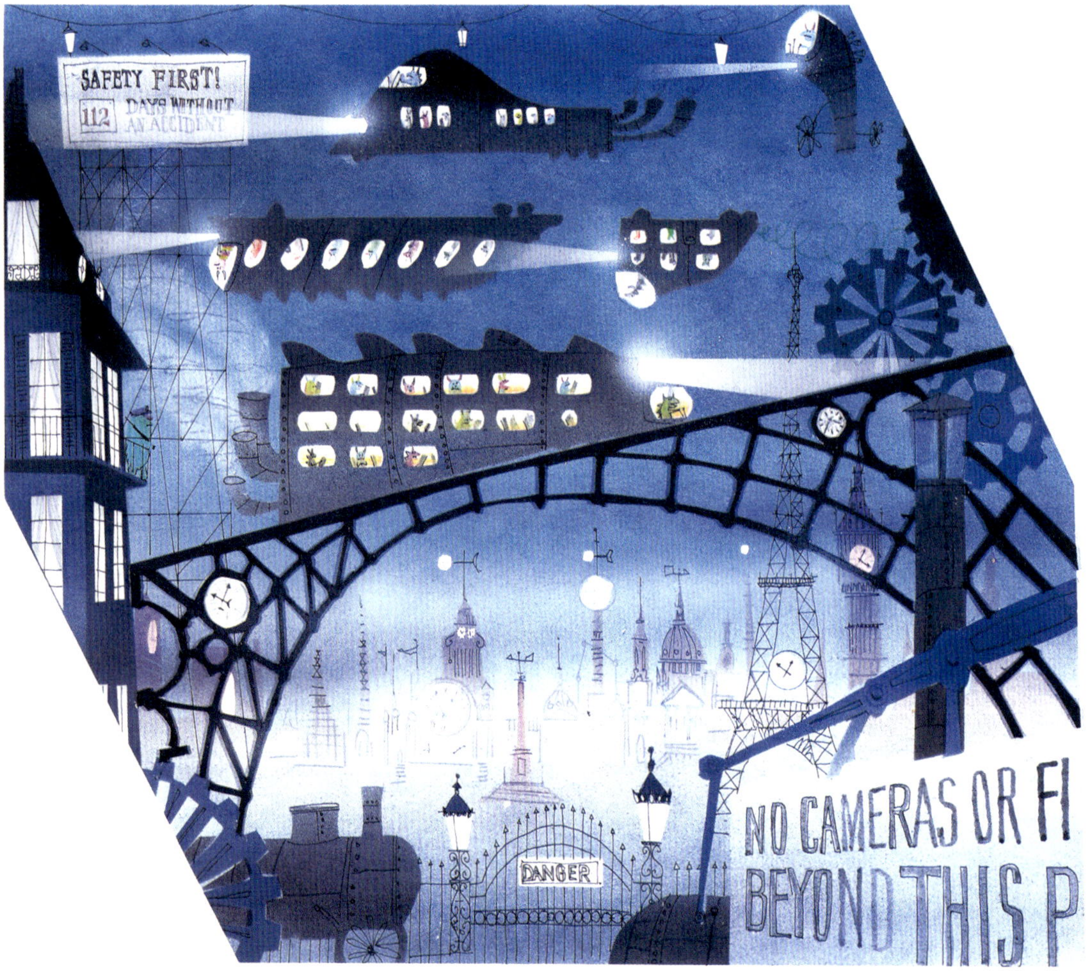

Harley Jessup
Monsters, Incorporated
MONSTERS, INC.
Mixed media
11 x 16

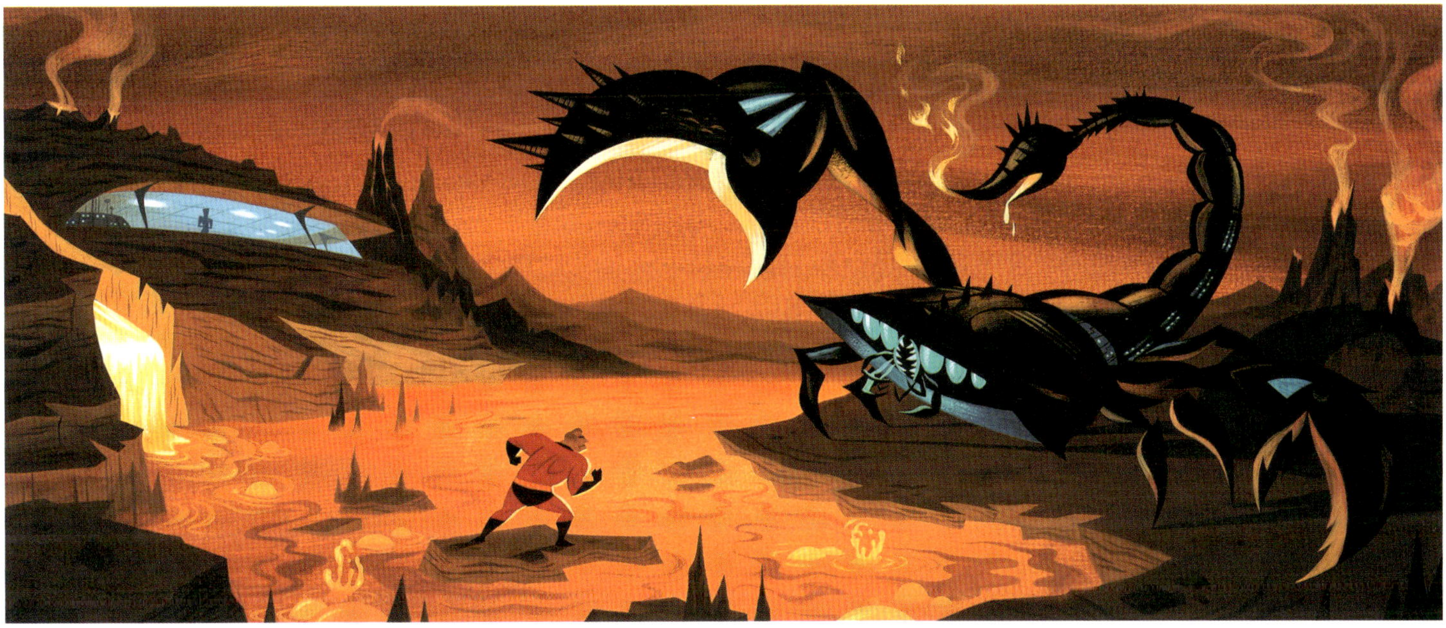

Lou Romano
Mr. Incredible vs. Omnidroid
Layout by Don Shank
THE INCREDIBLES
Gouache
7⅞ x 16¼

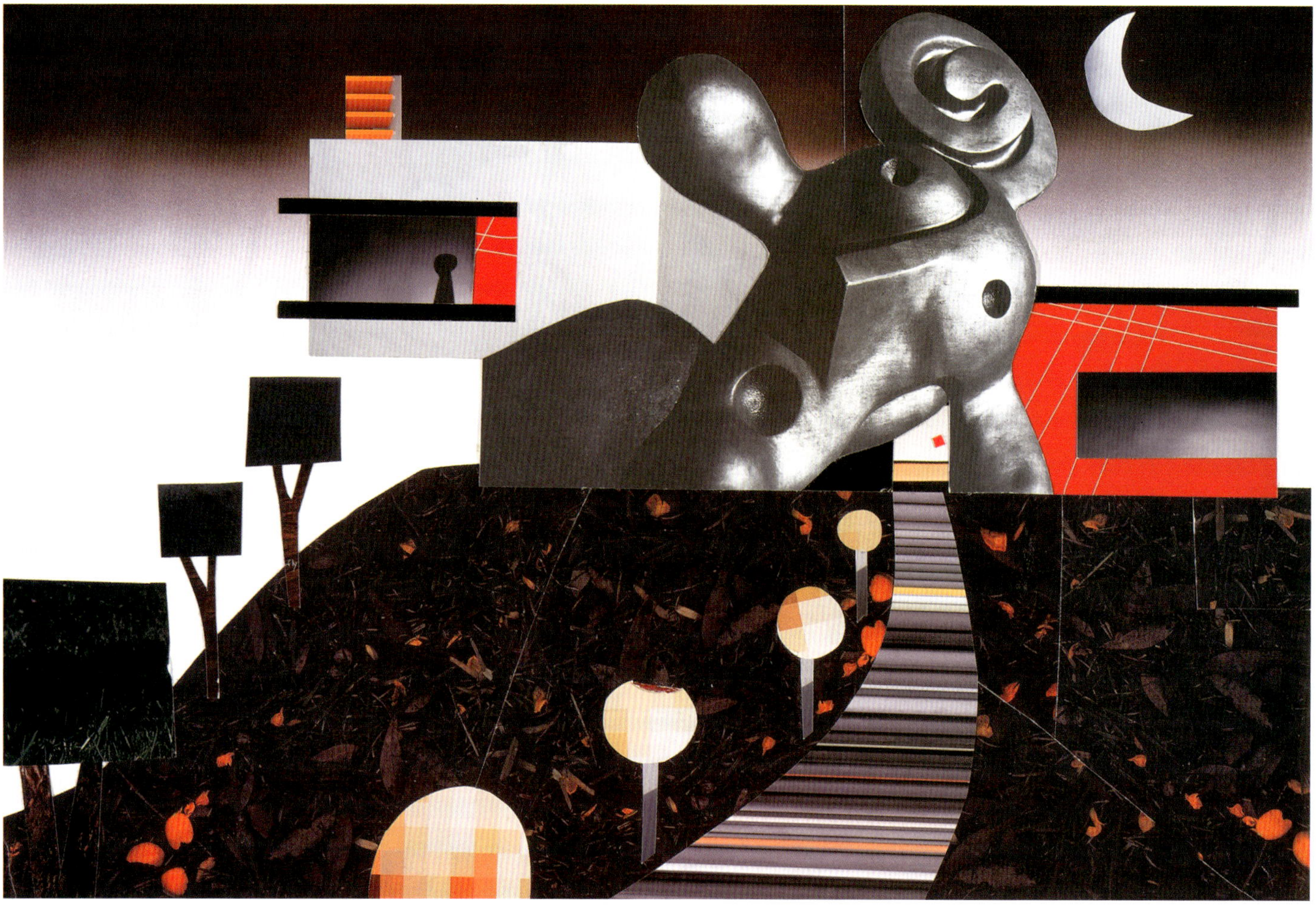

Teddy Newton
Edna Mode (aka "E") house
THE INCREDIBLES
Collage
13½ x 19½

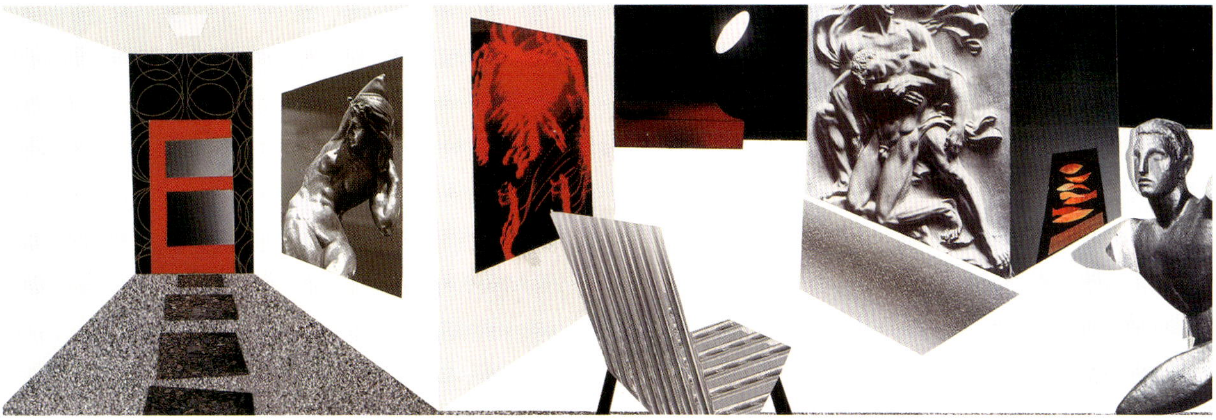

Teddy Newton
Edna Mode (aka "E") house
THE INCREDIBLES
Collage
10 x 29¾

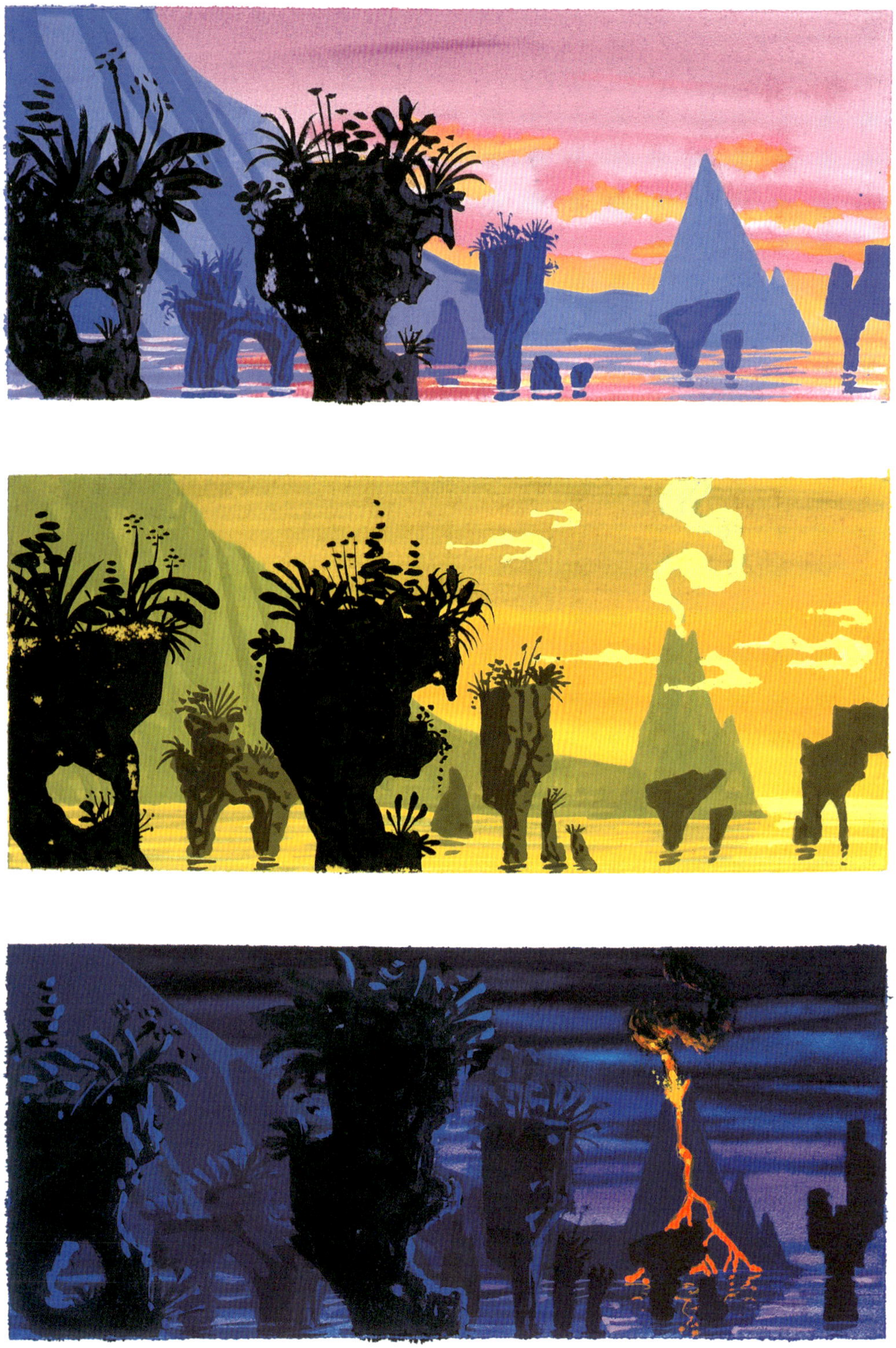

Geefwee Boedoe
Lagoon colors
THE INCREDIBLES
Gouache
9¾ x 7

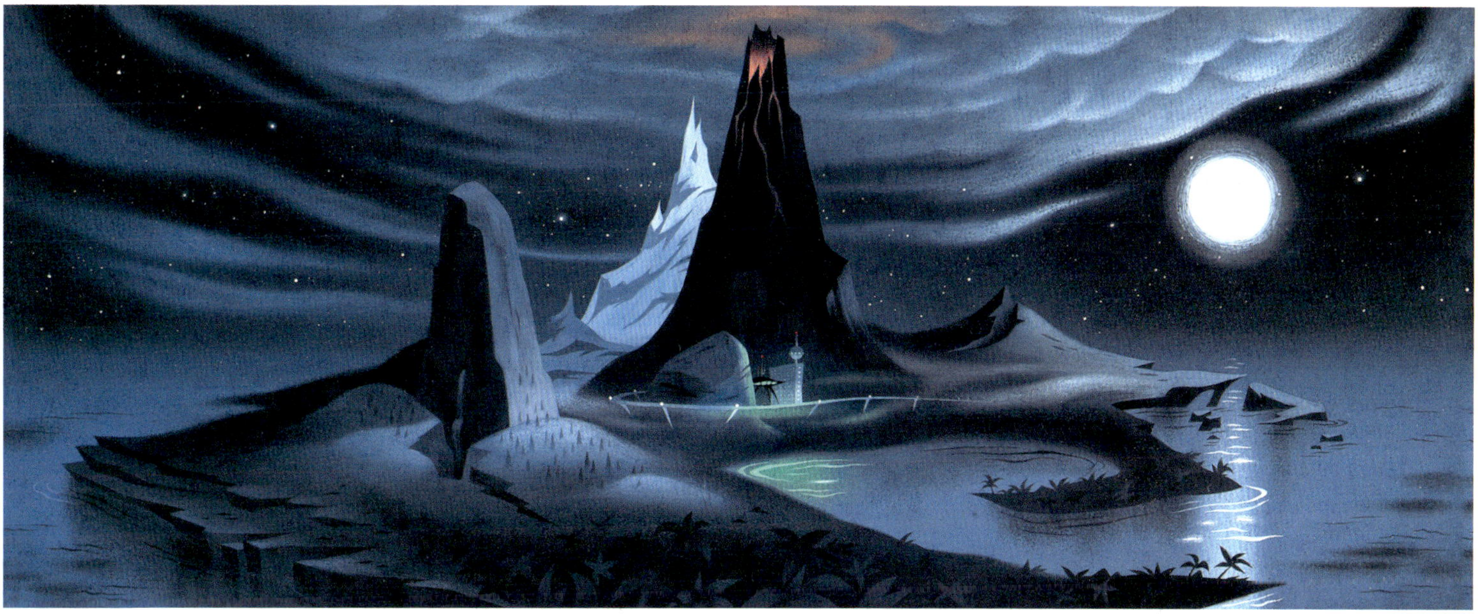

Lou Romano
Nomanisan Island
Layout by Don Shank
THE INCREDIBLES
Gouache
7 x 15⅜

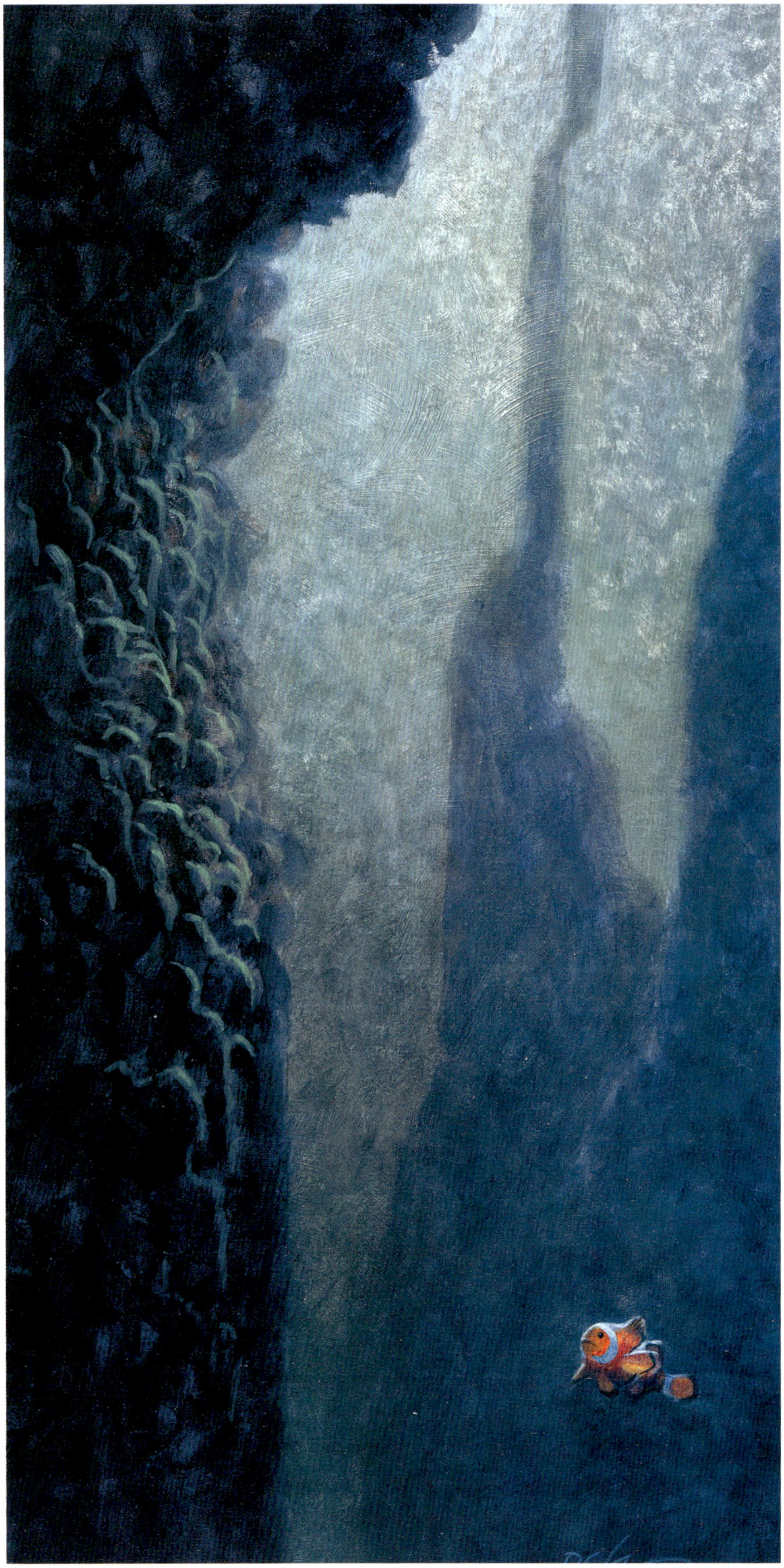

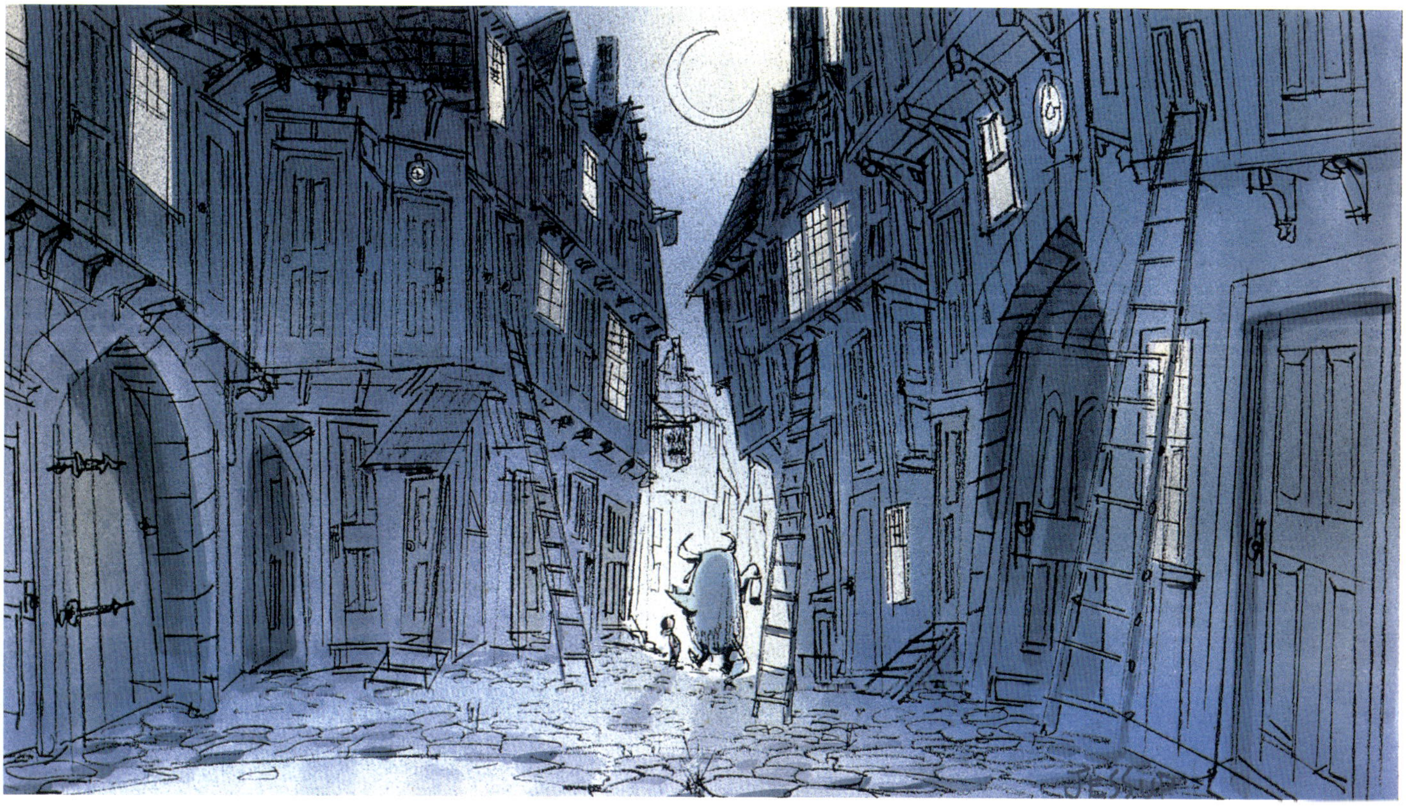

opposite:
D. J. Cleland-Hura
Ocean depths
FINDING NEMO
Acrylic
16 x 8

above:
Harley Jessup
Sullivan and Boo in Monstropolis
MONSTERS, INC.
Mixed media
11 x 8½

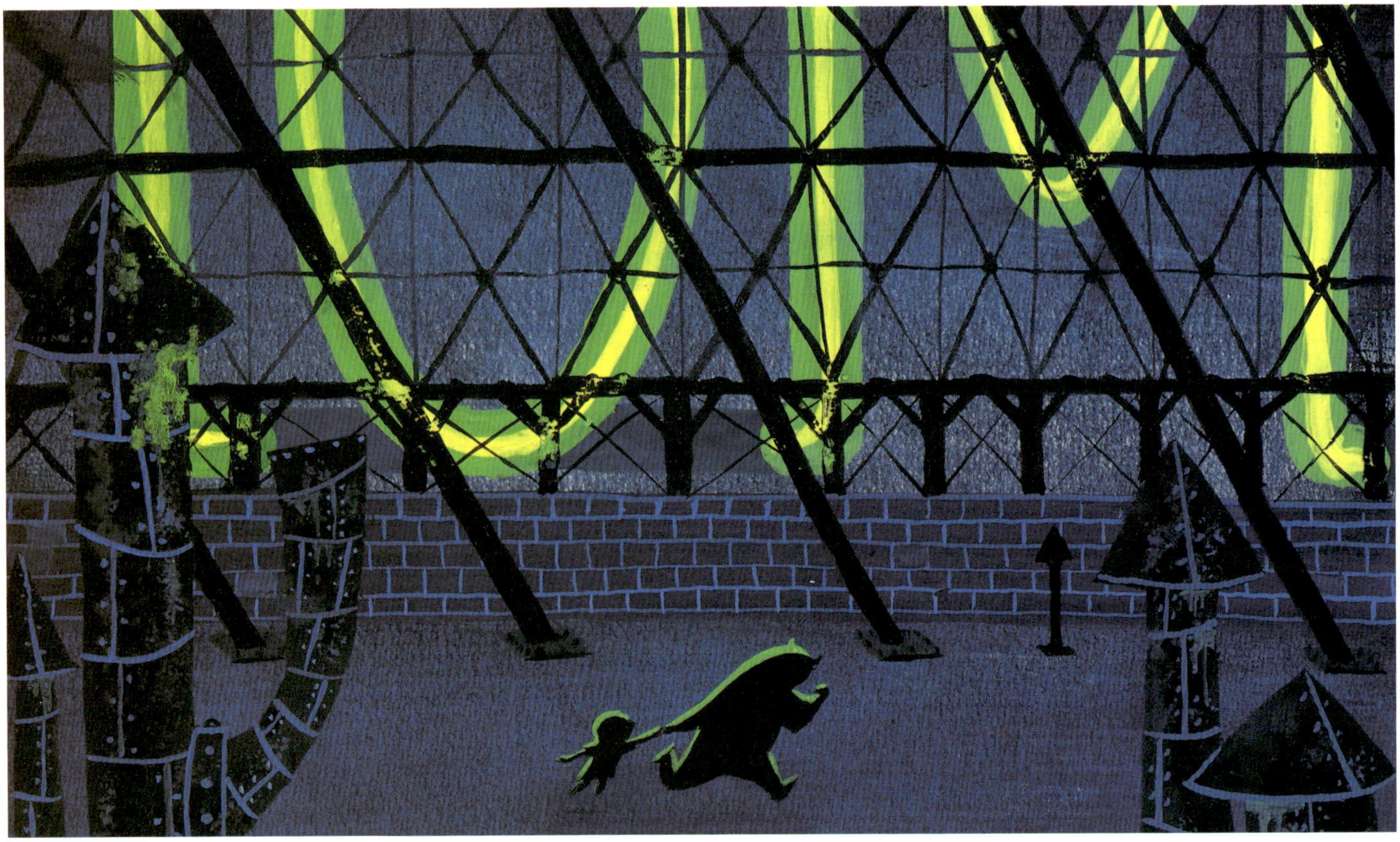

Ricky Nierva
Monsters, Incorporated
MONSTERS, INC.
Gouache
5 x 8

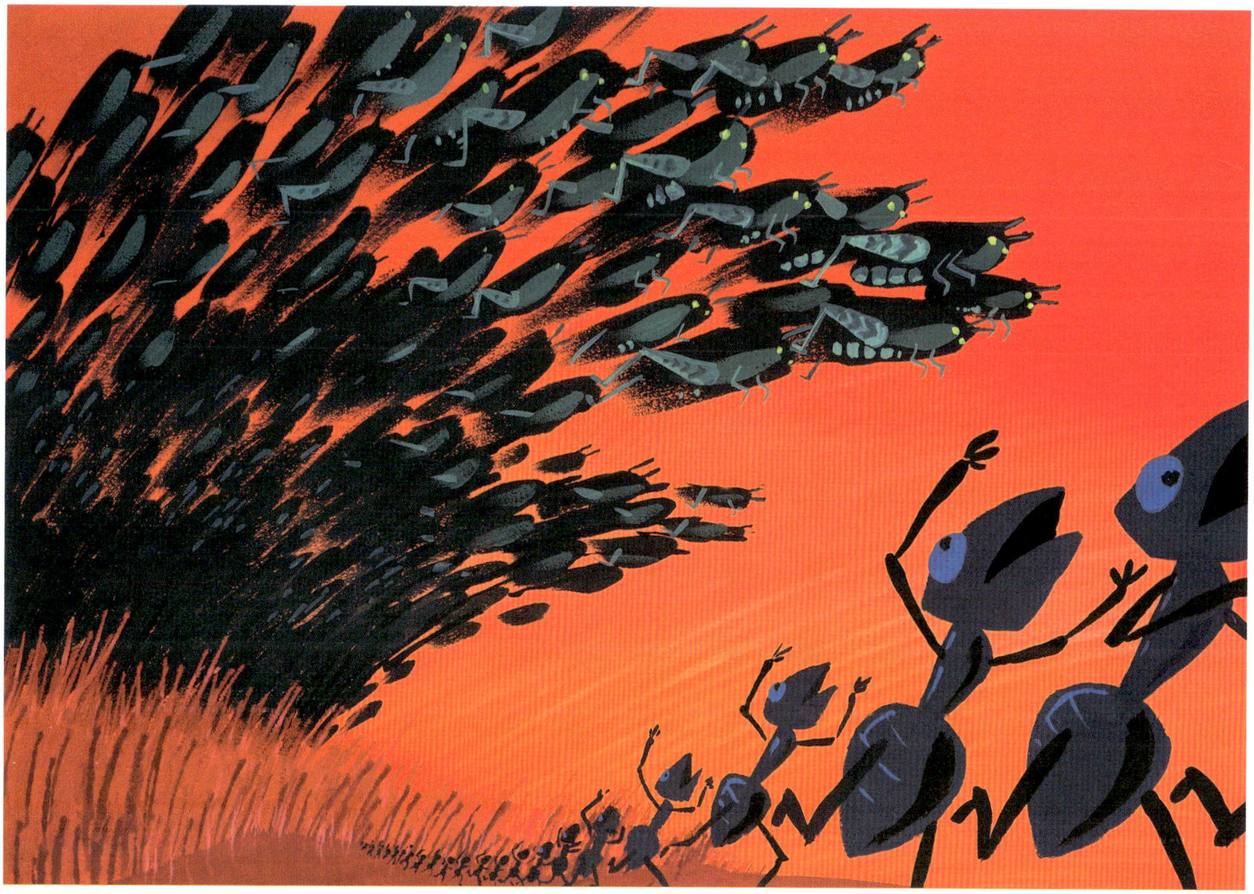

Geefwee Boedoe
Grasshopper attack
A BUG'S LIFE
Acrylic
11 x 17

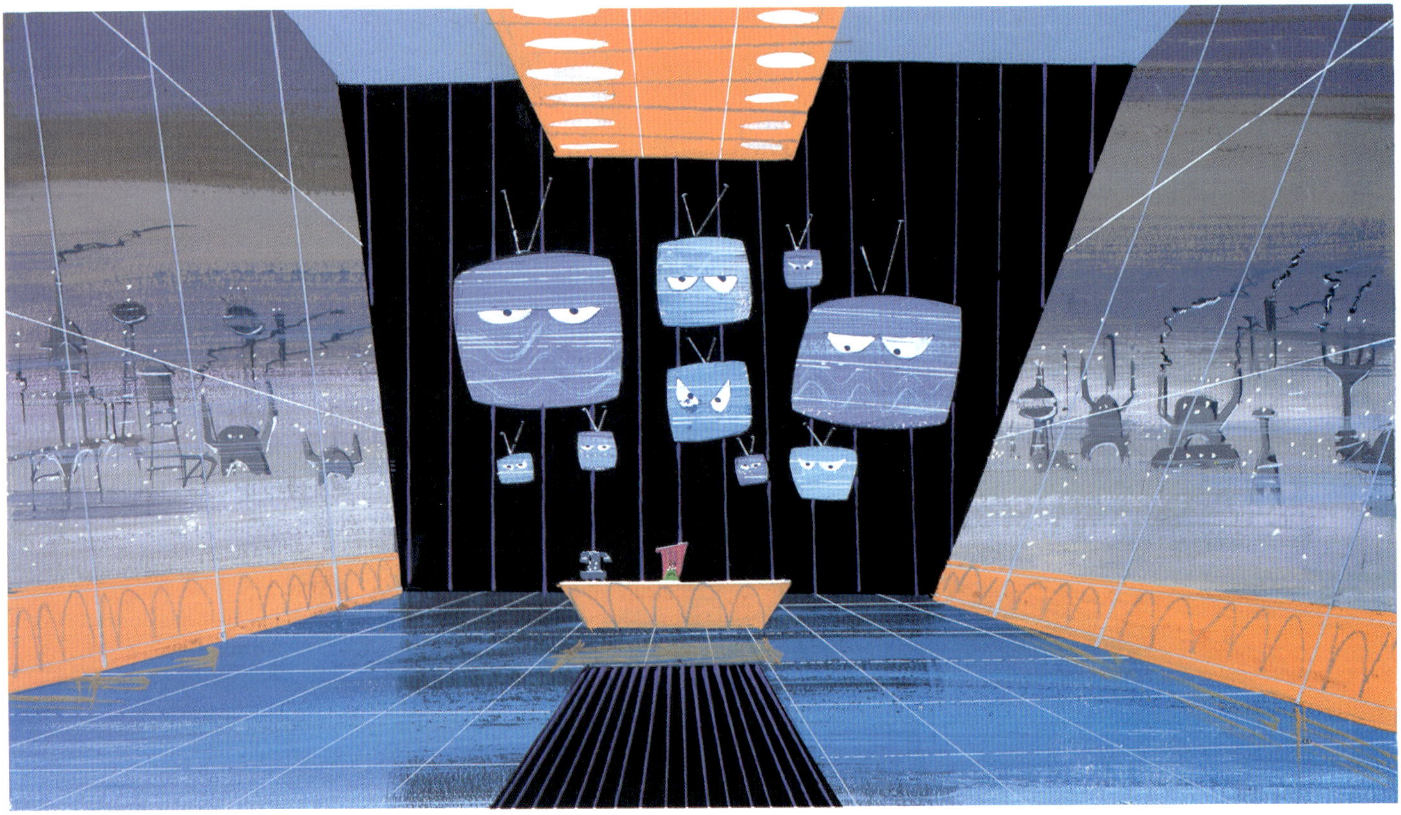

Harley Jessup
Waternoose's office
MONSTERS, INC.
Acrylic
8½ x 11

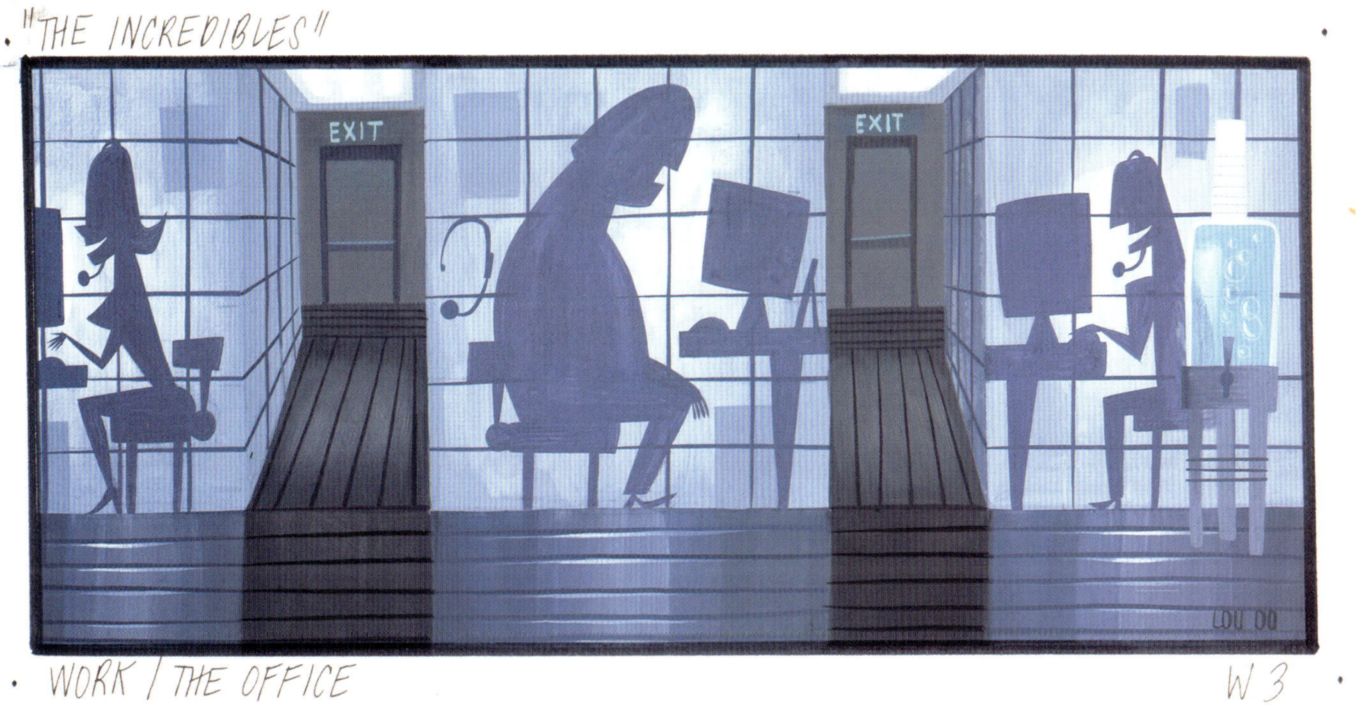

Lou Romano
Bob's cube
THE INCREDIBLES
Gouache
6⅛ x 12

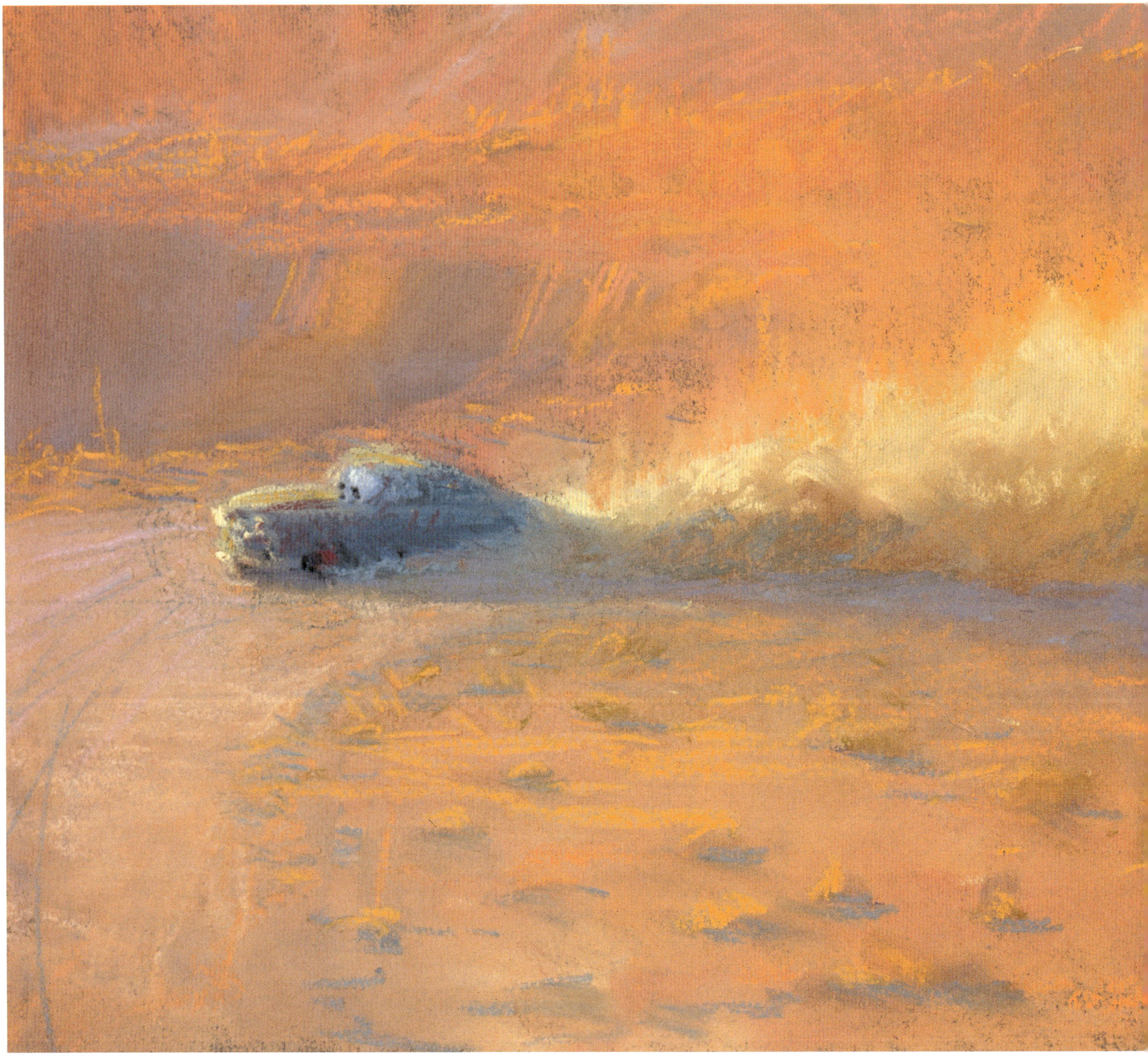

Bill Cone
Doc racing
CARS
Pastel
8 x 17⅞

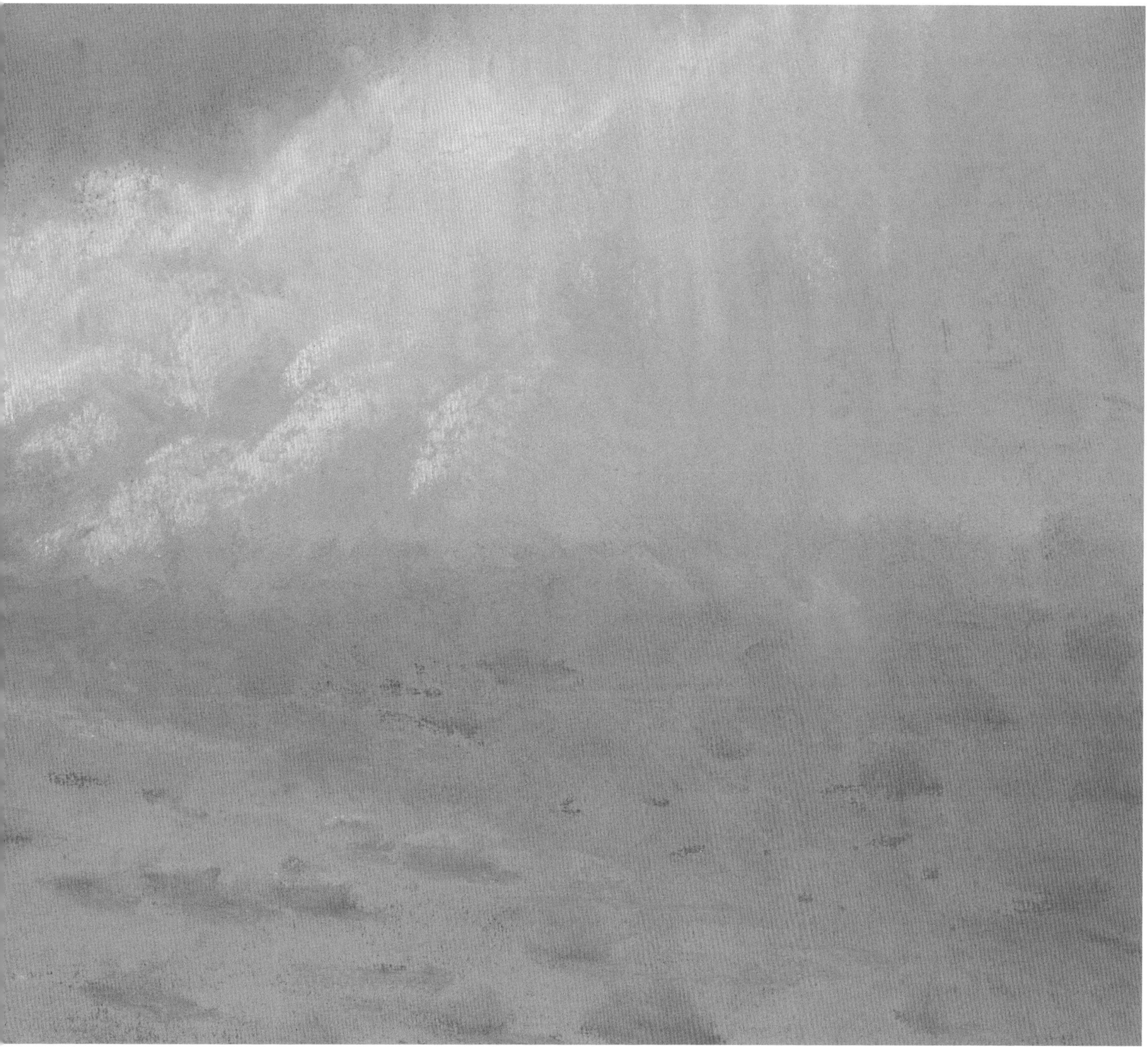

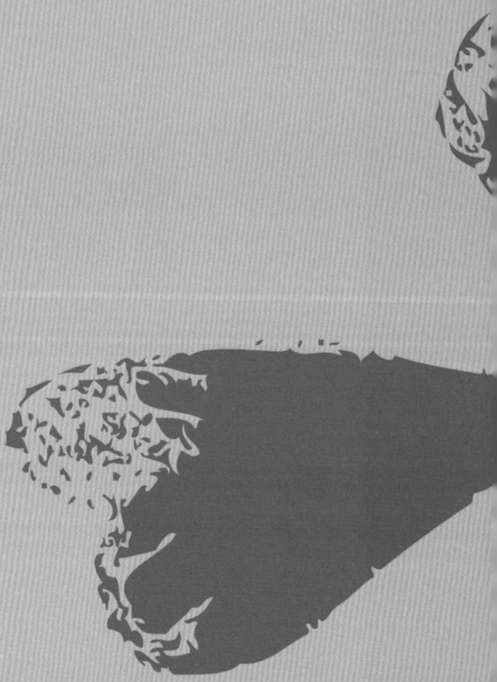

DeAnn Cobb
Clover
Based on *Clover Canopy*, by Tia Kratter
Digital. Original, acrylic

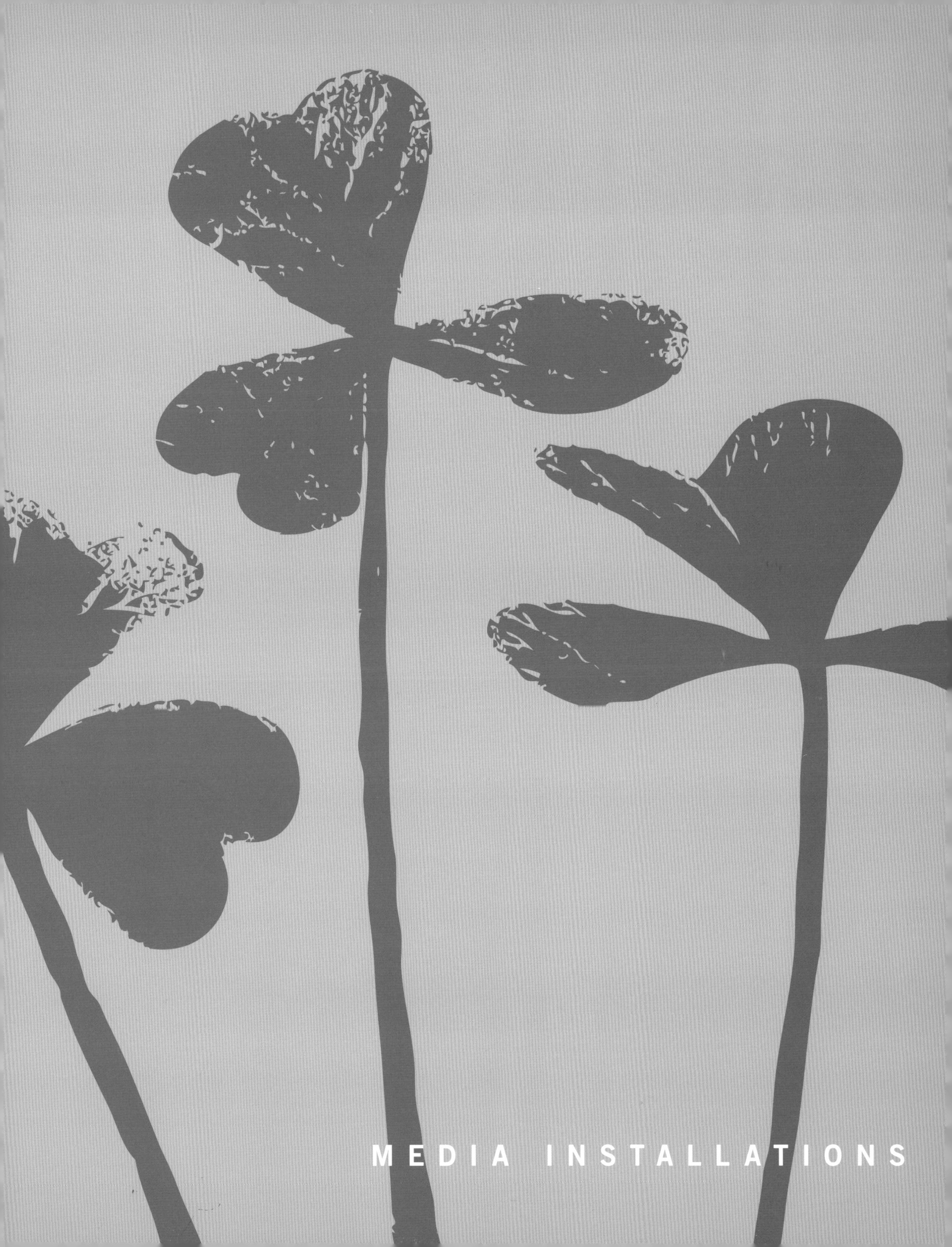

MEDIA INSTALLATIONS

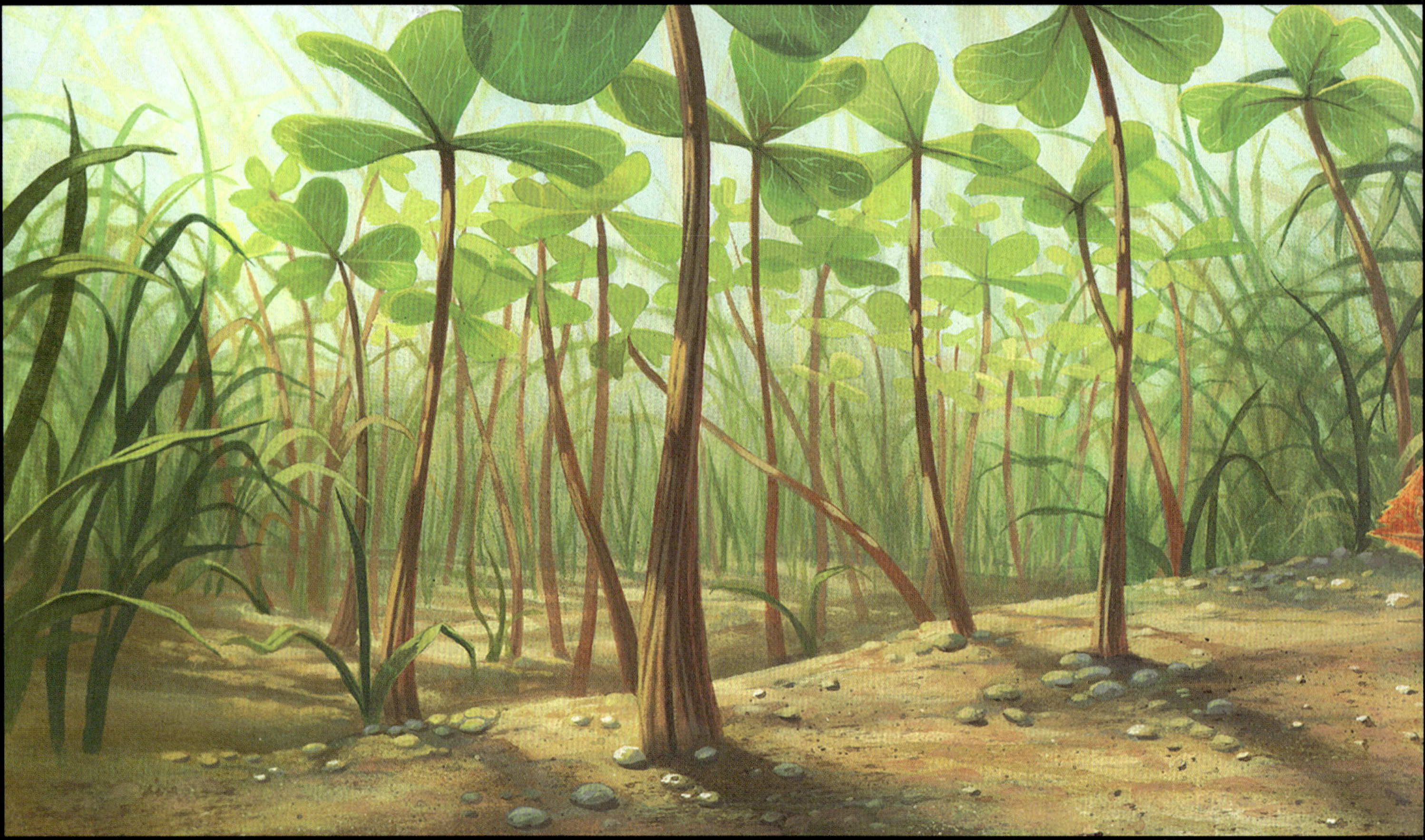

ARTSCAPE

The original drawings and paintings that form the basis of Artscape were created by various Pixar artists in traditional mediums such as pastels, charcoal, and gouache. Artist Andrew Jimenez used digital technology to explore this art in simulated 3-dimensional motion, in a large, high resolution format created especially for this exhibit. Sound designer Gary Rydstrom worked closely with Jimenez to create an immersive surround sound experience.

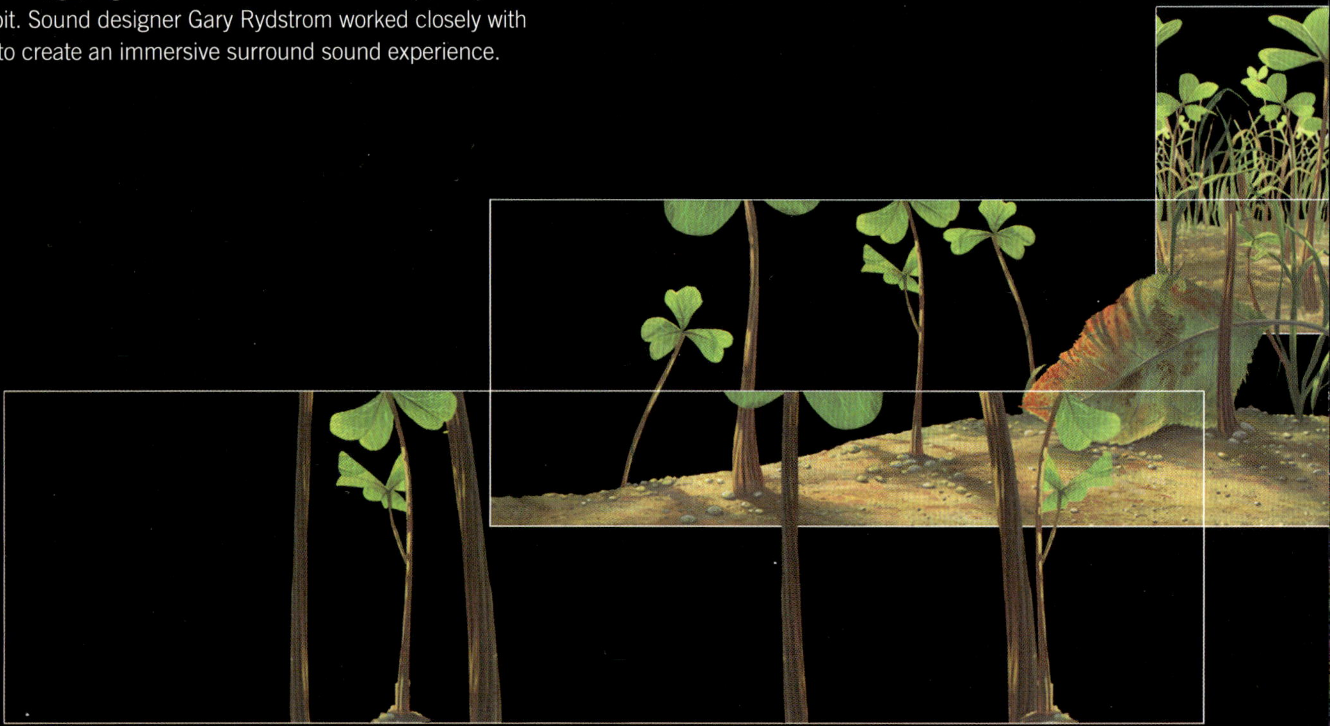

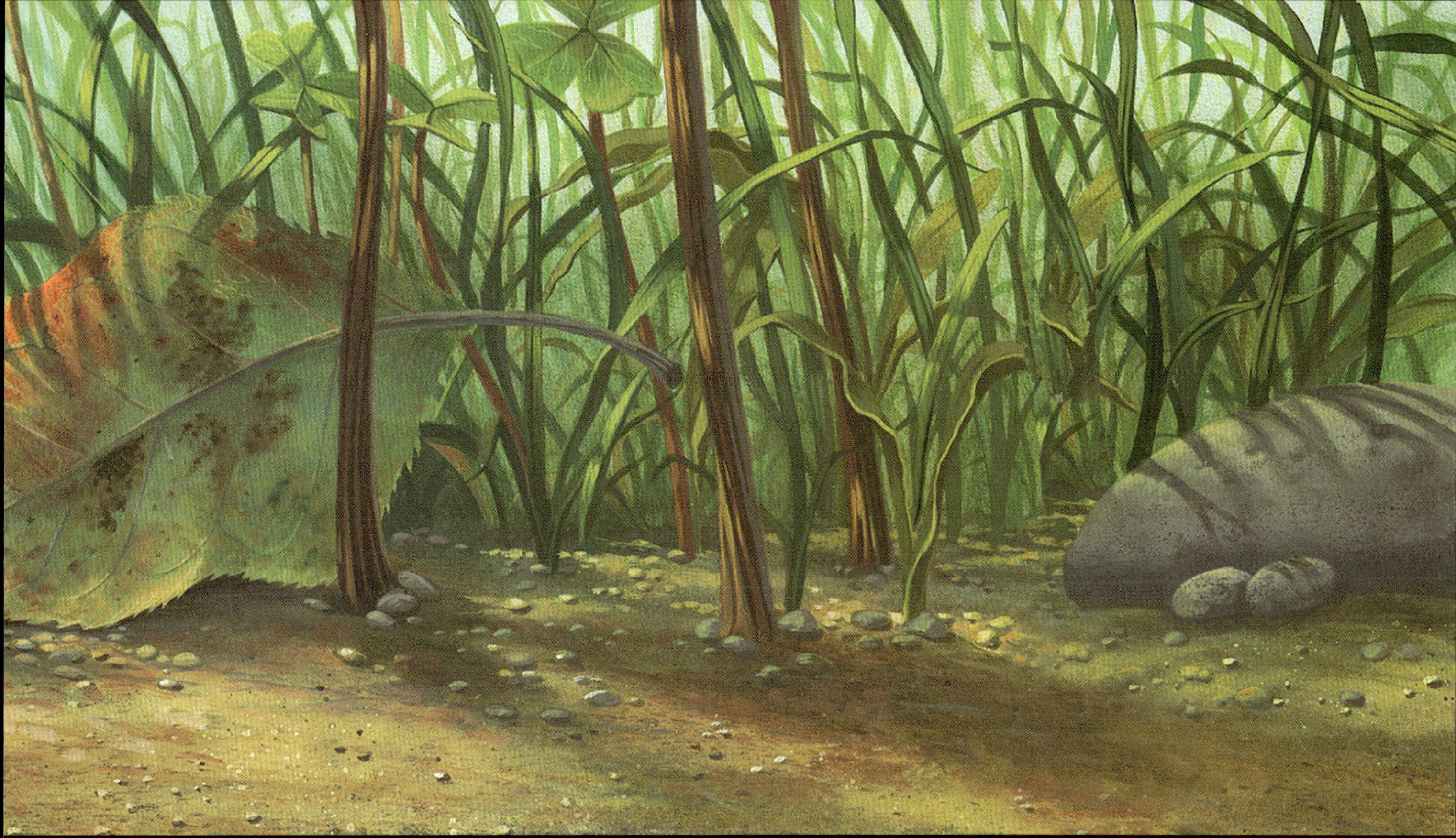

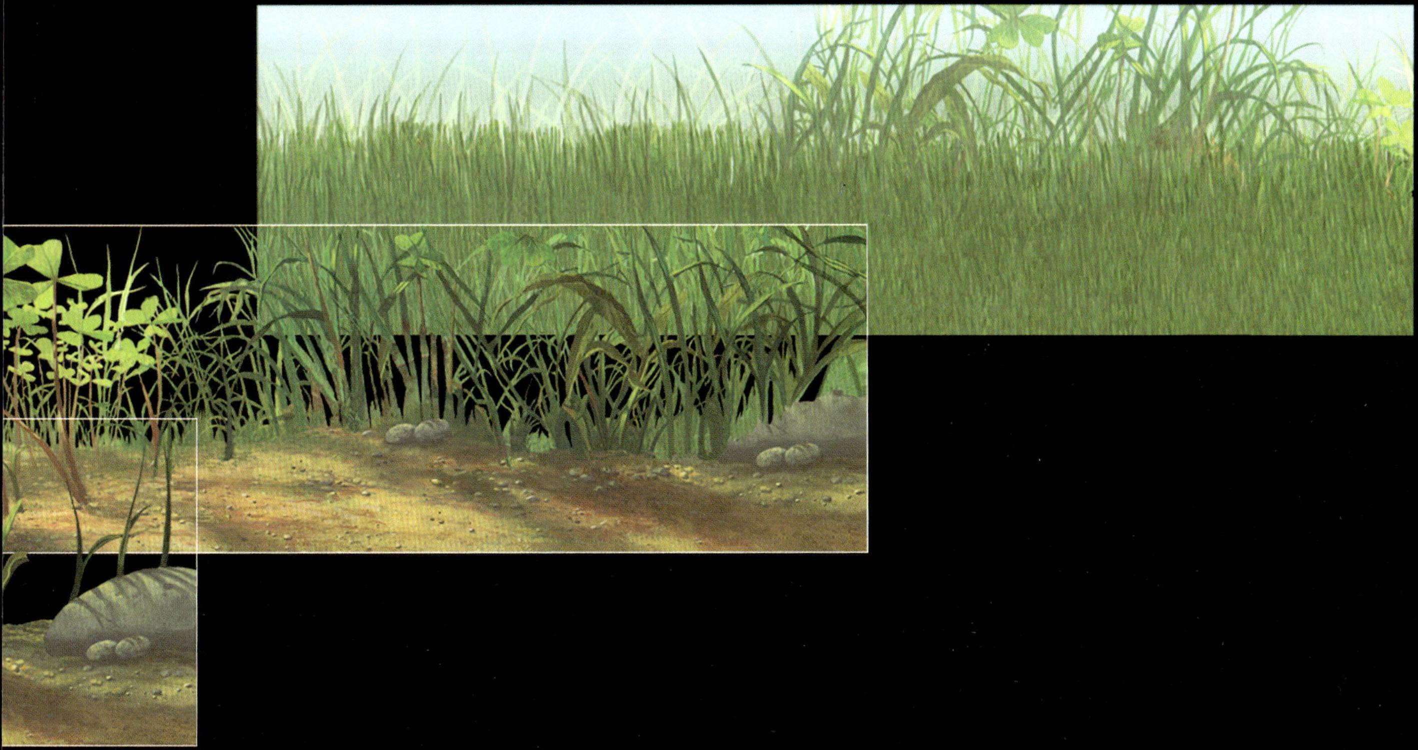

Andrew Jimenez
Artscape (detail)
Detail based on *Clover Canopy* by Tia Kratter
Media piece digital. Original, acrylic
Media piece 8' x 48'

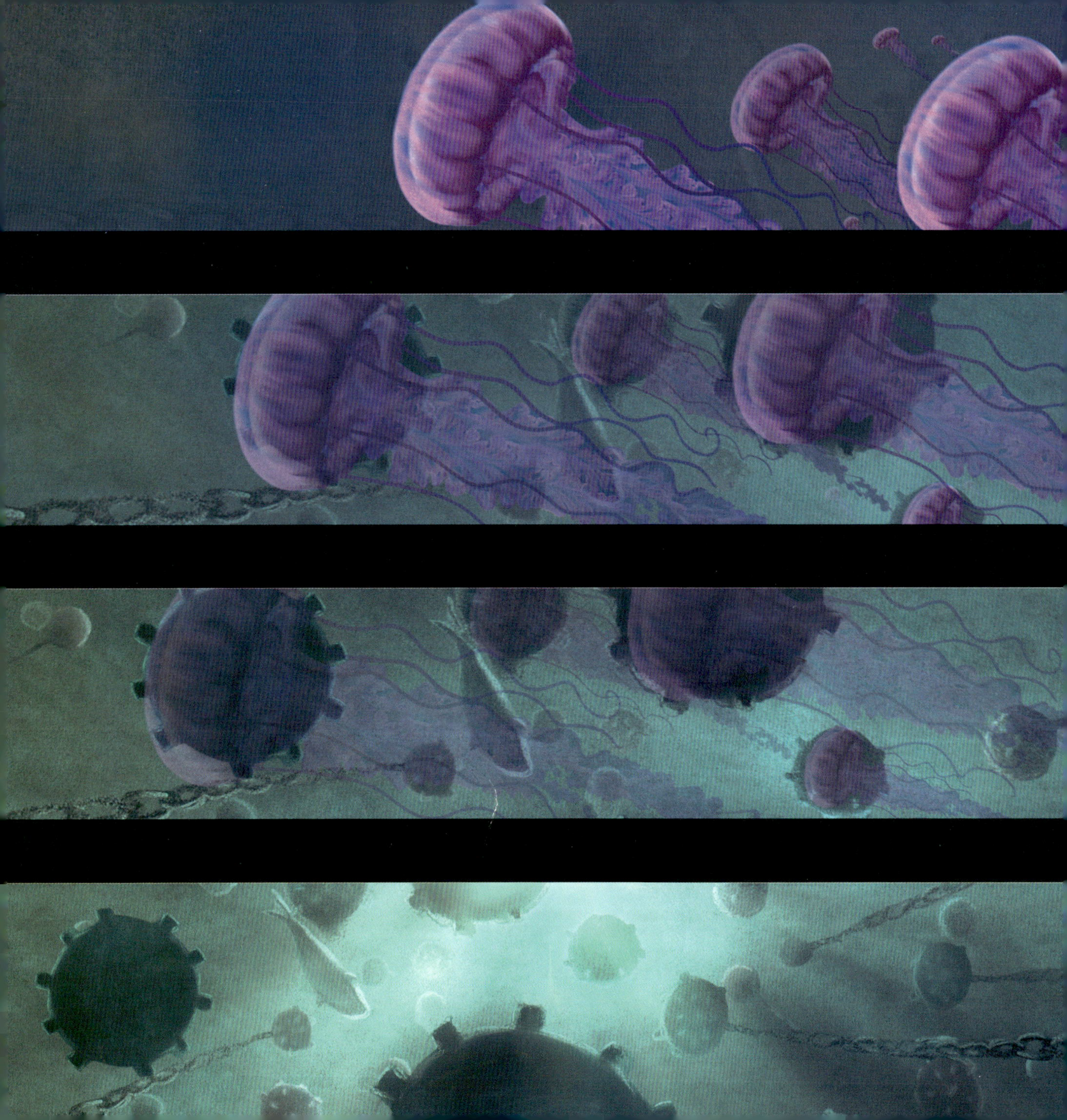

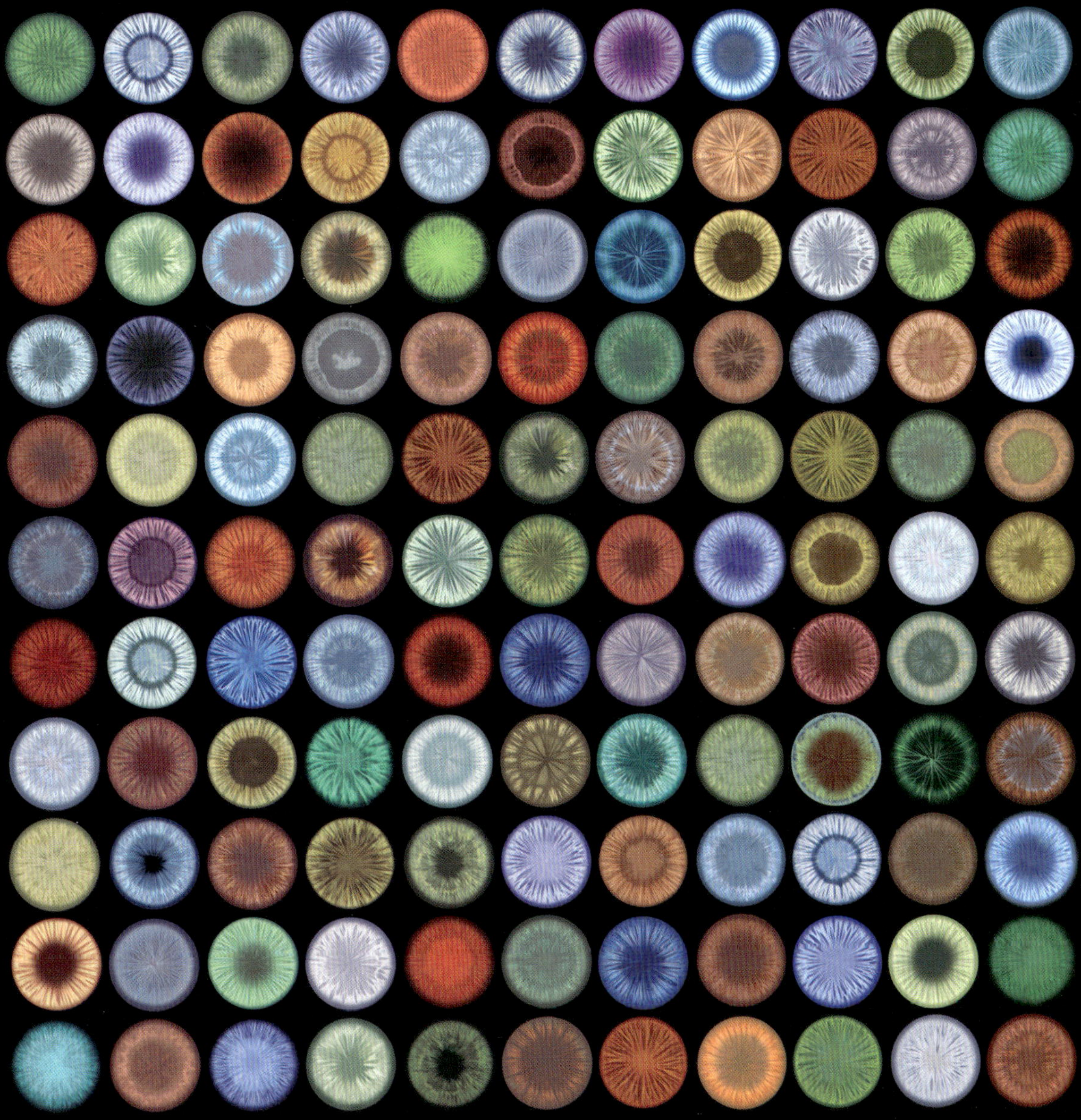

Becky Neiman
Digital collection (detail)
Iris paintings by Bert Berry, Robin Cooper, Jamie Frye,
Yvonne Herbst, Glenn Kim, Japeth Pieper
Digital

PIXAR FILMOGRAPHY

THE FOLLOWING list comprises all of the films, both short and feature-length, that have been produced by Pixar for theatrical or DVD release, and which will be shown at The Museum of Modern Art in conjunction with the gallery exhibition *Pixar* (December 14, 2005–February 6, 2006). The only exception is *Cars*, which will have its theatrical premiere in June of 2006; it is included here because so much of the artwork connected to its production will be included in the MoMA gallery show.

The Museum of Modern Art is grateful to Pixar for its generous donation of 35mm prints of all of these films to its permanent collection. By doing so, they will ensure the preservation of this body of work, in its original form, for generations to come.

The Adventures of André & Wally B. 1984. Character design and animation: John Lasseter. Concept/direction: Alvy Ray Smith. 35mm film, color, 2 minutes.

Luxo Jr. 1986. Director: John Lasseter. 35mm film, color, 2 minutes.

Red's Dream. 1987. Director: John Lasseter. 35mm film, color, 4 minutes.

Tin Toy. 1988. Director: John Lasseter. 35mm film, color, 5 minutes.

Knick Knack. 1989. Director: John Lasseter. 35mm film, color, 4 minutes.

Toy Story. 1995. Director: John Lasseter. 35mm film, color, 81 minutes.

Geri's Game. 1997. Director: Jan Pinkava. 35mm film, color, 4 minutes.

A Bug's Life. 1998. Director: John Lasseter. Co-director: Andrew Stanton. 35mm film, color, 95 minutes.

Toy Story 2. 1999. Director: John Lasseter. Co-directors: Lee Unkrich, Ash Brannon. 35mm film, color, 92 minutes.

For the Birds. 2000. Director: Ralph Eggleston. 35mm film, color, 3 minutes.

Monsters, Inc. 2001. Director: Pete Docter. Co-directors: Lee Unkrich, David Silverman. 35mm film, color, 93 minutes.

Mike's New Car. 2002. Directors: Pete Docter, Roger Gould. 35mm film, color, 4 minutes.

Finding Nemo. 2003. Director: Andrew Stanton. Co-director: Lee Unkrich. 35mm film, color, 100 minutes.

Boundin'. 2003. Director: Bud Luckey. Co-director: Roger Gould. 35mm film, color, 5 minutes.

The Incredibles. 2004. Director: Brad Bird. 35mm film, color, 115 minutes.

Jack-Jack Attack. 2005. Director: Brad Bird. 35mm film, color, 5 minutes.

One Man Band. 2005. Directors: Andrew Jimenez, Mark Andrews. 35mm film, color, 5 minutes.

Cars. 2006. Director: John Lasseter. 35mm film, color.

ACKNOWLEDGMENTS

A MUSEUM exhibition on the scale of *Pixar* requires the talents of numerous knowledgeable and dedicated collaborators.

At Pixar, we are grateful to Elyse Klaidman (Dean of Art and Film) and Osnat Shurer (Executive Producer, Shorts), who worked long hours with the MoMA team to help us realize our curatorial vision; Mary Conlin (Director of Marketing), who first set the project in motion; John Walker (Producer), who oversaw the big picture; and Kathleen Holliday, our indefatigable Exhibition Lead, whose experience kept the project on track and on time.

At MoMA, the exhibition could not have happened without the resourceful Jenny He, Celeste Bartos Research Assistant in the Department of Film and Media, who worked with tireless enthusiasm from the show's inception. We were also pleased for the opportunity to work closely with one of the world's best exhibition design teams: Lana Hum (Exhibition Design), Ed Pusz (Graphic Design), and Allegra Burnette (Digital Media).

We owe a special debt of gratitude to the teams of professionals at Pixar and MoMA who shared their ideas and matchless expertise:

At Pixar, we thank Christine Freeman, Lead Archivist, who is passionately dedicated to the preservation of the studio's history, and her colleagues Juliet Greenberg and Deborah Sadler, who opened countless storage boxes (and more than a few artist's desks) in their efforts to locate anything that we asked to see; Production team members Andrew Jimenez, Andy Dreyfus, Liz Gazzano, Karen Paik, Becky Neiman, and DeAnn Cobb for their imaginative solutions to countless questions of design and procedure; the wondrous Zoetrope design team of Warren Trezevant, Mike Krummhoefener, Guido Quaroni, Neftali Alvarez, and Loren Carpenter; and a special word of thanks to Jonas Rivera, Production Manager, and Darla K. Anderson, Producer, for their foresight in creating the Pixar Living Archives. In Marketing, our thanks to Michele Spane, Krista Swager, and Rosaleen O'Byrne. Indeed, we thank every single member of the Pixar family, whose generous spirit and infectious excitement for this project we sensed in every phase of our dealings with the studio.

At The Museum of Modern Art, in Exhibitions, we thank Maria DeMarco Beardsley, Carlos Yepes, Marci Regan Dallas, and Gael LeLamer. In the Registrar's office, we thank Ramona Bannayan and Kerry McGinnity. We thank Elan Cole and Claire Corey in the Department of Graphic Design. In Information Technology, we are thankful for the knowledge and expertise of Charles Kalinowski (Audio-Visual) and K Mita (Digital Media). In Development, we gratefully acknowledge the talents of Todd Bishop, Mary Hannah, and Nicole Goldberg. In the Department of Education, we thank Deborah Schwartz, Elizabeth Margulies, David Little, Sarah Ganz, Susan McCullough, Sara Bodinson, Heather Maxson, and Marine Putman. In Marketing and Communications we thank Ruth Kaplan, Kim Mitchell, Peter Foley, Paul Power, Mary Anisi, and Kim Donica. In the Department of Film and Media, our special thanks go to our colleagues Laurence Kardish, Charles Silver, and Natalie Hirniak. We would also like to thank Jerry Neuner, Lawrence Allen, Nicholas Apps, Karl Buchberg, Margaret Raimondi, and Julie Scherer for their help at various key stages of the project.

Our desire to organize the Museum's most comprehensive exhibition to date of animation art from a single studio, and to do so by making use of unorthodox exhibition space within our new Museum building, would not have been possible without the visionary support of the executive teams at both institutions. At Pixar, we thank Steve Jobs, Ed Catmull, John Lasseter, Sarah McArthur, Simon Bax, and Lois Scali; and at The Museum of Modern Art, we thank Glenn Lowry, Mary Lea Bandy, Jennifer Russell, and Michael Margitich.

Finally, we applaud Sarah Malarkey, Tera Killip, Kevin Toyama, and the experienced editorial staff at Chronicle Books for their determination to see this volume come to life.

STEVEN HIGGINS
RONALD S. MAGLIOZZI